Preface

This book is mainly targeted for the exam of Indian Administration for all Universities. It has been introduced in market after seeing the huge demand of ready to grasp material for exams with high level of quality, and its un-availability in market. We the GullyBaba Publishing House took a step ahead to publish the quality material focusing on exams at the same time giving you indepth knowledge about the subject.

GPH Book is the pioneer effort that provides a unique methodology so as to perform better in exams. If your goal is to attain higher grade use this powerful study tool independently or along with your text.

On the Web : **www.gullybaba.com** *is the vital resource for your exams acting as catalyst to boost up your preparation. Now you can access us on the net through* **www.doeacconline.com,** **www.ignouonline.com,** *and* **www.astrologyeverywhere.com.**

We gratefully acknowledges the significant contributions of Mr. S.K. Goel, Mr. Dinesh Verma, Mr. Mahesh Chand, Mrs. Bimla Devi, Mrs. Bhawna Verma and our experts in bringing out this publication.

New Delhi

Dear Reader, You are welcome in the world of GullyBaba Publishing House.

By long, in deep study & Research, we assure / guarantee you the most reliable, latest & accurate information on the subject.

We still believe that there is always a scope for improvement.

You a reader can be our best guide in making this book more interesting & user friendly.

We welcome your valuable suggestions.

Feedback about the book can be sent at **feedback@gullybaba.com.**

Publisher.

TOPICS COVERED

Block — 1	**Historical Context**	

Unit-1   Administrative System at the Advent of British Rule
Unit-2   Reforms in British Administration: 1858 to 1919
Unit-3   Administrative System under 1935 Act
Unit-4   British Administration: 1757-1858
Unit-5   Continuity and Change in Indian Administration: Post 1947

Block — 2   Central Administration

Unit-6   Constitutional Framework
Unit-7   Central Secretariat: Organisation and Functions
Unit-8   Prime Minister's Office and Cabinet Secretariat
Unit-9   Union Public Service Commission/Selection Commission
Unit-10   All India and Central Services
Unit-11   Planning Process

Block — 3   State Administration

Unit-12   Constitutional Profile of State Administration
Unit-13   State Secretariat: Organisation and Functions
Unit-14   Patterns of Relationship Between the Secretariat and Directorates
Unit-15   State Services and Public Service Commission

Block — 4   Field and Local Administration

Unit-16   Field Administration
Unit-17   District Collector
Unit-18   Police Administration
Unit-19   Municipal Administration
Unit-20   Panchayati Raj

INDIAN ADMINISTRATION

BPAE-102

For

Bachelor of Arts [BA]

Useful For

Delhi University (DU), IGNOU, Berhampur University (Odisha), University of Kashmir, Sambalpur University (Odisha), University of Kalyani (West Bengal), Gurukula Kangri Vishwavidyalaya (Uttarakhand), Himachal Pradesh University, Cooch Behar Panchanan Barma University (West Bengal), Ranchi University, University of Culcutta, Pune University, University of Mumbai, Andhra University, School of Open Learning (DU), Gondwana University (Maharashra), Babasaheb Bhimrao Ambedkar University (Lucknow), Dr. Babasaheb Ambedkar Marathwada University (Aurangabad), University of Madras, Netaji Subhas Open University (Kolkata), Odisha State Open University, all other Indian Universities.

Closer to Nature   We use Recycled Paper

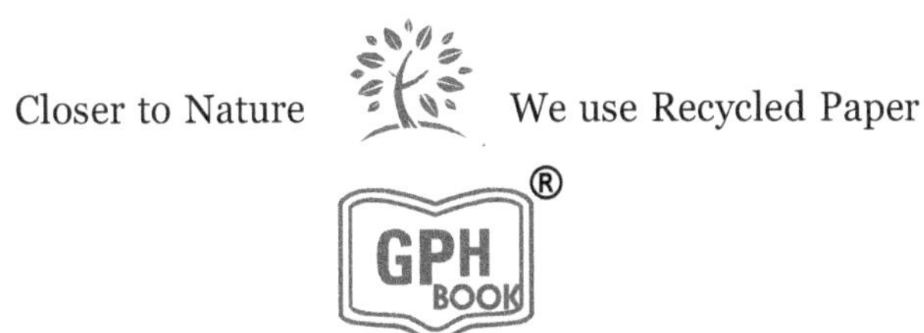

GULLYBABA PUBLISHING HOUSE PVT. LTD.
ISO 9001 & ISO 14001 CERTIFIED CO.

Published by:

GullyBaba Publishing House Pvt. Ltd.

Regd. Office:
2525/193, 1st Floor, Onkar Nagar-A,
Tri Nagar, Delhi-110035
(From Kanhaiya Nagar Metro Station Towards
Old Bus Stand)
Ph. 011-27387998, 27384836, 27385249

Branch Office:
1A/2A, 20, Hari Sadan,
Ansari Road, Daryaganj,
New Delhi-110002
Ph. 011-23289034
011-45794768

E-mail: hello@gullybaba.com, Website: GullyBaba.com

New Edition

Author: Gullybaba.Com Panel
ISBN: 978-93-81690-27-7
Copyright© with Publisher

FREE HOME DELIVERY of GPH Books

You can get GPH books by VPP/COD/Speed Post/Courier.
You can order books by Email/SMS/WhatsApp/Call.
For more details, visit gullybaba.com/faq-books.html

Contents

Question Papers

Historical Context

Q1. Discuss the features of Gupta administration.

Ans. The two hundred years of Gupta rule may be said to mark the climax of Hindu imperial tradition. From the point of view of literature, religion, art, architecture, commerce and colonial development, this period is undoubtedly the most important in Indian history. The Guptas inherited the administrative system of the earlier empires. The Mauryan bureaucracy, already converted into a caste, had functioned with impartial loyalty under succeeding empires. Under the Guptas we have direct allusions to viceroys, governors, administrators of provinces, and of course to ministers of the imperial government. The Mahamatri or provincial viceroys go back to the Mauryan period and continue, in fact, up to the twelfth century as the highest ranks in official bureaucracy. The position of Kumaramatyas, of whom many are mentioned, is not clear as we know of them in posts of varying importance. The gramikas or the village headmen formed the lowest rung in the ladder. Uparikas or governors were also appointed to provinces. In the Damodarpur plates, we have mentioned of an uparika named Arata Datta who was governing like police chief, controller of military stores, chief justice (Mahadanda Nayak), leave no doubt about the existence of an organised hierarchy of officials exercising imperial authority in different parts of the country.

1. Monarchs took high-sounding titles: The king assumes titles like Supreme Lord and Great King of Kings. The empire had a philosophy called imperialism but unfortunately, it only touched the social and cultural fields. It had no political objectives.

2. King was at the apex: Princes were often Viceroys. Queens were learned. Kumaradevi of Chandragupta I and Dhruvadevi of Chandragupta II, appear o the coins.

3. Council of Ministers were often hereditary: Harisena and Saba of Chandragupta II were military generals. Very often, ministers combined many offices. Some ministers accompanied the king to the battles. Chief Ministers headed the Ministry.

4. Central Government: Each department had its own seal. There were number of Mahasenapatis to watch over feudatories. The foreign ministers like Sandhi probably supervised the foreign policy towards the feudatory states.

5. Bureaucratic Organisation: The whole organisation was bureaucratic as in the case of Mauryas. To some extent, the administration mellowed with the Guptas. Police regulations were less severe. Capital punishment was rare.

Glowing tributes were paid to the Gupta administration by Fahien. There was no needless interference of the government in the lives of people. It was temperate in the repression of crime and tolerant in matters of religion.

Fahien could claim that he pursued his studies in peace wherever he chose to reside.

6. Provincial administration: Provinces were known as Bhuktis. Officers were very often of royal blood. They maintained law and order and protected people against external aggression. They also looked after public utility services. Bhuktis were divided into groups of districts called Pradeshas. Pradeshas were divided into Vishyas or districts. The head of the districts was Vishayapati. Probably, various officials assisted the provincial head.

Damdoar plate inscription mentions number of functionaries like chief banker, Chief Merchants, Chief Artisan, Chief of the writer class etc.

Whether they formed part of the non-official council of the districts or were elected is not known. Districts divided into number of villages. Being the last unit, villages looked after houses, streets, temples, and banks etc.

Each village had its own weavers, blacksmiths and goldsmiths, carpenters etc. A council called Panchamandali assisted village headman known as Gramika. Each village had its own seal. Towns looked after by Purapalas - town councils.

7. Payment of grants: A very revealing feature of the administration was the payment of grants in land instead of salaries. Only personnel of the military service were paid cash salaries. The grants in land were of two kinds. The agrahara grant was only to brahmins and it was tax-free. The second variety of land grant was given to secular officials either as salary or as reward for services. Both these practices were widely used as the time passed by. These grants definitely weakened the authority of the king.

Although technically the king could cancel the grants, he could not do so as the time passed by.

8. Not enough evidence on taxation: Officials on tour were provided free rice, curd, milk, flowers, transport, etc. Perhaps they were like modern day officials at the district level. Local people paid the expenses for apprehending criminals.

9. Three varieties of land: Wasteland belonging to State was donated very often. The crown land was rarely donated. The third was the private land.

Land revenue and various taxes were paid from the land and from various categories of produce at various stages of production.

10. Administration was highly decentralized: In Gupta administration, the authority was decentralised among Police, control of military stores, chief justice, etc. There was parallelism of power. It had highest concentration and extensive decentralisation. Such an administration required a good standing army and complicated system of checks and counter-checks.

Q2. Discuss the major characteristics of Mughal administration.

Ans. The legacy of the Mughal Empire lingers in the wide connotation of the word "Mughal" (Persian), or "Mogul" in the recent times. We crown the eminent, great personages with the aura of the title, "Moguls". Indeed, the Mughals were a magnificent breed of people. The Mughal Emperors are famous for the creation and management of one of the greatest empires, the Mughal empire, from the early sixteenth century to the mid-nineteenth century. They had set a glorious example of "unity in diversity". We wonder at their outstanding organisation of the teeming millions of the then India and the different warring states into one integrated whole. And even when the empire no longer exists today, physically, memories of Babur, Akbar, Shah Jahan, Aurangzeb will never fade into the darkness of oblivion.

The Mughal upheld the earlier traditions in political and administrative matters. The Mughal emperor was a perfect autocrat and the administration was 'a centralised autarchy'. The king symbolised the state and was the sources and centre of all power agencies. The Mughal did succeed in building up a 'monolithic administration.'

When compared to the Mauryas, the Mughals moved in the direction of greater centralisation. They did not pay much attention to social services of health and welfare as also morals which were areas of special concern for the Mauryan kings. But the Mughals had an efficient civil service. They recognised merit and accepted Hindu intelligentsia in the higher civil service. Its only drawback was that it was 'land-based'. It means it was mainly concerned with revenue functions and was a 'highly urbanised institutions.'

1. Role of the King: Administration was personalised. It has aptly been described as paternalistic. The entire administrative machinery revolved around the king who was viewed as a 'father figure' or a 'despot' by his people. Most of the time, the king was seen as a benevolent despot who worked for the welfare of his people. The theory upheld was that of absolute monarchy based on the divine right to rule. The king was everything to his people. He was the source of authority and the fountain-head of justice. The administrative system was highly centralised and personalised. Everything, therefore, depended on the character and person of the king. Hence, when Aurangzeb showed himself as a religious bigot and indulged in religious persecution of the worst kind, while indulging in endless wars in the South, central authority weakened, efficiency suffered and administration collapsed. Rajputs, Marathas, Jats, Sikhs and other local elements sought their independence and thus, forces of disintegration set into motion.

2. Bureaucracy: Organisation of the administrative machinery was unstable. It depended on the whims and fancies of the king. Recruitment was on the basis of caste, kin, heredity and personal loyalty to the king. Administration was based on fear of force. In the name of the king, the officials struck terror in the hearts of people. They wielded much awe and respect among the people. Officials were primarily engaged to maintain law and order, safeguard the interests of the king from internal uprisings and revolts, defend and extend the boundaries of the empire and collect revenue and other taxes.

Every officer of the State held a mansab or official appointment of rank and profit and was expected to supply a certain number of troops for the military service of the State. Hence, bureaucracy was essentially military in character. Officials or mansabdars were classified into 33 grades, ranging from Commanders of 10 to those of 10,000 soldiers. Each grade carried a definite rate of pay, out of which its holder had to provide a quota of horses, elephants, etc. State service was not by hereditary succession, nor was it specialised.

Officers received their salaries either in cash or through jagirs for a temporary period. The officers did not have ownership of lands in their jagirs, but only the right to collect the revenue equivalent to his salary. The jagir system provided scope for exploitation of the masses and gave undue power and independence to the holders of jagirs. These evils were difficult to check when the Emperor was weak.

3. Army: The army must be understood largely in terms of the Mansabdari system. In addition, there were the supplementary troopers and a special category of "gentlemen troopers" who were horsemen owing exclusive allegiance to the king. The army had cavalry which was the most important unit, the infantry, made up of townsmen and peasants and artillery with guns and navy.

The Mughal army was a mixture of diverse elements. As it grew in numbers, it became too heterogeneous to be manageable. The soldiers did not own direct allegiance to the Emperor but were more attached to their immediate recruiters or bosses and as such were busy with their bitter rivalries and jealousies. Above all, the pomp and splendour of the army proved to be its undoing. The army on the move was like a huge moving city, with all its paraphernalia of elephants, camels, harem, bazaars, workshops, etc. Soon indiscipline set in and the inevitable deterioration was fully manifest at the time of Jahangir. No longer capable of swift action, the Marathas, under Shivaji, could score over the Mughals in battles.

4. Police: In the rural areas, policing was undertaken by the village headman and his subordinate watchmen. This system continued well into the 19th century. In the cities and towns, police duties were entrusted to Kotwals. Among their many duties, Kotwals had to arrest burglars, undertake watch and ward duties, regulate prices and check weights and measures. They had to employ and supervise work of spies and make an inventory of property of deceased or missing persons. However, the Kotwal's main job was to preserve peace and public security in urban areas. In the districts, law and order functions were entrusted to Faujdars.

Q3. Explain the Mansabdari system.

Ans. Mansabdari system was a system of ranking introduced by Akbar, the Mughal emperor of India. The term is derived from Mansab, meaning 'rank'. Hence, Mansabdar literally means rank-holder. This system was introduced to strengthen the Army. Under this system, every officer was assigned a rank (mansab). The lowest rank was 10, and the highest was 5000 for the nobles. Princes of the blood received higher ranks. Towards the end of Akbar's reign, the highest rank a noble could attain was raised from 5000 to 7000.

Under the Mansabdari system contingents with nobles of mixed groups (Mughal, Pathan, Hindustani and Rajput) was the general rule. This rule was introduced to weaken tribalism and parochialism. The Mansabdari system, as it developed under the Mughals, was a distinctive and unique system, which did not have any parallel outside India. The system became the basis of Mughal military organisation and civil administration.

ZAT and SAWAR: The Mansabdars were differentiated by the Zat and the Sawar Rank. The Zat referred to the number of troops maintained by the mansabdar and the Sawar referred to the number of horses maintained by the mansabdar. It was dependent on whether the king ordered the mansabdar to maintain more horses than his rank. The categories are shown below:

-No. of Sawar = No. of Zat => 1st Class Mansabdar

-No. of Sawar = 1/2 the No. of Zat => 2nd Class Mansabdar

-No. of Sawar < 1/2 the No. of Zat => 3rd Class Mansabdar

A Mansabdar was in the service of the state and was bound to render service when asked. Additionally, they were graded on the number of armed cavalrymen, or sowars, which each had to maintain for service in the imperial army. Thus, all mansabdars had a zat, or personal ranking, and a sowar, or a troop ranking. All servants of the empire whether in the civil or military departments were graded in this system. There were thirty-three grades of mansabdars ranging from 'commanders of 10' to 'commanders of 10,000'. Till the middle of Akbar's reign, the highest rank an ordinary officer could hold was that of a commander of 5000; the more exalted grades between commanders of 7000 and 10,000 were reserved for the royal princes. During the period following the reign of Akbar, the grades were increased up to 20,000 or even more generally Rs. 20-25 per horse were paid to a mansabdar.

Appointment, promotion, suspension or dismissal of mansabdars rested entirely with the emperor. No portion of a mansabdar's property was hereditary, a mansabdar's children had to begin life anew. A mansabdar did not always begin at the lowest grade. The emperor, if satisfied, could and did grant higher or even the highest grade to any person. There was no distinction between civil and military departments. Both civil and military officers held mansabs and were liable to be transferred from one branch of the administration to another. Each mansabdar was expected to maintain prescribed number of horses, elephants, equipment, etc., according to his rank and dignity. These rules, though initially strictly enforced, were later slackened.

Senior mansabdars were awarded a jagir (personal fief) rather than a salary. Rates of remuneration, which included both the mansabdar's salary and so much per sowar, were matched by jagirs affording a similar aggregate yield. If their specified yield came to more, the surplus was due to the imperial treasury; if the jagirdar extracted more than the specified yield, he kept it.

Q4. Write a short note on following:
1. Mahalwari
2. Zamindari
3. Ryotwari

Ans. 1. Mahalwari System: This was the system in North India. There was zamindari system in Northern India. Their land and crops were inspected, their rights and customs were observed and then Taxes were charged. "Mahal" meant a village. So, this system became to be known as Mahalwari System. Mahal in British Revenue sources, it is a village or a group of Villages.

2. Zamindari System: In the Mughal Era, the Zamindari system was begun to ensure proper collection of taxes during a period when the power and influence of the Mughal emperors was in decline. With the Mughal conquest of Bengal, "zamindar" became a generic title embracing people with different kinds of landholdings, rights and responsibilities ranging from the autonomous or semi-independent chieftains to the peasant-proprietors. All categories of zamindars under the Mughals were required to perform certain police, judicial and military duties. Zamindars under the Mughals were, in fact, more the public functionaries than revenue collecting agents. Although Zamindari was allowed to be held hereditarily, the holders were not considered to be the proprietors of their estates.

The territorial zamindars had judicial powers. Naturally, judge-magistracy, as an element of state authority conferred status with attendant power, which really made them the lords of their domains. They held regular courts, called Zamindari adalat. The courts fetched them not only power and status but some income as well by way of fines, presents, and perquisites. The petty Zamindari also had some share in the dispensation of civil and criminal justice. The Chowdhurys, who were Zamindars in most cases, had authority to deal with the complaints of debts, thefts, and petty quarrels and to impose paltry fines.

3. Ryotwari System: The ryotwari system, instituted in some parts of British India, was one of the two main systems used to collect revenues from the cultivators of agricultural land. These revenues included undifferentiated land taxes and rents, collected simultaneously. Where the land revenue was imposed directly on the ryots — the individual cultivators who actually worked the land — the system of assessment was known as Ryotwari. Where the land revenue was imposed indirectly — through agreements made with Zamindars — the system of assessment was known as Zamindari. In Bombay, Madras, Assam and Burma, the Zamindar usually did not have a position as a middleman between the government and the farmer.

An official report by John Stuart Mill in 1857 explained the Ryotwari land tenure system as follows. As John Stuart Mill was himself working for the British East India Company, the following quote will see the system from the British perspective:

Under the Ryotwari System every registered holder of land is recognised as its proprietor, and pays direct to Government. He is at liberty to sublet his property, or to transfer it by gift, sale, or mortgage. He cannot be ejected by Government so long as he pays the fixed assessment, and has the option annually of increasing or diminishing his holding, or of entirely abandoning it. In unfavorable seasons remissions of assessment are granted for entire or partial loss of produce. The assessment is fixed in money, and does not vary from year to year, in those cases where water is drawn from a Government source of irrigation to convert dry land into wet, or into two-crop land, when an extra rent is paid to Government for the water so appropriated; nor is any addition made to the assessment for improvements effected at the Ryot's own expense. The Ryot under this system is virtually a Proprietor on a simple and perfect title, and has all the benefits of a perpetual lease without its responsibilities, in as much as he can at any time throw up his lands, but cannot be ejected so long as he pays his dues; he receives assistance in difficult seasons, and is irresponsible for the payment of his neighbours. The Annual Settlements under Ryotwari are often misunderstood, and it is necessary to explain that they are rendered necessary by the right accorded to the Ryot of diminishing or extending his cultivation from year to year. Their object is to determine how much of the assessment due on his holding the Ryot shall pay, and not to reassess the land. In these cases where no change occurs in the Ryots holding a fresh Potta or lease is not issued, and such parties are in no way affected by the Annual Settlement, which they are not required to attend.

The Ryotwari system is associated with the name of Sir Thomas Munro, who was appointed Governor of Madras in 1820. Subsequently, the Ryotwari system was extended to the Mumbai area. Munro gradually reduced the rate of taxation from one half to one third of the gross produce, even then an excessive tax. The levy was not based on actual revenues from the produce of the land, but instead on an estimate of the potential of the soil; in some cases more than 50% of the gross revenue was demanded.

In Northern India, Sir Edward Colebrook and successive Governor-Generals had implored the Court of Directors of the British East India Company, in vain, to redeem the pledge given by the British Government, and to permanently settle the land-tax, so as to make it possible for the people to accumulate wealth and improve their own condition.

Payment of the land tax in cash, rather than in kind, was instituted in the late 1700s when the British East India Company wanted to establish an exclusive monopoly in the market as buyers of Indian goods. Critics asserted that in practice the requirement of cash payments was ruinous to the cultivator, exposing him to the demands of moneylenders as an alternative to the loss of his land and starvation when crops failed. They also asserted that lean years resulted in regional famines, as the cultivators could not accumulate capital or invest in the productive development of their landholdings

Q5. Explain the structure of the Mughal administrative/judiciary system.
[June-07, Q.1]

Ans. The Central Government: First of all, it should be recognised that the Mughals drew heavily on the past, for the organisation of their government was on essentially the same lines as that of the sultanate. The principal officers of the central government were four: i) diwan; ii) mir bakhshi; iii) mir saman; and iv) sadr. The first of these dignitaries, the diwan, often called the wazir (the chief minister), was mainly concerned with revenue and finance, but as he had a say in all matters where any expenditure was involved, the work of other departments also came under his control. All the imperial orders were first recorded in his office before being issued, and the provincial governors, district faujdars, and leaders of expeditions came to him for instructions before assuming their duties. All the earning departments were under his direct control, and could spend only what was allotted to them by the diwan.

The mir bakhshi performed those duties which had been the responsibility of the ariz-i-mamalik during the earlier period. Owing to the organisation of the civil services on military lines, his power extended far beyond the war office, and some foreign travellers called him the lieutenant-general or the captain-general of the realm. The main departure from the sultanate was in respect to work relating to state karkhanas, stores, ordinance, and communications, now so important that the dignitary dealing with it, called the mir saman, ranked as an important minister often senior in rank to the sadr. The sadr (or, more fully, sadr-i-jahan) was, as in the earlier period, director of the religious matters, charities, and endowments.

Occasionally a higher dignitary, superior to the wazir and other ministers, was also appointed. He was called the vakil, and functioned like the naib (deputy) of the sultanate period. This appointment, as under the sultanate, was sporadic, depending on the wish of the monarch and the requirements of the situation. During the reigns of Akbar, Jahangir, and Shah Jahan, a period of ninety-seven years (1560–1657), there were ten vakils whose terms of service totaled about thirty-nine years. Ibn Hasan, the author of the Central Structure of the Mughal Empire, argues that the post was primarily for show and honor, with the vakil as the head of the nobility but not of the administration. To a large extent this is true, and normally the vakil was less effective than the wazir, who controlled the purse, but theoretically the vakil was the king's deputy and even the wazir referred to him whatever was "beyond his own ability." Abul Fazl calls him "the emperor's lieutenant in all matters connected with the realm and the household," adding that "although the financial offices are not under his immediate superintendence, yet he receives the returns from heads of all financial offices and wisely keeps abstracts of their return."

The splendor and stability of the Mughal rule was due to a succession of very capable rulers who attempted to build up an efficient administrative system, choosing their principal officers on the basis of merit. The most famous diwan under Akbar was Raja Todar Mal, who for a time acted as the chief minister of the realm, but the contribution of Khwaja Mansur and Mir Fathulla Shirazi to the building up of Akbar's revenue administration was perhaps equally great. Under Jahangir, Itimad-ud-Daula, the father of Nur Jahan, who was a diwan even before his daughter married the emperor, remained the chief wazir and diwan until his death. He was succeeded by his son, Asaf Khan, who became the vakil just before the death of Jahangir. Itimad-ud-Daula and Asaf Khan were able, efficient officers. Asaf Khan maintained his position until his death, but his successors were selected on the basis of their scholarship and technical efficiency. Allami Afzal Khan remained Shah Jahan's diwan for ten years, and the office was held from the nineteenth to the thirtieth years of Shah Jahan's reign by the celebrated Saadulla Khan who, like his predecessor, had won his post because of his learning, wisdom, and resourcefulness.

The diwan, who can perhaps be called the finance minister, had under him two principal officers, called diwan-i-tan and diwan-i-khalsa, who were in charge of salaries and state lands respectively. It is interesting that all the assistants of the diwan-i-khalsa under Shah Jahan's reign were Hindus, and five out of the seven under the diwan-i-tan belonged to the same community. Raja Raghunath Rai, who had been diwan-i-khalsa for some years, became sole diwan in the thirty-first year of Shah Jahan's reign, and maintained this position until his death, during the reign of Aurangzeb. Aurangzeb's principal wazir, who held office for thirty-one years, was Asad Khan, originally his mir bakhshi. Next to him, the most famous mir bakhshi of the Mughal period was Shaikh Farid, who played a decisive role in the enthronement of Jahangir.

The organisation of public services was perfected during Akbar's reign, and was based on the mansabdari system, borrowed originally from Persia. Every important officer of state held a mansab or an official appointment of rank and emoluments, and, as members of an imperial cadre, were liable for service anywhere in the empire. In 1573–74 Akbar classified the office holders in thirty-three grades, ranging from commanders of ten to commanders of ten thousand. The principal categories of Mughal mansabdars, however, were three: those in command of ten to four hundred were commonly styled mansabdars (officers); those in command of five hundred to twenty-five hundred were amirs (nobles); and those in higher ranks belonged to the category of umara-i-kabir or umara-i-azim (grandees). The highest amir in the third category was honored with the title of amir-ul-umara. In the eighteenth century this title was usually given to the mir bakhshi. Until the middle of Akbar's reign, the highest rank which any ordinary officer could hold was that of a commander of five thousand; the more exalted grades between commanders of seven thousand and ten thousand were reserved for princes of royal blood. Toward the end of his reign and under his successors these limits were relaxed. Originally each grade carried a definite rate of pay, out of which the holders were required to maintain a quota of horses, elephants, beasts of burden, and carts. But even in Akbar's days and in spite of safeguards introduced by him, the number of men actually supplied by the mansabdars rarely corresponded to the number indicated by his rank, and under Akbar's successors greater latitude was allowed. The mansabdars were paid either in cash or by temporary grant of jagirs. Theoretically, the mansabdars received enormous salaries, which appear all the more excessive when it is realised that they did not normally maintain all the troops expected of them. It was probably an awareness of this that led Shah Jahan to introduce the practice of paying salaries to the mansabdars for only four months of the year instead of twelve, the implication being that the actual income for part of the year was equivalent to what the emperor had originally intended for the whole year. Even with this reduction, the mansabdars lived extravagantly. The tendency to luxurious expenditure was undoubtedly heightened by the mansabdar's knowledge that on his death, his whole property would be taken over by the state, pending satisfaction of any outstanding claims by the treasury. But while there may have been little incentive to save within the system, the high scale of salaries enabled the state to attract the ablest and most ambitious individuals from almost the whole of southern and western Asia.

Appointment to the ranks of mansabdars was made by the emperor, usually on the recommendation of military leaders, provincial governors, or court officials. In addition to the mansabdars, there was a class known as ahadis, who though holding no official rank, were employed in posts in the palace. They were usually young men of good families, who were not fortunate enough to secure a mansab on their first application. Given an opportunity to show their worth, they could then be promoted to the ranks of mansabdars. These mansabdars have been compared to the Civil Service during British rule in that they formed an all-India cadre of officials, liable to transfer anywhere in the empire and providing the personnel for all major offices. The existence of a single imperial cadre undoubtedly gave a cohesion and unity to the Mughal empire that was lacking during the sultanate.

Provincial Administration: Provincial administration was greatly improved under Akbar, and in this respect the Mughal period differs substantially from the Sultanate. The boundaries of the provincial units were more definitely fixed; and a uniform administrative pattern, with minor modifications to suit local conditions, was developed for all parts of the empire. Further, drawing upon the experiments introduced by Sher Shah, the provincial administration was strengthened, and each province was provided with a set of officials representing all branches of state activity. By the introduction of a cadre of mansabdars, liable to be transferred anywhere at the behest of the central government and by the introduction of other checks, the control over the provinces was made more effective.

The principal officer was the governor, called sipah salar under Akbar and nazim under his successors, but popularly known as subahdar and later only as subah. Next to him in official rank, but not in any way under his control, was the provincial diwan, who was in independent charge of the revenues of the province. He was usually a mansabdar of much lower status than the governor, but he was independent of the governor's control and was directly under the imperial diwan.

The next provincial functionary was the bakhshi, or the paymaster. He performed a number of duties, including, occasionally, the functions of the provincial newswriter. The diwan-i-buyutat was the provincial representative of the khan-i-saman, and looked after roads and government buildings, supervised imperial stores, and ran state workshops. The sadr and the qazi were entrusted with religious, educational, and judicial duties.

The faujdar and the kotwal were the two other important provincial officials. The faujdar, who was the administrative head of the sarkar (district), was appointed by the emperor but was under the supervision and guidance of the governor. The kotwals were not provincial officers, but were appointed by the central government in the provincial capitals and other important cities, and performed a number of executive and ministerial duties similar to the Police Commissioners during British rule in Bombay, Calcutta, and Madras. The ports were in charge of the mir bahr, corresponding to the modern Port Commissioner, but with powers over customs also.

The Mughals interfered very little with the local life of the village communities, for they had no resident functionary of their own in the villages. The muqaddam was normally the sarpanch (head of the village panchayat, or council) and these panchayats continued to deal with local disputes, arrange for watch and ward, and perform many functions now entrusted to the local bodies.

Finances: The tax structure of the Mughal empire was relatively simple in its theoretical formulation, however much it was complicated by changing needs and local circumstances. Both revenue and expenditure were divided between the central and the provincial government. The central government reserved for itself land revenue, customs, profits from the mints, inheritance rights, and monopolies. Land revenue was the most important source of income, as it has been throughout Indian history, and more than doubled in value between the reigns of Akbar and Shah Jahan. The principal items of expenditure for the central government were defense, the general civil administration of the empire (including the religious organisations), maintenance of the court and the royal palace, and the cost of buildings and other public works. The provincial sources of income were the assignments of land revenue granted to the provincial governor and his officials as a remuneration for their services, a variety of local taxes and cesses, transit dues and duties, and fines and presents.

The Mughal revenue system was based on the division of the empire into subas or governorships, sarkars or districts, and parganas, consisting of number of villages which were sometimes styled mahals. (These were replaced during British rule by the somewhat large tehsils or talukas.) The revenue staff had also to perform miscellaneous administrative duties, including the keeping of the public peace, and recruitment of the military forces. The suba was modeled after the central imperial structure. The sarkar was in the charge of the faujdar, or military commander, who combined the functions of the modern district magistrate and superintendent of police. The revenue work in the sarkar was looked after by the amalguzar, who would correspond to the modern afsar-i-mal (revenue officer).

The levy of land revenue was based on survey settlements calculated after a detailed measurement and classification of the cultivated areas. The nature of the crops grown and the mean prevailing market prices were also taken into consideration in fixing the final assessment. This assessment system, evolved after many experiments, became the basis of the survey settlement of the British period. Akbar's revenue system in most areas was raiyatwari, the revenue being collected directly as far as possible from the individual cultivator, and was payable in cash. Akbar introduced the system in the greater part of northern India, and during the viceroyalty of Aurangzeb, it was extended to the Deccan. The revenue system as evolved under Akbar was thoroughly sound, but the government demand was heavy and amounted to one-third of the produce. Abul Fazl tried to justify it by referring to the abolition of many miscellaneous cesses and taxes, but it is not certain whether all the cesses abolished by royal order were given up by subordinate officials. In the settlement of the Deccan during Aurangzeb's viceroyalty, the state share was reduced to one-fourth.

Mughal emperors, particularly Akbar and Aurangzeb, continued to make cautious experiments and improvements in the land-revenue system. The basic data was collected by detailed measurement of land and assessment of the yield and estimates of productivity of each pargana or assessment area. When sufficient data had been collected the system of group assessment was introduced, with the alternatives of measurement and sharing being held in reserve.

That the Mughal rulers wanted the revenue system to operate fairly is evident from the guidance to collectors of revenue given in the Ain-i-Akbari. "The Collector was directed to be the friend of the agriculturist; to give remissions in order to stimulate cultivation to grant every facility to the raiyat, and never to charge him on more than the actual area under tillage; to receive the assessment direct from the cultivator and so avoid intermediaries; to recover arrears without undue force; and to submit a monthly statement describing the condition of the people, the state of public security, the range of market prices and rents, the conditions of the poor and all other contingencies.

The specifications were high—at least on paper, but anyone who studies the procedure for giving relief to the raiyats in case of hardships, the general instructions to the collectors, and the details of the assessment system and mode of recovery is bound to be struck by the professional competence of men like Todar Mal, Shah Mansur, and Amir Fathullah Shirazi, as well as the statesman like benevolence motivating the state's basic policy. The British paid special attention to revenue administration, and introduced many significant improvements, but it can be said without injustice that on certain points the Mughal system compared favorably with the one that evolved over a long period in British India. As an example, one may take the assessment of lands newly brought under cultivation or reclaimed after having fallen out of cultivation. A variety of scales of assessment was applied to such lands, such as a low initial rate, rising to the full amount after five years. The collector was also able to vary the revenue demands to encourage wasteland being cultivated. Regulations under the British were neither so liberal nor so flexible for this particular kind of cultivation.

Another important difference between the British and the Mughal systems was the position of the village accountant, or patwari. Throughout the Mughal period the patwari, who was responsible for the maintenance of the financial records, was an employee of the village, not of the revenue administration. Under the British system, however, he became an employee of the government. This altered his relationship to the people, because previously he had been an agent for the people, but now he became an instrument of government. This was one factor that led to the weakening of village autonomy.

The Mughal theory and practice of revenue administration must be seen as the essential elements underlying the later administrative structure of India. The great memorial to Mughal rule is not so much the great architectural monuments that fill the subcontinent, but the governments of the great successor states, India and Pakistan, which following the model of the period of British rule, have maintained an administrative pattern that derives from the Mughals. "The District system with the district officer as head of the public services and general factotum or Poo Bah, the erection of an administrative hierarchy upon the basis of land revenue collection, and the development of an involute maze of office procedure, these features of Mughal rule were all accepted as the foundation of British rule; and, indeed, to an astonishing degree, in India and Pakistan today local administration is Mughal in spirit."

Military Organization: The weakest part of Mughal administration was the military organisation, precisely the area where one might have expected the most efficient centralised control. But instead of a large standing army, the emperors depended upon four different classes of troops for the maintenance of order and the defense of the empire's borders. There were, first of all, the soldiers supplied by the mansabdars; the number a mansabdar was expected to provide upon the demand of the emperor were specified in his warrant of appointment or were indicated by his rank. Another class of troops under the command of a mansabdar was known as dakhili, whose services were paid for by the state. A third class were the ahadis, or "gentlemen troopers," drawing higher pay than those in the ordinary service; according to the Ain-i-Akbari, they might get as much as five hundred rupees a month, in contrast to the seven or eight rupees of the regular troopers. Finally, the chiefs who had been permitted to retain a degree of autonomy were required to provide contingents under their own command.

The artillery was paid wholly out of the imperial treasury. Recognising its importance, Akbar had given it his special attention, but his efforts to secure from the Portuguese some of their better pieces were unsuccessful. European gunners were employed later on in appreciable numbers, but no permanent improvement was effected. During the eighteenth century the Mughal army shared in the decline of the other imperial institutions, and little advantage was taken of technical improvements in weaponry. When Nadir Shah invaded India in 1739 the jazair or swivel guns employed by his troops were superior to anything the Mughals could bring against them.

There are no existing statistical records of the strength of the Mughal army. The best estimate is probably that of Sir Jadunath Sarkar, who concluded from evidence from the reign of Shah Jahan that in 1648 the army consisted of 440,000 infantry, musketeers, and artillery men, and 185,000 cavalry commanded by princes and nobles. The army could still count on the personal valor of the commander of an individual contingent, but pitted against disciplined European soldiers, or hardy, resourceful Maratha horsemen, it did not prove effective. The loose organisation of the army, the paucity of officers, the failure to build up a well-knit and active pyramidical organisation, reduced the efficiency of the army. There were no uniforms, and discipline was poor, particularly in lower ranks. The cavalry was the only branch which was considered respectable and fit for a gentleman to join, while the ordinary "Indian foot soldier was little more than a night watchman and guardian over baggage." The Mughal practice of taking along a great number of camp followers, including occasionally the families of the soldiers and the royal harem, made the army a very cumbersome, slow-moving organisation.

Descendants of a people who knew nothing of the sea, the Mughals had little success in creating a navy. They had no large fighting vessels, and the ships that they maintained were primarily for the furtherance of the commercial operations of the state. After the conquest of Gujarat, the Mughal army reached the shores of the Indian Ocean, but Akbar failed to build a navy. He tacitly acquiesced in the Portuguese supremacy by making no effort to challenge their authority, and by taking out licenses from them for the ships which he sent to the Red Sea. To deal with the pirates in the Bay of Bengal, and also for the purpose of communication over the vast river system of Bengal, a river flotilla was maintained at Dacca. Under Akbar it consisted of 768 small armed vessels and boats, estimated to cost about 29,000 rupees a month. It was not effective against the Magh and Portuguese pirates, but it was reorganised under the efficient administration of Mir Jumla and Shayista Khan, and in 1664 the latter was able to inflict a decisive blow against the pirates.

A few years later Aurangzeb had an opportunity to make at least tentative arrangements for the defense of the seas along the west coast of India. A coastal chieftain known as the Sidi of Janjira had provided protection for the ships and ports of the sultan of Bijapur. When the Sidi's territories were attacked by Shivaji, however, the sultan did not come to his assistance, and in 1670 the Sidi offered his services to Aurangzeb. Since Aurangzeb needed all the help he could get in the Deccan, he took the Sidi into his service, placing him under the Mughal governor of Surat, and subsidising his fleet. The Sidi was assisted by another fleet based on Surat, and in every way treated as an official of the empire, but the Mughal command of the sea was too slight to make supervision of so independent a force possible. In course of time his descendants established themselves as the rulers of the state of Janjira south of Bombay.

THE JUDICIARY: The judicial system of the Mughals was very similar to that of the sultanate. It became more systematic, particularly under Aurangzeb, but as compared with the judicial structure of British India, it was very simple, being based on a different approach to many categories of disputes. Normally no lawyers were allowed to appear. The disputes were speedily settled, often on the basis of equity and natural justice, though of course in the case of Muslims, the injunctions and precedents of Islamic law applied where they existed. Many crimes—including murder—were treated as individual grievances rather than crimes against society. The complaints in such cases were initiated by the individuals aggrieved, rather than by the police, and could be compounded on payment of compensation. The aim of the judicial system was primarily to settle individual complaints and disputes rather than to enforce a legal code, as is indicated by the fact that the criminal court was normally known as the diwan-i-mazalim, the court of complaints.

All foreign travellers have commented on the speedy justice of the Mughal courts and the comparatively few cases coming before them. The latter was partly due to the general prejudice against litigation, but even more to the fact that a large number of disputes, particularly those affecting the Hindus, were settled by the village and caste panchayats, and did not come before the official courts. The Hindus were not debarred from taking cases before the qazi or the governor—and frequently did so where other arrangements did not prove effective—but normally they had their own arrangements for settling their disputes. Badauni has recorded that according to Akbar's orders the cases of Hindus were to be decided by the Hindu judges and not by the qazis. The Jesuit Father Monserrate says that "Brachmane (Brahmans) governed liberally through a senate and a council of the common people" —referring presumably to the administration of justice by these agencies. Local usage and custom ruled in most rural areas, and, according to one estimate, perhaps not one person out of a hundred in the Punjab, for example, was governed by the provisions of either the classic Hindu or Muslim law.

The judicial courts provided by the Mughals were principally of two types—

secular and ecclesiastical. Except during the reign of Aurangzeb, the principal courts for settlement of disputes were presided over by the emperor, the governors, and other executive officers. Akbar used to spend several hours of the day disposing of judicial cases, and governors followed the same procedure in the provinces. In the Ain-i-Akbari, we find the instructions issued to a governor detailing the judicial procedure he should follow.

Apart from the secular courts and the panchayats, the principal agency for the settlement of disputes was the qazis' court. The qazi, being the repository of Muslim law, attended the hearing of cases by the executive authority, whether governor, faujdar or kotwal, and assisted the latter in arriving at a decision consonant with Quaranic precepts. Presumably the civil disputes of Muslims were, as a rule, left to the qazis to be settled according to the canon law. When both parties in a dispute were Hindus, the point at issue was referred to Hindu pandits for an opinion. This principle was supported by the Fatawa-i-Alamgiri, the authoritative digest of Islamic law, where it is held that "Dhimmis ... do not subject themselves to the laws of Islam either with respect to things which are merely of religious nature, such as fasting or prayer, or with respect to such temporal acts, as though contrary to [Islam], may be legal by their own, such as sale of wine or of swine's flesh, because we [Muslim jurists] have been commanded to leave them at liberty in all things, which may be deemed by them to be proper according to the precepts of their own religion." These provisions presumably related to religious matters. In the case of Muslims, the secular types of criminal suits went to the kotwal, while the religious and civil cases, such as concerning inheritance, marriage, divorce, and civil disputes went to the qazis' courts.

The death penalty normally had to be confirmed by the emperor, but there seem to have been departures from the rule. A Dutch resident of India states that fines represented the normal mode of settling all disputes in Mughal India. Capital punishments and mutilations were frequent, and there are records of impaling, dismemberment, and other cruel punishments. They were, however, limited in their incidence and were inflicted only under the royal orders. Furthermore, they were confined to those cases where an example was to be made of the individual concerned. Imprisonment was not a method of punishment that appealed to the Mughals. It was seldom used as a sentence in private cases, though it was sometimes resorted to for preventive purposes. Whipping was commonly used. The Muslim punishment of parading the offender in an ignominious condition seems to have been frequently used, as it coincided with the Hindu tradition as well.

The assessments made by two acute British observers on Mughal government as they saw it in a period of decline may serve as summary of the Mughal achievement as administrators. Luke Scrafton, who was resident for the East

India Company at the capital of Bengal in 1758, declared that until the invasion of Nadir Shah in 1739 "there was scarce a better administered government in the world. The manufactures, commerce, and agriculture flourished exceedingly; and none felt the hand of the oppression but those who were dangerous by their wealth or power." Mughal government was despotic, and official corruption increased from the reign of Jahangir, but on the whole, the judgment of the English historian, Sidney Owen seems just: "Whatever its defects, it was ... a grandly conceived, well-adjusted, and beneficent structure of government. ... Taxation was light; and its most productive source, the land revenue, was moderately assessed, and equitably adjusted. Foreign commerce was protected and favoured; and the English East India Company throve, and multiplied its factories, under the shadow of the Imperial authority. The judicial system, though what we should consider crude and capricious, as well as too often corruptly exercised, was not liable like our own to the tedious delays which have been its reproach, and which have so much tended to obstruct, and even defeat, the course of justice. And the right of appealing to the Emperor from inferior tribunals, though too generally a futile privilege, was sometimes really remedial, and probably was a standing check to judicial iniquity. Much the same may be said as to the provincial Governors."

Q6. Explain the Regulating Act of 1773.

Ans. By 1773, East India Company of Britain was facing terrible financial straits. The company had a great significance to Britain as it was doing monopoly business in India and east and many influential people of Britain were attached with the company as shareholders. The company paid four hundred thousand pounds annually to British Government so that their monopoly was maintained. But the time came when the company was unable to meet its commitments to the government because of the loss of tea sales to America since the year 1768. About eighty five percent of the tea sold to America was smuggled tea from Holland. The East India Company owed money both to the Government and Bank of England. Fifteen million lbs of tea was being wasted in the British warehouse and more tea was on the way from India. There were also some other reasons behind the decision of undertaking Regulating Act of 1773.

The conditions that persisted on the region of Bengal, Bihar and Orissa reflected the irresponsibility of the East India Company since it acquired the Diwani and the Nizamat. After these incidences British Parliament was convinced of the incompetence of the Company in any given circumstances and settled to undertake the Regulating Act. The conditions can be narrated in a more detailed way-

• After the battles of Plassey (1757) and Buxar (1764), Company won over

Diwani and Nizamat and established its military domination in Bengal, Bihar and Orissa. These areas were acquired without any proper law for the greed for wealth of company's employees. The company's servants were totally corrupted and exploited the common people so that they could gather much wealth in order to return quickly to England. After returning to England, the Employees of East India Company took part in politics and bought the seats in the House of Commons with the huge wealth they had accumulated in India. They also purchased the share of the company and tried to become influential in political world. This uncouth display of wealth caused them to earn the nickname 'Nabobs'.

• The British Rulers realised that East India Company was gradually becoming the source of political and territorial power instead of being a mere commercial farm. The British politicians understood that it should not be wise to leave the East India Company beyond any Parliamentary control. It was becoming more dangerous as the members of the Company had no training or experience in handling Politics as they were specialised in commerce. This was supported by the mess they created in the Bengal and its surrounding region. Thus, public opinion in England was in the favor of interference of British Parliament in company's affair.

• As a consequence of this corruption, company's servants were getting more affluent while East India Company itself was suffering from monitory loss. The directors of the Company voted for increased profits to shareholders but the Company had to borrow a loan from the British Parliament to meet the increasing demand for Company shares. The company was already committed to pay the British Treasury four hundred thousand pounds annually as 'Share in the Indian Spoil'. The incidence of Bengal famine and other things already reached the British Parliament and granting the loan was difficult without supporting the requirement of the loan with proper reason.

• The House of Commons appointed a Select Committee and a Secret Committee to investigate and report the deficiencies in the Management of East Indian Company in the Indian region. The report was condemning in all the aspects and it became obvious that company could no longer be an independent body and must be subdued to the parliament.

Lord North decided to overtake the management of the East India Company with the Regulating Act. This was the first incidence of British Government interference in India. The Act set up such a system that the Government supervised or regulated East India Company but did not undertake the whole power.

The East India Company was basically a trading farm that made business over a vast area of India but also maintained an army to protect its interests. North decided to start Governmental control, as East India Company had no experience in ruling and it conquered few areas. East India Company had a very powerful lobby in Parliament in spite of the financial crises of the Company. The Shareholders along with this lobby of Parliament opposed the act.

However, British Parliament passed the Regulating act of 1773. The Government at Calcutta was reorganised and Supreme Court was established in Calcutta. The Regulating Act of 1773 was the first instance where Parliamentary Acts deviated from its royal charters. The Regulating Act, 1773 might have various defects but it was the turning point in the constitutional history of India as it protested against the putrefaction of East India Company.

The Regulating Act, 1773 said that:

1. The Government of the presidency of Fort William in Bengal should have a Governor General and a Council, which consists of four councilors with the general democratic rule that the Governor General would consider decision of the majority of the councilors.

2. Warren Hastings shall be the first Governor General and Lt. General John Clavering, George Monson, Richard Barwell, and Philip Francis shall be the first four Councilors.

3. His Majesty shall establish a supreme court of judiciary, which would have a Chief Justice and three subordinate judges at Fort William. The Court's jurisdiction shall be applied to all British subjects residing in the subdivision of Bengal and to their native servants.

4. The Company shall pay the salaries to the designated persons out of its revenue in the rate of : the Governor General twenty five thousand sterling, Councilors ten thousand sterling each, Chief Justice eight thousand sterling and the judges six thousand sterling a year.

The fifth, sixth and seventh sections of the act state that: The Governor General, Councilors, Judges, Persons from military and civil establishments, collectors and other district officials are refrained from taking gifts, present or reward and any monetary advantages from the Indian kings, princes, zamindars or any other native subjects.

The provision of the Regulating Act of 1773 clearly indicates that it was enacted to stop the malpractice of law and to control corruption among Company officials. However, it failed to stop the corruption and degeneracy became a common practice for all officials, from the top level to the lowest subordinate. The major charges were brought against the first Governor General, Warren Hastings and he was impeached in the trial for corruption. Infact, the whole council was divided into two factions based on the corruptions- the Hastings Group and the Francis Group. They fought against each other on the issues of corruption charges alleged on them. Consequently, Pitt's India act, 1784 was passed to prevent corruption and an uncorrupted person, Lord Cornwallis, was appointed in order to bring a corruption free environment in the company.

Q7. Discuss the features of Pitt's India Act 1784.

Ans. After the Regulating Act of 1773 to regulate the affairs of the Company in India, the second important step taken by the British Parliament was the appointment of a Board of Control under Pitt's India Bill of 1784. It provided for a joint government of the Company (represented by the Directors), and the Crown (represented by the Board of Control).

A Board of six members was constituted with two members of the British Cabinet and four of the Privy Council. One of them was the President and who soon became, in effect, the minister for the affairs of the East India Company. The Board had all the powers and control over all the acts and operations, which related to the civil, military and revenues of the Company.

Lord Cornwallis

The Council was reduced to three members and the Governor General was empowered to overrule the majority. The Governors of Bombay and Madras were also deprived of their independent powers. Calcutta was given greater powers in matters of war, revenue, and diplomacy, thus becoming in effect the capital of Company possessions in India.

By a supplementary the Bill passed in 1786 Lord Cornwallis was appointed as the first Governor General, and he then became the effective ruler of British India under the authority of the Board of Control and the Court of Directors. The constitution set up by the Pitt's India Act did not undergo any major changes during the existence of the Company's rule in India.

The Charter Act of 1813 abolished the trading activities of the Company and henceforth became purely an administrative body under the Crown. Thereafter, with few exceptions, the Governor General and the Council could make all the laws and regulations for people (Indians and British).

The salient features relating to the governance of the kingdom of Bengal were:

1. There shall be a Board of Control consisting of maximum six parliamentarians headed by a senior cabinet member to direct, superintend and control the affairs of the company's territorial possessions in the East Indies.

2. The Court of Directors shall establish a Secret Committee to work as a link between the Board and the Court.

3. The Governor General's council shall consist of three members one of whom shall be the commander-in-chief of the King's army in India. In case the members present in a meeting of the council shall any time be equally divided in opinion, the Governor General shall have two votes (one his own and another casting vote).

4. The government must stop further experiments in the revenue administration and proceed to make a permanent settlement with zamindars at moderate rate of revenue demand. The government must establish permanent judicial and administrative systems for the governance of the new kingdom.

5. All civilians and military officers must provide the Court of Directors a full inventory of their property in India and in Britain within two months of their joining their posts.

6. Severe punishment including confiscation of property, dismissal and jail, shall be inflicted on any civilian or military officer found guilty of corruption.

7. Receiving gifts, rewards, presents in kind or cash from the rajas, zamindars and other Indians are strictly prohibited and people found guilty of these offences shall be tried charged with corruption.

Parliament directly appointed Lord Charles cornwallis to implement the Act. Immediately after his joining as Governor General in 1786, Cornwallis embarked upon the responsibility of reform works reposed on him by parliament. In 1793 he completed his mission. He introduced permanent settlement, announced a judicial code, established administrative and police systems and then left for home in the same year.

Q8. Describe the functions of board of Revenue.

Ans. British administration in its initial stages had a number of Provincial Revenue Councils at work and above them was a Secretariat at Calcutta. These Provincial Revenue Councils came to be replaced by a Board of Revenue which came to assume tremendous importance both in revenue collection and general administration for nearly 140 years. The jurisdiction of the Board extended to the whole field of revenue administration including settlement, collection and receipt of public revenues.

In 1788, Cornwallis revised the constitution to the Board of Revenue. The Board was concerned with the deliberation, superintendence and control. The details of management of revenue were left to Collectors who were responsible to the Board. In the exercise of its powers, the Board could summon any officer to explain his conduct, fine him or even suspend him with the final consent of Government.

The Collectors became very important because they supplied, in the first instance, all the data on the basis of which the Board's report to Government would be prepared. Once decisions were taken and instructions issued, the execution of details was left to the Collectors who with the discretionary power they wielded, became supreme in district administration.

Two more reforms were affected in the Board of Revenue on the recommendations of John shore in 1788. They sought to affect the total control of revenue administration by the covenanted civil servants.

In 1970, a regulation was passed which empowered the Board to Act as a Court of review as well as appeal in all revenue cases. In the same year the Governor General in Council, constituted the Board of Revenue into a Court of Wards. This was to bring under the Board, the affairs of all such estates as belonged to females, minors, idiots, lunatics and persons of doubtful character. From time to time, regulations, were issued to guide the Board in this activity. Subsequently, Divisional Commissioners came to be appointed.

In the history of the Board of Revenue from 1786, one sees two main developments – one jurisdictional and the other functional in character. Jurisdictionally, the extent of territories under its control increased progressively till 1807, when it covered Bengal, Bihar, Orissa, Banaras as well as the conquered Provinces. It was followed by a process of decentralisation which has first marked by the establishment of the Board of Commissioners for the ceded and conquered Provinces. This process continued until two district Boards of revenue came to be established in 1831 with a number of Commissioners of Revenue to take care of local supervision.

Functionally, the controlling and supervisory character of the Board of Revenue remained unchanged. As for judicial powers, the Cornwallis principle (which favoured separation of judicial from revenue work) was reversed. This was necessitated by the exigencies of periodical assessment in the ceded and conquered Provinces where frequent judicial matters came up.

A third development was the tendency of the government to reduce the number of Board members or to vest in a single member, the powers and authority exercised by the Board as a whole. This was done for the sake of speedy conduct of business, economy, and the want of trained men.

Q9. Discuss about the administration of criminal justice and police in India under the British rule.

Ans. The Mughal administration of criminal Justice and Police was based on Quranic law which was applied to Muslims and non-Muslims alike. With the collapse of the Mughal Central authority, there was a breakdown of the law and order machinery. Zamindars, farmers and other agents of revenue took over control though they did not have the right to do so. However, they prevented a situation of anarchy.

Hastings had the following four objectives when he sought to improve criminal administration:

1) To reconstitute the criminal courts.

2) To establish an efficient machinery of supervision and control.

3) To offset the inadequacies of Muslim criminal law.

4) To restore power of Faujdars.

Hastings, as per his plan in 1772, had a criminal court in each district and a superior court of criminal jurisdiction at Murshidabad. The Collector had to exercise supervision and control and keep an eye on judicial proceedings.

In 1781, the Governor General and Council abolished the office of Faujdars and transferred their duties to the Company's covenanted servants acting primarily as judges of the Courts of diwani adalat. They were designated as Magistrates. In 1787, on orders from the Directors, Cornwallis united in the office of Collector, the duties of Magistrate and Civil judge. In addition, he conferred on the magistracy, part of the authority exercised by the criminal courts themselves. Though contrary to Islamic jurisprudence, police and judicial functions were for the first time united in the officer of the Magistrate on a general plan.

Cornwallis wanted the authority of the Magistrate to be more effective and complete. But the administration of criminal justice remained practically unaltered. It was still outside the sphere of the Company's responsibility.

Cornwallis Europeanised and functionalised the Civil Service. He did not have faith and trust in Indians especially in the administration of Criminal justice. He set up four courts of circuit, one for each of the four divisions of Calcutta, Murshidabad, Dacca and Patna in place of the *darogas* of criminal courts. Each of these courts of circuit was under two covenanted civil servants who were designated Judges of the Court of Circuit. They were assisted by a qazi and a mufti as law officers. The police duties of the Magistrate continued. He was to apprehend criminals and peace breakers and have them tried before the Judges of Circuit.

Cornwallis introduced measures to reform the administration of police in 1792. These had three features:

1) Landholders and farmers who maintained *thanedars* and *chowkidars* were divested of their entire police authority.

2) Districts were divided into *thanas* or police jurisdictions. At the head of each was an officer of Government called *daroga* of police.

3) Duty of rural police like *chowkidars* and others was to assist the *daroga* in the apprehension of criminals and to undertake intelligence work.

In his police reforms of 1792, Cornwallis had been guided by administrative and political considerations.

Administratively, police administration at the hands of the zamindars was unsound in principle. There was much exploitation and personal revenge. Politically, the *thanedary* system was risky because it meant continuance of small pockets of local influence which was prejudicial to the Company's interests. Cornwallis' *daroga* system was hailed as an innovation which strengthened the Magistracy.

But after 1793, the crime rate steadily increased. Bengal was known for gang robbery. Thugs operated in the Upper Provinces. Many more social evils increased considerably. The police system of Cornwallis suffered because it did not have roots in society. Moreover, the resumption of the whole or part of the lands previously adjusted in the rentals of the zamindars for the support of their police establishments was resented. The resumption of service lands of village watchmen and zamindari servants led them to combine with the zamindars and make common cause against the *darogas* of Police. A gap developed between the official police under Magistrate and rural police under zamindars with their roots in society.

The *darogas* of police were unfit and negligent. But they had extensive powers. Ill-paid, they indulged in corrupt practices. The administration of police suffered in addition from the union of the Magistracy with the office of the Judge.

Between 1793 and 1813, several measures of reforms were designed to:

1) seek the cooperation of zamindars,

2) remove the inadequacy of the stipendiary police,

3) to impart efficiency and speed to criminal administration, and

4) to modify Muslim criminal law well as the established mode of trial.

Responsible Hindus and Muslims were appointed as amins and commissioners of police who could assist a *daroga* in maintenance of law and order. The police amins were to preserve peace, help suppress crime, control village watchmen and the like. The idea was to unite the influence of zamindars with the power of *darogas* through the police amins.

The government increased the establishment of the Kotwali and Thana police. Apart from a general increase in the establishment of the stipendiary force, provisions were made to meet local exigencies. Also, not only was there an increase in the powers of the Magistrates, Joint and Assistant Magistrates were appointed. Above all, modifications were introduced in criminal law.

The necessity of decentralising the powers of superior courts arose mainly because of increase in the bulk of crime. Magistrate's powers were increased, courts of circuit appointed and later on in their place, divisional commissioners assigned tasks.

By and large in administration of criminal justice and police, an attempt was to have an effectual administration of justice and liberalise criminal law by reducing severity of punishment, by having trial by jury and bringing dangerous social customs under purview of law. In short, the effort was to make the law conform to principles of liberalism and natural justice.

Q10. What was the contribution of Wellesley to improve the civil service in India?

Ans. With responsibilities of ruling territorial possessions in India, the British Governors and Councillors needed assistants in the Central offices and in districts. They also had to study the manners and customs of the people, collect necessary facts and make timely recommendations. To begin with, the men to fill this important role in public service were drawn from the ranks of writers, factors and merchants of the company. It was not till 1769 that some of these offices were appointed supervisors over large areas and charged with responsibilities. Though most of the men did not prove equal to their tasks there were a few like John shore, Charles Stewart, Charles Grant and Jonathan Duncan who did outstanding work. The Court of Directors continued to send every year fresh batch of writers without realising that a revolutionary change had taken place in the Company's role and functions and, therefore, better equipped men required. None of the Acts of Parliament between 1773 and 1793 looked into the education and training of civil servants in India.

To the open question as to whether administration would be efficiently conducted by only Indians, a mixed agency or exclusively by the British, Cornwallis provided the answer by deciding on the policy of complete Europeanisation. All higher positions in Government service were filled by the Company's British covenanted servants. The Charter Act of 1793 took care of this and provided the Charter of rights of civil servants. Promotion was by seniority. Duties of different departments were defined. Salaries were proportionate to responsibility.

Wellesley realised that civil servants of the Company had to discharge functions of Magistrates, Judges, ambassadors, etc. To discharge these duties efficiently they had to be not only well acquainted with the languages, laws and usages of the people but be well informed on the British Constitution and be well versed in Ethics, Civil Jurisprudence, the laws of nations and general history. To provide all these, Wellesley set up the College of Fort William in Calcutta. The civil servants of Bombay and Madras had to undergo training at the College like those of Bengal for three years.

The three year course provided for instruction in liberal arts, classical and Modern History and Literature, Law of Nations, Ethics and Jurisprudence. The syllabus also include Indian languages, different codes and regulations. The college aroused mental and intellectual powers of the civil servants and improved their morals to a considerable extent. But the College was short-lived. After seven years it continued as only a language school.

In 1805, the Haileybury college was set up in England and that really spelt the end of the College at Fort William. The young recruits to the covenanted Civil

Service had to spend two years at Haileybury and for the next 50 years the ICS was the product of the Haileybury College.

The syllabus drawn up by Wellesley for his College was followed at the Haileybury College. The young civil servants had to continue their mathematical and classical education for two years under expert guidance. They had also to read Political Economy, Principles of jurisprudence, elements of Indian history and rudiments of Indian legal codes and regulations and Indian languages.

But admission was still on the basis of patronage. Each of the Company's Directors could nominate one candidate while Chairman and Deputy Chairman could nominate two candidates each. Though there was an entrance test, it was so simple, that no one ever failed it. Though candidates did equip themselves with liberal education, the standard at Haileybury was not really high or else it would have resulted in a high rate of failures. The admission system, though modified later, was at best, one of qualified patronage.

Despite this, the College had a good name and its products were known for their corporate outlook and spirit comradeship which they brought to India. These men in far-flung parts of India still upheld old Haileybury ties. They set healthy traditions especially in honesty and integrity. But at the same time they felt high and mighty and some did become despotic in outlook and dictatorial in behaviour.

In 1837, an arrangement was made for the preliminary examinations to Haileybury College. Yet it did not achieve the expected results. The men who came out to India were not of the level of competence demanded by the work. Meanwhile, opposition was developing in England against patronage since 1833, when the Company lost the last vestige of commercial monopoly. The Northcote Trevelyan report submitted to Parliament in 1854 suggested that patronage must give place to open competitive examination. Among those happy to promote merit system was Macaulay. Once the principle of competition was accepted, the necessary regulations had to be framed. For this an expert body was appointed of which Macaulay was Chairman. The committee recommended that candidates be between ages 18 and 23 and the examination should be in subjects of liberal study. The introduction of the competitive test meant the end of the Hailerybury college.

First competitive examination was held in 1855. From 1858 the exams were conducted by the British Civil Service Commission.

It must be noted that the Civil Service established a great reputation for itself as a most efficient, honest and upright organ of government. But civil servants had limited functions to perform. They were essentially concerned with law and order and revenue administration.

Q11. Discuss the features of Indian councils Acts, 1861 and 1892.

[Dec-08, Q.6]

Ans. The Indian Council Act of 1861: The Act for the Better Government of India in the year 1858 led to the introduction of several significant changes in the Home Government. But these changes had nothing to do with the administrative set up of India. There was a strong feeling that there were sweeping changes in the Constitution of India after the great crisis of 1857-58. Apart from these there were several other reasons, which necessitated the changes of the constitution of India. The charter Act of 1833 had centralised the legislative procedures. The Legislative council (Center) had the sole authority to legislate and passing decrees and implementing them for whole of the Country. The workings of the Legislative Council set up by the Charter Acts of 1833, were not fulfilled properly. The council had become a sort of debating society or a Parliament on a small scale. It had claimed all the functions and privileges of the representative body. Trying to act as an independent legislature, it did not work properly with the Home Government. In such circumstances, after an exchange of views between the Home Government and the government of India, the first Council Act was passed in 1861.

The Indian Councils Act of 1861, in the first place added to the Viceroy's executive council fifth member who was to be a gentleman of legal profession, a jurist rather than a technical lawyer. The Act empowered the Governor General to make rules for more convenient transactions of business in the Council. This power was used by Lord Canning to introduce the portfolio system in the Government of India. Upto that time theoretically, it was the rules that the government of India was the government by entire body of the executive council. As a result, all the official papers had to be brought to the notice of the members of the council. By the provisions declared by the council Act of 1861, Canning divided the government between the members of the Council. In this way, the foundation of the Cabinet Government in India was established. It had been declared through this Act, each branch of administration had its spokesman and head in the Government, who was responsible for its administration and defence. Under the new system the daily matters of administration were placed by the member-in-charge. In cases of important matters, the member concerned presented the matters before the Governor General and decided in consultation with him. The decentralisation of business undoubtedly made for efficiency but it was not achieved however.

The Indians councils Act of 1861 also introduced reforms in the legislative purpose. For the convenience of legislation, the viceroy's executive council was expanded by the addition of members. It was declared that the additional members should not be less than six and not more than twelve. These members were directly nominated by the governor General, who held their office for tenure of two years. It was made obligatory that not less than half of the members were to be the non-official members. The Council Act of 1861 made no statutory provisions made for the admissions of the Indians. However, in actuality some of the non-official seats were offered to the natives of high rank. The functions of the Legislative council were declared strictly to be confined only with the legislative affairs. It would have no control over the administration, finance or the right of interpretation.

The Indian councils Act of 1861 restored the legislative powers of making and amending laws to the provinces of Madras and Bombay. However, no laws were passed by the provincial councils were to be valid until those receive the assent of the Governor General. Further in certain matters, the prior approval of the Governor General was made obligatory. Following the provisions declared by the Councils Act of 1861, legislative council were established in Bengal, the North Western Provinces and Punjab in the years 1862, 1886 and 1889 etc. Moreover, the Governor General was empowered by the Act of 1861, to issue without the concurrence of the Legislative Council, ordinances, which were not to remain in force for more than six months.

The significance of the Indians Councils Act of 1861 lies in the fact that it laid down the gradual construction and consolidation of the mechanical framework of the government. Due to this Act three separate presidencies were brought into a common system. The legislative and the administrative authority of the Governor General in Council, was asserted over all the provinces and extended to all the inhabitants. By this act the local needs and the growth of the local knowledge were emphasised.

The Act of 1861 vested the legislative authority in the Governments of Bombay and Madras. It also laid the provision for the creation of similar legislative council in other provinces too. As a result, it laid the foundation of legislative devolution culminating in the grants of autonomy to the provinces by the Government of India Act, 1935. However, it should be noted that by the Council Act of 1861, no attempts were made to demarcate the jurisdiction of the Central and the Local Legislature as in the federal constitution.

However, the character of the Legislative Councils established by the Act of 1861, was not fulfilled properly. Moreover, the Legislative Councils could not function like the true legislatures neither in the composition nor in the function. The Council Acts of 1861, in no way established representative government in India on the model of the government prevalent in England. By the Act of 1861, it was declared that in the colonial representative assemblies there would be the discussions of the financial matters and taxation. Regarding this, Sir Charles Wood, the Secretary of the state, while introducing the Bill made it clear in the unequivocal terms that Her Majesty's Government had no intentions to establish a representative law making body normally. However, the Indian council Act of 1861 led widespread public dissatisfaction and agitation.

The Indian Councils Act, 1892: The Indian Constitution came into existence after the Act of 1861. The growth of the Indian Constitution following the Act of 1861 caused political dissatisfaction and agitation alternating the Council reforms.

The Legislative reforms introduced by the Act of 1861, failed to meet the aspirations and the general demands of the people of the country. The group of non-officials, though small in number, however, did not represent the people. The group members belonged to the upper section or the aristocratic class of the Indian society. They were generally big zamindars, retired officials, or Indian princes. These aristocrats were completely ignorant of the problems of the common people in India.

During the later half of the 19th century, the current of nationalist spirit began to emerge in India. The setting up of the universities in the presidencies led to the development of education. The use of English by the educated Indians brought them close to one another. The gulf between the Indians and the British in the field of the Civil Services incited the rage of the Indians. Moreover, the repressive Acts made by Lord Rippon, the Vernacular Press Act and the Indian Arms Act in the year 1878, greatly exasperated the feelings of the Indians. The controversy between the Government of India and the Government of England over the abolition of 5% cotton duties made the Indians aware of the injustice of the British Government. As a whole the hollowness and the insincerity of the British Government was revealed to the Indians. It was under these circumstances, the Indian National Congress was formed in the year 1885. The sole motto of the Congress was to organise the public opinions in India, thereby ventilate their grievances, and demand reforms constitutionally.

In the beginning though the attitudes of the British Government to the Indian National Congress was friendly, yet by 1888, that attitude changed when Lord Dufferin made a frontal attack on the Congress. Lord Dufferin tried to belittle the importance of the representative character of Congress. Even so, he did not understand the significance of the movement launched by the Congress. He secretly sent to England the proposals for liberalising the Councils. He also appointed a committee of his council to prepare plans for the enlargement of the provincial councils, for enhancement of their status, the multiplication of their functions, and introduction of elective principles in the councils and the liberalisation of their general character as political institutions. The report of the Committee was sent to the Home authorities in England proposing for the changes in the composition and functions of the Councils. The main aim of the report was to give the Indian people wider share in the administration.

The Conservative Ministry in England, introduced in the year 1890, a bill in the

House of Lords based on this proposal. But, the measures adopted in the Bill were preceded very slowly and was passed two years later as the Indian Councils Act in the year 1892.

The Indian Councils Act of 1892, dealt exclusively with the powers, functions and the compositions of the Legislative Councils in India. With regard to the Central Legislature, the Councils Act of 1892 provided that the number of additional members must not be less than ten or more than sixteen. The increase of the members of the Central Legislature was described as a very paltry and miserable addition. But Curzon defended it on the ground that the efficiency of the deliberative body was not necessarily to be commensurate with the numerical strength. The Council Act of 1892 upheld that two fifth of the total members of the Council would to be non-officials. It had also declared that non-officials would be partly nominated and partly elected.

The principle of election was conceded to a limited extent. The Indian Councils Act of 1892 increased the members of the Legislatures. These members were entitled to express their views upon the financial statements.

The statement on the financial affairs henceforth was decided to be prepared in the Legislature. But these legislative members were not entitled to move resolutions or divide the houses in respect of any financial question. These legislative members were empowered to put questions with certain limits to the government on matters of interest after giving a six days notice.

For the provincial legislatures, the Council Act increase the number of additional members to not less than eight or more than twenty in case of Bombay and Madras. It also fixed the maximum number of members for Bengal at twenty. But for the northwestern province and Oudh, the number was fixed at fifteen. The members of the provincial legislatures had to perform several functions. Their Chief function was to secure the interpretation of the executive in the matters of the general public interest. They could also discuss the policy of the government and ask questions, which required a thorough previous notice. However, the central government if necessary could also reject their questions without assigning any reason.

The Indian Councils Act of 1892 introduced several new rules and regulations. However, the significant feature of this Indian Council Act was the procedure of election it introduced, though the word election was very carefully avoided in it. The Act envisaged that apart from the elected official members, there should be elected non-official members, whose number was to be five. The four out of five non-official members of the Council were to be elected by each of the non-official member of the four Provincial legislatures of Bombay, Madras, Calcutta and the Northwestern province and one by the Calcutta Chamber of Commerce. The Governor General nominated the other five non-officials himself. In cases of Provincial Legislatures, the bodies permitted to elect the members of   Municipalities, District Boards, Universities and the Chamber of Commerce. The methods of election, however, were not mentioned in the clear terms. The "elected" members were officially declared as "nominated" although after taking into consideration the recommendation of each body. These Legislative bodies met in several sessions in order to prepare recommendations to the Governor General or head of the Provincial Government. The person favoured by the majority was not described as the "elected", rather they were directly recommended for nomination.

The Indian Councils Act of 1892 was undoubtedly an advance on the Act of 1861. The Act of 1892 widened the functions of the legislature. The members could ask questions and thus obtain information, which they desired, from the executive. The Councils Act of 1892 made it obligatory that the financial accounts of the current year and the budget for the following year should be presented in the legislature. The members were permitted to make general observations on the budget and make suggestions for increasing or decreasing revenue and expenditure.

Apart from these, the recognition of the principle of election introduced by the Act of 1892, was a measure of constitutional significance. However, there were several defects and shortcomings in the Act of 1892 by the reason of which the Act failed to satisfy the Indian nationalists. The Act was criticised at successive sessions of the Indian National Congress. Critics opined that the procedure of election was a roundabout one. This was so because though theoretically the process of election was followed, in actuality these local bodies were the nominated members. Moreover, the function of the legislative councils was strictly circumscribed. In conclusion, it can be said that despite the fact that the Indian councils Act of 1892 fell far short of the demands made by the Indian National Congress, yet it was undoubtedly a great advance on the existing state of things.

Q12. Explain the important features of Montague Chelmsford Reforms.
[Dec-09, Q.5]

Ans. The Montagu-Chelmsford Reforms were reforms introduced by the British Government in India to introduce self-governing institutions gradually to India. The reforms take their name from Edwin Samuel Montagu, the Secretary of State for India during the latter parts of World War I and Lord Chelmsford, Viceroy of India between 1916 and 1921. The reforms were outlined in the Montagu-Chelmsford Report prepared in 1918 and formed the basis of the Government of India Act 1919. Indian nationalists considered that the reforms did not go far enough while British conservatives were critical of them.

Background: Edwin Montague became Secretary of State for India in June 1917 after Austen Chamberlain resigned after the capture of Kut by the Turks in 1916 and the capture of an Indian army staged there. He put before the British Cabinet a proposed statement containing a phrase that he intended to work towards the gradual development of free institutions in India with a view to ultimate self-government. Lord Curzon thought that this phrase gave too great an emphasis on working towards self-government and suggested an alternative phrase that the Government would work towards increasing association of Indians in every branch of the administration and the gradual development of self-governing institutions with a view to the progressive realisation of responsible government in India as an integral part of the British Empire. Cabinet approved the statement with Curzon's phrase incorporated in place of Montagu's original phrase.

The report: In late 1917, Montagu went to India to meet up with Lord Chelmsford, the Viceroy of India, to meet with leaders of Indian community such as Mohandas Karamchand Gandhi and Muhammed Ali Jinnah to discuss the introduction of limited self-government to India and protecting the rights of minority communities such as Muslims and Sikhs.

The Report went before Cabinet on 24 May and 7 June 1918 and was embodied in the Government of India Act of 1919. These reforms represented the maximum concessions the British were prepared to make at that time. The franchise was extended, and increased authority was given to central and provincial legislative councils, but the viceroy remained responsible only to London.

The changes at the provincial level were significant, as the provincial legislative councils contained a considerable majority of elected members. In a system called "dyarchy," the nation-building departments of government — agriculture, education, public works, and the like — were placed under ministers who were individually responsible to the legislature. The departments that made up the "steel frame" of British rule — finance, revenue, and home affairs — were retained by executive councillors who were nominated by the Governor. They were often, but not always, British and who were responsible to the governor. In 1921, another change recommended by the report was carried out when elected local councils were set up in rural areas, and during the 1920s urban municipal corporations were made more democratic and "Indianised."

Reception in India

The 1919 reforms did not satisfy political demands in India. The British repressed opposition, and restrictions on the press and on movement were reenacted in the Rowlatt Acts introduced in 1919. These measures were rammed through the Legislative Council with the unanimous opposition of the Indian members. Several members of the Council including Jinnah resigned in protest. These measures were widely seen throughout India of the betrayal of strong support given by the population for the British war effort.

Gandhi launched a nationwide protest against the Rowlatt Acts with the strongest level of protest in the Punjab. An apparently unwitting example of violation of rules against the gathering of people led to the massacre at Jalianwala Bagh in Amritsar in April 1919. This tragedy galvanised such political leaders as Nehru and Gandhi and the masses who followed them to press for further action. Montagu ordered an inquiry into the events at Amritsar by Lord Hunter. The Hunter Inquiry recommended that General Dyer, who commanded the troops, be dismissed, leading to Dyer's sacking. Many British citizens supported Dyer, whom they considered had not received fair treatment from the Hunter Inquiry. The conservative Morning Post newspaper collected a subscription of £26,000 for General Dyer and Sir Edward Carson moved a censure motion in Montagu which was nearly successful. Although Montagu was saved largely due to a strong speech in his defence by Winston Churchill, Lloyd George's secretary reported that some of the Tories could have assaulted him (Montagu) physically they were so angry.

The Amritsar massacre further inflamed Indian nationalist sentiment ending the initial response of reluctant co-operation. At the grass roots level, many young Indians wanted faster progress towards Indian independence and were disappointed by lack of advancement as Britons returned to their former positions in the administration. At the Indian National Congress annual session in September 1920, delegates supported Gandhi's proposal of swaraj or self rule — preferably within the British empire or outside it if necessary. The proposal was to be implemented through a policy of non-cooperation with British rule meaning that Congress did not stand candidates in the first elections held under the Montagu-Chelmsford reforms in 1921.

The Montagu-Chelmsford report stated that there should be a review after 10 years. Sir John Simon headed the committee (Simon Commission) responsible for the review which recommended further constitutional change. Three roundtable conferences were held in London in 1930, 1931 and 1932 with representation of the major interests. Gandhi attended the 1931 roundtable after negotiations with the British Government. The major disagreement between Congress and the British was separate electorates for each community which Congress opposed but which were retained in Ramsay MacDonald's Indian Communal Award. A new Government of India Act 1935 was passed continuing the move towards self-government first made in the Montagu-Chelmsford Report.

Q13. Write in brief about Simon commission and Nehru Report.

Ans. Simon Commission: The Indian Statutory Commission was a group of seven British Members of Parliament that had been dispatched to India in 1927 to study constitutional reform in that colony. It was commonly referred to as the Simon Commission after its chairman, Sir John Simon. Ironically, one of its members was Clement Attlee, who subsequently became the British Prime Minister who would oversee the granting of independence to India and Pakistan in 1947. The Government of India Act 1919 had introduced the system of dyarchy to govern the provinces of British India. However, the Indian public clamoured for revision of the difficult dyarchy form of government, and the Government of India Act 1919 itself stated that a commission would be appointed after 10 years to investigate the progress of the governance scheme and suggest new steps for reform. In the late 1920s, the Conservative government then in power in Britain feared imminent electoral defeat at the hands of the Labour Party, and also feared the effects of the consequent transference of control of India to such an "inexperienced" body. Hence, in November of 1927, Prime Minister Stanley Boldwin appointed seven MPs (including Chairman Simon) to constitute the Commission that had been promised in 1919 that would look into the state of Indian constitutional affairs. The people of the Indian subcontinent were outraged and insulted, as the Simon Commission, which was to determine the future of India, did not include a single Indian member in it. The Indian National Congress, at its December 1927 meeting in Chennai, resolved to boycott the Commission and challenge Lord Birkenhead, the Secretary of State for India, to draft a constitution that would be acceptable to the Indian populace. A faction of the Muslim League, led by Muhammad Ali Jinnah, also decided to boycott the Commission. In Burma (Myanmar), which was included in the terms of reference of the Simon Commission, there was strong suspicion either that Burma's unpopular union with India would continue, or that the constitution recommended for Burma by the Simon Commission would be less generous than that chosen for India; these suspicions resulted in tension and violence in Burma leading to the rebellion of Saya San. Almost immediately with its arrival in Mumbai on February 3, 1928, the Simon Commission was confronted by throngs of protestors. The entire country observed a *hartal* (strike), and many people turned out to greet the Commission with black flags. Similar protests occurred in every major Indian city that the seven British MPs visited. However, one protest against the Simon Commission would gain infamy above all the others. On October 30, 1928, the Simon Commission arrived in Lahore where, as with the rest of the country, its arrival was met with massive amounts of protestors. The Lahore protest was led by Indian nationalist Lala Lajpat Rai, who had moved a resolution against the Commission in the Legislative Assembly of Punjab in February 1928. In order to make way for the Commission, the local police force began beating protestors with their *lathis* (sticks). The police were particularly brutal towards Lala Lajpat Rai, who later that day declared, "The blows which fell on me today are the last nails in the coffin of British imperialism." On November 17, Lajpat Rai died of his injuries on his head. The Commission published its 17-volume report in 1930. It proposed the abolition of dyarchy and the establishment of representative government in the provinces. It also recommended that separate communal electorates be retained, but only until tensions between Hindus and Muslims had died down. Noting that educated Indians opposed the Commission and also that communal tensions had increased instead of decreased, the British Government opted for another method of dealing with the constitutional issues of India. Before the publication of the report, the British Government stated that Indian opinion would henceforth be taken into account, and that the natural outcome of the constitutional process would be dominion status for India. The outcome of the Simon Commission was the Government of India Act 1935, which established representative government at the provincial level in India and is the basis of many parts of the Indian Constitution. In 1937, the first elections were held in the provinces, resulting in Congress Governments being returned in almost all provinces. In September 1928, Mr. Motilal Nehru presented his Nehru Report to counter British charges that Indians could not find a constitutional consensus among themselves, it advocated that India be given dominion status of complete internal self-government.

The Nehru Report: The constitution outlined by the Nehru report was for Indian enjoying dominion status within the British Commonwealth. Some of the important elements of the report:

• Unlike the eventual Government of India Act 1935 it contained a Bill of Rights;

• All power of government and all authority - legislative, executive and judicial

• are derived from the people and the same shall be exercised through organisations established by, or under, and in accord with, this Constitution;

• There shall be no state religion; men and women shall have equal rights as citizens;

• There should be federal form of government with residuary powers vested in the center;

• It included a description of the machinery of government including a proposal for the creation of a Supreme Court and a suggestion that the provinces should be linguistically determined;

• It did not provide for separate electorates for any community or for weightage for minorities. Both of these were liberally provided in the eventual Government of India Act 1935. However, it did allow for the reservation of Muslim seats in provinces having a Muslim minority of at least ten percent, but this was to be in strict proportion to the size of the community;

• The language of the Commonwealth shall be Hindustani, which may be written either in Nagari or in Urdu character. The use of the English language shall be permitted.

The Nehru Report, along with that of the Simon Commission was available to participants in the three Indian Round Table Conferences 1931-1933. However, the Government of India Act 1935 owes much to the Simon Commission report and little, if anything to the Nehru Report.

With few exceptions League leaders rejected the Nehru proposals. In reaction Mohammad Ali Jinnah drafted his Fourteen Points in 1929 which became the core demands the Muslim community put forward as the price of their participating in an independent united India. Their main objections were: Separate Electorates and Weightage - the 1916 Congress-Muslim League agreement provided these to the Muslim community whereas they were rejected by the Nehru Report; Residuary Powers – the Muslims realised that while they would be a majority in the provinces of the North-East and North-West of India, and hence would control their provincial legislatures, they would always be a minority at the Centre. Thus, they demanded contra the Nehru Report, that residuary powers go to the provinces. The inability of Congress to concede these points must be considered a major factor in the eventual partition of India. This was the major historical significance of the Nehru Report

Q14. What are the features of Government of India Act, 1935?
[June-07, Q.10]

Ans. After the failure of the Third Round Table Conference, the British government gave the Joint Select Committee the task of formulating the new Act for India. The Committee comprised of 16 members each from the House of Commons and House of Lords, 20 representatives from British India and seven from the princely states. Lord Linlithgow was appointed as the president of the Committee. After a year and a half of deliberations, the Committee finally came out with a draft Bill on February 5, 1935. The Bill was discussed in the House of Commons for 43 days and in the House of Lords for 13 days and finally, after being signed by the King, was enforced as the Government of India Act, 1935, in July 1935.

The main features of the Act of 1935 were:

1. A Federation of India was promised for, comprising both provinces and states. The provisions of the Act establishing the federal central government were not to go into operation until a specified number of rulers of states had signed Instruments of Accession. Since, this did not happen, the central government continued to function in accordance with the 1919 Act and only the part of the 1935 Act dealing with the provincial governments went into operation.

2. The Governor General remained the head of the central administration and enjoyed wide powers concerning administration, legislation and finance.

3. No finance bill could be placed in the Central Legislature without the consent of the Governor General.

4. The Federal Legislature was to consist of two houses, the Council of State (Upper House) and the Federal Assembly (Lower House).

5. The Council of State was to consist of 260 members, out of whom 156 were to be elected from the British India and 104 to be nominated by the rulers of princely states.

6. The Federal Assembly was to consist of 375 members; out of which 250 were to be elected by the Legislative Assemblies of the British Indian provinces while 125 were to be nominated by the rulers of princely states.

7. The Central Legislature had the right to pass any bill, but the bill required the approval of the Governor General before it became Law. On the other hand, Governor General had the power to frame ordinances.

8. The Indian Council was abolished. In its place, few advisers were nominated to help the Secretary of State for India.

9. The Secretary of State was not expected to interfere in matters that the Governor dealt with the help of Indian Ministers.

10. The provinces were given autonomy with respect to subjects delegated to them.

11. Diarchy, which had been established in the provinces by the Act of 1919, was to be established at the Center. However, it came to an end in the provinces.

12. Two new provinces Sindh and Orissa were created.

13. Reforms were introduced in N. W. F. P. as were in the other provinces.

14. Separate electorates were continued as before.

15. One-third Muslim representation in the Central Legislature was guaranteed.

16. Autonomous provincial governments in 11 provinces, under ministries responsible to legislatures, would be setup.

17. Burma and Aden were separated from India.

18. The Federal Court was established in the Center.

19. The Reserve Bank of India was established.

Both the Indian National Congress and the Muslim League opposed the Act, but participated in the provincial elections of winter 1936-37, conducted under stipulations of the Act. At the time of independence, the two dominions of India and Pakistan accepted the Act of 1935, with few amendments, as their provisional constitution.

Q15. What are the reasons behind the failure of All India federations?
Ans. The proposed All India Federation did not materialise. It was conceptually inadequate and structurally defective. It could convince nobody – the Indian National Congress, the Muslim League, the Hindu Mahasabha or the Princely States. Muslims opposed the majority rule. Princes opposed the force of democracy and Congress opposed Federation by courtesy. It thus remained 'a lost ideal'. Federation is a political mechanism. The members entering into a union should

be independent, legally equal and should voluntarily form the union. Here the Princely States had an option to join the Federation and also to decide their relations with the Federal Government through the provisions of the Instrument of Accession. Also undue weightage was given to the Princely States. They could send their nominees (and not elect representatives like British provinces) and the representation was proportionately larger than their geographic or demographic strength. With roughly one-fourth of the population of British India, the princely states had 104 seats out of 260 in the Council of State and 125 out of 375 in the House of Assembly. This created a reactionary block in the legislature as the Princely States were lagging behind the provinces in the introduction and practice of democratic reforms.

In a federation, Constitution is supreme. But in the Act, supremacy of the British Parliament was retained. The Secretary of State for India and the Governor General were the ultimate authority and they were above the Act. The Act gave area of discretion, area of individual judgement and special responsibility to the Governor General. This made the Governor General not responsible to the legislature. As the diarchy was introduced at the Centre, his control over reserved subjects was absolute and over transferred subjects very effective. All the Governors and ICS officers acted under his instructions. Federal constitution on the other hand, tries for a balance in power in its different organs and levels. Provincial autonomy was also restricted in practice in the context of safeguards provided in the Act. Such provincial governments with an unrepresentative and powerless Central legislature made negation of the spirit of Federalism. Though the distribution of power through the Three-list system could be condoned as being the first attempt and could have been improved upon, keeping residuary powers with the Governor General was harmful. The Act could have developed some healthy conventions and certain powers given to executive been accepted as natural if the executive would have been responsible to the legislature and the legislature supreme, in its field. Both these aspects were missing. Atlee called, therefore, the keynote of act as 'mistrust and distrust'. The line of thinking now changed and Congress felt that the struggle for self-government could not further be carried within a constitutional frame but need to be carried on a mass base. This indicated the full decline of the liberals and the endorsement of Mahatma Gandhi's mass agitational movements. The logic of Quit India thus becomes clear.

Q16. Explain the features of administrative structure under the Act of 1935.

Ans. The Administrative Structure under the Act 1935:

1. Organisation of Departments: In the reorganisation of departments, natural grouping of subjects and administrative branches was the main consideration. The workload of the department also was a factor in reorganisation. The whole administration was established in 1929. In 1937, the Foreign and Political Department as divided into two departments. Similarly, Department of Industries and Labour was bifurcated into two separate departments. In 1942, there was reorganisation in food department and also three separate Departments of Education, Health and Agriculture were established. However, departmental reshuffling was not always rational but influenced by economy considerations and the exigencies of war. In 1947, there were nineteen departments; Home, External Affairs and Commonwealth relations, Finance, Transport, Railways, Education, Health, Agriculture, Food, Industries and Supplies, Political (States), Legislative Works, Mining Power, Labour and Information, and Broadcasting.

Procedural changes aimed at reducing delay in administrative process. The Secretariat Procedure Committee, 1919 advocated delegation of power (Financial delegation), simultaneous circulation of papers to concerned levels and information communication between the Member, Secretary and Deputy Secretaries in a Department. The Maxell Committee (1937) looked into the Minister-Secretary relationship in the context of administrative continuity. Gorawala Committee (1951) looked into the question of administrative integrity while Appleby Committee (1953) focused on training needs of officials especially the middle level officials and the need to establish Organisation and Method Department for continuous appraisal of administration structures and processes.

2. The Public Service: The 1935 Act classified services as superior and other services. The Indian Civil Service, Indian Police and Indian Medical (Civil) Services were classified as superior services and controlled by the Secretary of State. These continued to enjoy social rights and privileges (No adverse order against a member of the superior service could be passed without concurrence of the governor. They had right to appeal to the Secretary of State against an adverse order.) The 1919 Act had recommended for the establishment of the Federal Public Service Commission and through it, Indianisation of Services was realised. The profile of service that developed was that of a generalist associated with the formulation of policies and their implementation. As a whole Public Service retained an All India character.

3. Administration of Finance: The financial arrangements under the Government of India Act 1935 were based on the recommendations of the Niemeyer Committee. Revenue sources followed the list system. As such receipts from provincial subjects formed the main income source for provinces. Provinces were given some additional sources of revenue too; for example, share in succession duty other than landed property, share in income tax, grant in aid, etc. The provinces were also given power to raise loans on the security of their resources. The Centre to secure financial stability for itself could for a period retain such sums as might be prescribed in the form of a fixed percentage of income tax assigned to the provinces. The Auditor General of India occupied a key position in financial administration. He controlled the accounts both of the Centre as well as the provinces. The Reserve Bank of India was established in April 1935. Financial control over expenditure was exercised through the Public Accounts Committee of the legislature. The centralised machinery of finance has been a feature of the Indian system since the Charter Act of 1833. The position of the office of the comptroller and Auditor General in India, a statutory office in our present constitution, derives strength from this historic fact.

4. Administration of Justice: The Government of India Act 1935 established the Federal Court to interpret the provisions of the Act and also to deal with inter-province conflicts. It is a prerequisite of a federal form of government. The Privy Council still continued as the highest court of appeal for India (it indicates uneasy compromise). The Federal court made substantial contribution to the constitutional development of India. Much credit for this goes to Sir Maurice Gwyer, as the first Chief Justice in the formative period of its working. It established the cardinal principle of independence of Judiciary in the critical period of its functioning. The immediate aim was to protect the autonomy of provinces and to emphasis order in the politically activated atmosphere.

5. Local Administration: Local governments were more representative and popularly controlled. The legislation also provided for representation for backward and depressed classes and for labour class. But as local bodies were drawn in the nationwide political surge through civil disobedience movement, they lost the priority of attention. The traditional panchayat system had long been defunct and the new local government could not take firm roots. The fact is that local government, rural or urban, grew as administrative necessity of managing local funds. Ripon's objective of political education was lost in executive directions that followed the Resolution. Older village panchayat system was based on a corporate spirit and British tenancy legislation affected this base. The British administration of Justice was also centralised. The defunct panchayats, therefore, became a sink of localism and a den of narrow mindedness (Ambedkar). The Decentralisation Commission also looked at the problem from administrative angle. It was only with the experiment of community Development Movement and its subsequent development in Panchayati Raj that the rural government structure became meaningfully involved in the larger process of participative development.

Q17. Discuss about the departmental structure adopted by the Government of India after getting independence.

Ans. The pre-independence era saw the administrative organisations of the

Central and the State (then called 'Provincial') governments intact. This was a factor contributing to the undisturbed transfer of power from the British to the Indian hands. The administration of the country's security, law and order, finances, communication system, educational organisation and other elements of the infrastructure after 1947 continued as before.

At independence on 15 August 1947, the following eighteen departments (redesignated as 'Ministeries') functioned under the Government of India: **(1)** External Affairs and Commonwealth Relations, **(2)** Defence, **(3)** Finance, **(4)** Home **(5)** States, **(6)** Legislative (Law) **(7)** Commerce, **(8)** Industries and Supplies, **(9)** Railways, **(10)** Transport, **(11)** Communication, **(12)** Labour, **(13)** Agriculture, **(14)** Food, **(15)** Education, **(16)** Health, **(17)** Information and Broadcasting, **(18)** Works, Mines and Power.

From five departments in 1858, at the transfer of the government in India from the charge of the East India Company to the Control of the British Parliament (actually handled by British Government), to eighteen in 1947 indicated an enormous increase in the administrative activity. These nine decades of the British rule witnessed the beginning of the elementary social services like primary education, health and medicine, agricultural research, fiscal incentives for industries, etc. Legislative activity had commenced. The two World Wars introduced price and physical controls over the essential supplies including food, cloth, petrol and kerosene, etc., besides growth in armed services, war industries and supplies. In 1921, the number of departments stood at nine, which were increased to twelve in 1937. After 1919 the main administrative activities in agriculture, education, health, and labour were conducted by the provincial governments, due to decentralisation under the 1919 and 1935 government of India Acts.

The following are the typical present-day secretariat departments in the State governments: **(1)** General Administration, **(2)** Home, **(3)** Revenue and Forests **(4)** Agriculture, Food and Cooperation, **(5)** Education and Social Welfare, **(6)** Urban Development and Public Health, **(7)** Finance, **(8)** Buildings and Communication, **(9)** Irrigation and Power, **(10)** Law and Judiciary, **(11)** Industries and Labour, **(12)** Rural Development.

Though the volume and variety of the administrative activities in the State have increased after independence, the number of Secretariat departments has not grown much. The administration in the States has changed in nature and size in rural development, in education, agriculture, health and medicine and related matters.

The administrative work both at the Centre and State levels has, after Independence, become more complex and challenging. New forms of organisation of these administrative activities have come up which did not exist before independence. The types of knowledge and skills require among the administrative personnel have also become more complex. The new economic social welfare, scientific and technical activities assumed by the state in India account for their variety and complexity. The growing international and defence responsibilities of the Indian state have also partly contributed to the strengthening and speeding up of this process. The low levels of literacy and awareness of numerous people have also added to the responsibilities and tasks of the administration.

Usually, the ministries at the central level will be having one or more departments, depending on the need for specialisation. For instance, the Ministry of Personnel, Public Grievances and Pension, as the name suggests, has three departments. The number of Ministeries and their constituent departments go on increasing on both political and administrative grounds. Need to accommodate many ministries leads to proliferation of Ministries and Departments. Also, specialisation asks for creation of new ministries and departments. Science and technology, Atomic Energy, Non-Conventional Energy are such instances of new needs. In short terms, the ministry of Social Justice and Empowerment exemplifies the need for new administrative set up to deal with social justice and empowerment. The new economic activities undertaken by the Union Government are reflected in the departments of coal, power and non-conventional energy sources in the Ministry of Energy, departments of chemicals and petrochemicals, Industrial development and public enterprises in the Ministry of Industry, departments of planning and statistics in the Ministry of Planning and Ministers of Petroleum and Natural Gas, Programme Implementation and Steel and Mines. Nationalised banks are looked after by the Finance Ministry. Concerns for the development of Science and Technology are imbibed by the Ministries of Science and Technology and Department of Atomic Energy, Electronics and Space. The electronic media and the computers have brought about a change in methods of information, storage and retrieval, and communication. The forum of Parliament and State legislatures have brought in the Ministry of Parliamentary Affairs and increased the work of the Ministry of Law and Justice. The tremendous growth in the strength of personnel in administration has led to the creation of the new Ministry of Personnel, Public Grievances and Pension. The new Departments of Family Welfare, Youth Affairs and sports and Women and Child Development mark the compulsions of a social awakening among the families, youth and women and the awareness of the social responsibilities towards them, after independence. The Planning Commission, though not a department in the strict sense of the term, belongs to that species.

The innovated forms for public corporations, government companies and joint companies have appeared on the post-independence administrative scene, giving rise to the demand for new categories of administrators. Attached offices like the National Academy of Administration at Mussoorie and subordinate offices like the National Fire Service College at Nagpur are new off-shoots of administration. Scientific laboratories and research stations have broadened the scope of administration. Numerous advisory bodies like the Central Board of Education and the Central Labour Advisory Board evoke the participation of concerned interest groups in the policy-making in those areas.

In terms of internal organisation and relationships within the departments and outside, the working of the Departments has not changed much after independence. Hierarchy and importance of the written word and communication have continued. Red-tapism and delay still haunt the administration. Pre-independence manuals prepared during the colonial rule still govern in most of the other departments with modification here and there. The Chief Secretary of provincial administration before 1947 continues today; but at the Centre, the Cabinet Secretary, de facto head of administration, is an innovation.

Another recent development is the growth of independent regulatory agencies like TRAI in telecommunication, SEBE in shares and stock exchanges, etc. These agencies have been set up to lend a degree of independence, away from normal executive departments, to quasi-judicial arbitration, rate-fixation and conflict resolution functions of the government.

Feedback is the breakfast of Champions.

Ken Blanchard

You can Help other students.
"Inform any error or mistake in this book."

We and Universe
will reward you for Your Kind act.

Email at : feedback@gullybaba.com
or
WhatsApp on 9350849407

Central Administration

Q1. Explain the basic features of Indian constitution.

[Dec-09, Q.6][Dec-08, Q.1]

Ans. Following are the basic features of Indian constitution:

1. Written, Lengthy and Detailed Constitution: Our Constitution is written, lengthy and detailed. Written constitution is that which is based on written laws duly passed by a representative body elected for this very purpose. In other words, a written constitution is an enacted constitution. An unwritten constitution, on the other hand, is an evolved constitution. It is primarily based on unwritten conventions, traditions and practices. The Constitution of the U.S.A. is another example of a written constitution and that of England of an unwritten one. The Constitution of India is an elaborate document and is the most voluminous Constitution in the world. Our Constitution originally consisted of 395 Articles and eight Schedules. During the last forty-three years of its operation, seventy-six Amendments have been made to the Constitution. Two new Schedules have also been added, resulting in a further increase in its size and volume. An important reason for the extraordinary volume of the Constitution is that it contains detailed provisions regarding numerous aspects of governance. This was done to minimise confusion and ambiguity in the interpretation of the Constitution, another reason for its being unusual lengthy is the incorporation of the good points of various constitutions of the world. The vastness of our country and its peculiar problems has also added to the bulk of the Constitution. Thus, for example, the Indian Constitution envisages laws for the governance of the States too. Detailed provisions regarding the working of the Union Government and the State Governments have been given with a view to avoiding any constitutional problem which the newly-born Democratic Republic might experience in the working of the Constitution.

2. Partly Rigid and Partly Flexible Constitution: A flexible constitution is that which can be amended like an ordinary law of the country, i.e. by a simple majority of Parliament. On the other hand, a rigid constitution is the one which prescribes a difficult procedure for its own amendment. The Constitution of the U.S.A. is the best example of rigid constitution because it can be amended only if a proposal for constitutional amendment is passed by a two-third majority in each House of the Congress (the US Parliament) and ratified by at least three-fourths of the federal states. The Constitution of Great Britain, on the other hand, is highly flexible. This is so because it can be amended by a simple majority of its Parliament, much like the ordinary laws of the country. The Indian Constitution is neither very flexible nor very rigid. Some provisions of the Constitution can be amended by a simple majority of Parliament, like ordinary laws of the land while most of the provisions can only be amended by a two-thirds majority of Parliament. For very important provisions of the Constitution, such as the manner of election of the President and the extent of the legislative powers of the Union and the States, an amendment passed by a two-thirds majority of Parliament should also be ratified by at least one-half of the State legislatures. The Indian Constitution thus combines the flexibility of the British Constitution and the rigidity of the American Constitution. Jawaharlal Nehru, while justifying this nature of the Constitution, said, *"Our Constitution is to be as solid and permanent as we can make it, yet there is no permanence in a constitution. There should be a certain amount of flexibility. If you make anything rigid and permanent, you stop the nation's growth, the growth of a living vital organic people."*

3. Partly Federal and Partly Unitary: Our Constitution declares India a Union of States (federation). It prescribes dual set of governments-the Union Government and the State Governments. The subjects of administration have also been classified into three lists-the Union List, the State List and the Concurrent List. Whereas subjects of national importance like currency, defence, railways, post and telegraph, foreign affairs, citizenship, survey and census have been assigned to the Union Government and placed under the Union List, subjects of local importance like agriculture, law and order, health and entertainment have been assigned to the States and form a part of the State List. Both, the Union Government and the State Governments, operate within the spheres of their authority. The Union Parliament and the State Legislatures enjoy co-equal powers to make laws in regard to the Concurrent subjects. These subjects are of common importance such as marriage and divorce, adoption, succession, transfer of property, preventive detention, education, civil and criminal law, etc. However, if there is a conflict between a Union law and a law passed by one or many State Legislatures, the law made by the Union Parliament would prevail over the State law. The Indian Constitution possesses other features of a federation too, for example, supremacy of the constitution. This means that the Union and the State Governments both operate within the limits set by the Constitution. Both the governments derive authority from the Constitution itself. Similarly, in all federal countries, the authority of the Court is a well established fact. This means that in case of a dispute between the Union Government and State Governments or between two or more State Governments, the verdict of the Court will be final. Not only this, the Supreme Court is given the responsibility of interpreting the Constitution in case of dispute or confusion. The Supreme Court of India is the guardian of the Constitution and fulfils its role as a Federal Court too. The Indian Constitution, though federal in form, has a strong unitary bias. The Central Government possesses extensive powers compared to the State Governments. The exercise of these powers by the Centre gives the Constitution the strength of a unitary government. Let us look at those provisions of the Indian Constitution that make it partly unitary. The Union Government can supersede the authority of the States both in the normal and abnormal times. The President of India can declare three different types of emergency. During the operation of an emergency, the powers of the State Governments are greatly curtailed and the Union Government becomes all in all. Even in normal times, the Union Parliament can legislate upon a subject given in the State List, if the Rajya Sabha passes a resolution by a two-thirds vote that such legislation is necessary in the national interest. Moreover, the Indian Constitution, unlike the US Constitution, does not provide for double citizenship, division of public services or of the judiciary. Similarly, the States in India do not enjoy the right to secede from the Union nor do they enjoy equality of representation in the Council of States (Rajya Sabha). Another unitary feature of our Constitution is that it gives Union Parliament the power to alter the boundaries of the existing States or to carve out new States out of the existing ones. It is on account of these features that the Indian Constitution is said to be federal in form but unitary in spirit.

4. Parliamentary System: The Constitution of India adopts Parliamentary system of government at the Centre and in the States. In such a system of government, the executive power is wielded by the Council of Ministers which is collectively responsible to the legislature. The Ministers continue in office so long as they enjoy the confidence of a majority of Members in the legislature. The moment they lose this confidence, a vote of no-confidence is passed against them and they have to resign forthwith. The responsibility of the executive to the legislature is also ensured by the right of the Members of the legislature to put questions to the Ministers. The Members may table adjournment motions and call attention motions against the policies pursued by the Government. The Ministers are duty-bound to answer all such questions and satisfy the Members of the legislature.

5. Fundamental Rights: Certain rights are considered basic or fundamental as they provide suitable conditions for the material and moral upliftment of the people. The Indian Constitution guarantees a number of such rights to the citizens of India. The Fundamental Rights of India conferred by the Constitution are:

(i) The Right to Equality;

(ii) The Right to Freedom;

(iii) The Right against Exploitation;

(iv) The Right to Freedom of Religion;

(v) Cultural and Educational Rights; and

(vi) The Right to Constitutional Remedies.

The Right to Property was deleted from the list of Fundamental Rights by the Forty-fourth Constitution Amendment Act, 1978. The fundamental rights as envisaged in the Constitution of India are justiciable.

6. Directive Principles of State Policy: The Directive Principles of State Policy constitute another distinctive feature of our Constitution, These Principles embody certain ideals and objectives which should be kept in mind by the Union and State Governments while making laws and implementing policies. The implementation of these directives was not made compulsory due to the paucity of resources. The framers of the Constitution expected that as and when the future Governments would mobilise resources, they would do their best to implement these directives. Equitable distribution of wealth, employment for all, protection of health, compulsory education for children up to the age of fourteen and the establishment of village panchayats are some such principles. The Directive Principles of State Policy are non-justiciable. No legal remedy can be sought in a court of law if the Government fails to follow or implement any of these principles. In other words, the Directive Principles are non-justiciable rights of the citizen. However, these principles are considered important in the governance of the country. It becomes a moral duty of every government to follow them and realise the purpose behind them. Several amendments to the Constitution, together with some judgements of the Supreme Court have paved the way for the implementation of the Directive Principles.

7. Independence of the Judiciary: Our Constitution has taken special care to establish an independent and impartial judiciary. The judges of the Supreme Court and the State High Courts have been provided security of service. Once appointed, their salaries and allowances cannot be altered to their disadvantage by the Government during the course of their tenure. Nor can they be dismissed before the age of their retirement except in case of proven misconduct supported by a resolution of Parliament passed by a two-thirds majority. Security of service of judges is in keeping with the dignity and prestige of the highest judicial organs of the country. This provision has been made in the Constitution to keep the judges independent and immune from the control and influence of the Executive. The judges can exercise their discretion in the dispensation of justice even if their decisions go against the Government. The Supreme Court and the State High Courts are also the guardians of the rights and liberties of the citizens and protect them against arbitrary action on the part of all government agencies.

8. Official Language: In a country like India, with diverse cultural traditions and languages, it is essential to declare one language as the national language, symbolic of the unity of the different regions of the country. The Constitution declares Hindi in Devanagari script as the official language of the country. Besides, each State is authorised to adopt a regional language for all or some of its official purposes. English has also been allowed to be used along with other languages for official purposes.

9. Adult Franchise and Joint Electorates: The Constitution provides for Universal Adult Franchise. The citizens of India who are 18 years of age and above have been granted the right to vote irrespective of any qualification pertaining to education, possession of property or payment of income tax. The adoption of Universal Adult Franchise was indeed a very daring step taken by the Constituent Assembly in view of the fact that large sections of our people are illiterate. The manner and the orderliness, with which Indian masses have exercised their right to vote during ten general elections and many State Legislative Assembly elections, speak eloquently of the political maturity of our people. The Constitution has replaced the system of communal representation (introduced by the British in 1909) by that of joint electorates. The country is divided into territorial constituencies. From each constituency, members of different communities jointly elect a common candidate. The system of joint electorates promotes communal harmony and goodwill and discourages communal politics. To bring the Scheduled Castes and Tribes at par with the other communities of the country, some seats have been reserved for them in the Union Parliament, State Legislatures and local bodies. There are reserved parliamentary and assembly constituencies from where only the members of the Scheduled Castes or Tribes can contest elections.

10. Establishment of a Welfare State: The Preamble to the Constitution, as modified by the Forty-second Amendment Act, 1976 and the Directive Principles of State Policy aim at the establishment of a Welfare State in India. Keeping in view the inherent spirit of the Constitution, the successive governments at the Centre have been pursuing a policy of democratic socialism. Nationalisation of banks and general insurance, fixation of ceiling on urban and rural lands and abolition of privy purses of the rulers of the erstwhile native States, implementation of various poverty alleviation programmes are some of the measures which have been taken to remove gross inequalities of wealth and to usher in an era of social and economic equality.

Q2. What are the main features of a federal system?

Ans The most important aspect of a federal system is that it recognises that there are different types of political issues which need different types of institutions to deal with them. Some affect only a local area, others are more widespread in their scope. The institutions of government should reflect this. The idea that government should be based solely on strong central institutions is old-fashioned and out-of-date. In a federal system, the power to deal with an issue is held by institutions at a level as low as possible, and only as high as necessary. This is the famous principle of subsidiary. The second major feature of a federal system is that it is democratic. Each level of government has its own direct relationship with the citizens. Its laws apply directly to the citizens and not solely to the constituent states. In a federal system, power is dispersed but coordinated. For this reason, federalism is often seen as a means of protecting pluralism and the rights of the individual against an over-powerful government.

Q3. Explain the role of council of Ministers.   [June-09, Q.6]

Ans. India is one of the largest democracies enshrined as the Sovereign Socialist Secular Democratic Republic in the Constitution. After independence when the Constitution of India came into force, the country started to follow Republican system. The republic is governed in terms of the constitution and the sovereignty is shared in between the state and the federal governments with the domination of the central cabinet. Article 74 of the constitution of India lays down that there shall be a Council Of Ministers with the Prime Minister at the head to aid and advise the President who shall in exercise of his functions, act in accord to such advice.

Article 75 (1) states that "the Prime Minister shall be appointed by the President and the other Ministers shall be appointed by the President on the advice of the Prime Minister". It is also stated that the total number of Ministers, including the Prime Minister, in the Council of Ministers shall not exceed fifteen percent of the total number of members of the House of the People. It is also laid that the Ministers shall hold office during the pleasure of the President and the Council of Ministers shall be collectively responsible to the House of the People. Article 75 also states that before a Minister enters upon his office, the President shall administer to him the oaths of office and of secrecy according to the forms set out for the purpose in the Third Schedule of the constitution. A Minister who for any period of six consecutive months is not a member of either House of Parliament shall be at the expiration of that period cease to be a Minister. The salaries and allowances of Ministers shall be such as Parliament may from time to time by law determine and, until Parliament so determines, shall be as specified in the Second Schedule of the constitution. The Council of Ministers in India consist different categories which are as

follows:
• Cabinet Ministers
• Minister of States (often with independent charges)
• Deputy Ministers
The Prime Minister communicates any decision, issue or policy related to the Government to the Council of Ministers. The Prime Minister also conveys the Council of Ministers all the decisions in regard to the administration of affairs of the central Government and suggestions for approvals to the President of India. As per Article 79 of the Constitution of India, the council of the Parliament of the Union consists of the President and two Houses known as the Council of States (Rajya Sabha) and the House of the People (Lok Sabha). The president is the constitutional head of the Executive of the Union of India. The prime minister is responsible in communicating all the decisions of the Council of Ministers to the President. Usually each department has a designated officer as the secretary to the Government of India to mainly advise the Ministers on policy matters as well as to propose on general administration. The cabinet secretariat also plays an important role as a coordinator under the able direction of the Prime minister and takes the decision at the highest level.

Q4. Write a short note on followings:
1. The Comptroller and Auditor General of India
2. Attorney - General of India
3. The Election Commission
4. Finance commission
5. Official language commission
6. UPSC
7. National commission for scheduled castes   **[June-08, Q.13]**
8. National commission for scheduled Tribes
Ans. 1. The Comptroller and Auditor General of India: The duties and powers of the comptroller and Auditor General of India are enshrined in chapter V of part V of the Constitution of India is Article 148 to 151. There are two types of functions of the comptroller and Auditor General of India:
(i) Audit Functions
(ii) Accounting Functions
The duties of Comptroller and Auditor General includes audit of;
all expenditure from the Consolidated Fund of India of Union, of each State and of each Union Territory having a Legislative Assembly with the objective to ascertain whether the moneys shown in the accounts as having been disbursed were legally available for and applicable to the service or purpose to which they have been applied or charged and whether the expenditure conforms to the authority which governs it;

all transactions of the Union and of the States/Union Territory having a Legislature relating to Contingency Funds and Public Accounts;

all trading, manufacturing, profit and loss accounts and balance-sheets and other subsidiary accounts kept in any department of the Union or of a State and in each case, to report on the expenditure, transactions or accounts so audited by him;

receipts and expenditure of bodies or authorities substantially financed from Union or State revenues;

grants or loans given to other authorities or bodies;

revenue of the Union and of the State Governments;

accounts of stores and stock; Government Companies and Corporations under the Company's Act 1956 read with CAG's (DPC) Act, 1971 and accounts of other authorities or bodies as per their statute or upon request by the Governor of a State or the Administrator of a Union Territory having a Legislative Assembly.

Accounting Functions: The Accounts Offices are responsible for; Compilation of accounts of the State Government; preparation of the annual accounts of the States Governments and Union Territories having a Legislative Assembly; and rendering accounting information and assistance to the State Government.

2. Attorney General of India: The Constitution of India, under Article 76, states that the Attorney General should be appointed by the President of India. Elected by the ruling government of India, the Attorney General performs the function of a chief legal advisor. For being nominated as the Attorney General of India the concerned candidate should possess all the qualifications to take seat of the judge of the Supreme Court. During the sessions of the Parliament, the Attorney General of India has the right to participate in the same. However, he or she does not have any right to vote in the Parliament. In order to take various legal decisions in a smooth and faster way, one Solicitor General and four Additional Solicitor Generals assist the Attorney General of India. The Attorney General is also required to perform all legal functions that are delegated to him by the President of India.

3. The Election Commission: The Election Commission of India is an autonomous, extra constitutional body created to conduct free and fair elections. It was established on January 25,1950. The Commission comprises one Chief Election Commissioner and two Election Commissioners. At present, the Chief Election Commissioner is Navin Chawla and the other two Election Commissioners are S.Y. Quraishi and V.S. Sampath. Being an extra constitutional body, the Election Commission is independent and is protected from any kind of executive interference. The Commission also functions as a quasi-judiciary body in case of electoral disputes and other matters involving the conduct of elections. It is responsible for planning and executing a whole range of complex operations that are required for conducting elections. During the elections, the entire Central and State Government machinery, including paramilitary forces and the police force under the stewardship of the Election Commission is stationed for the successful completion of the electoral process. The National Elections held after every five years, has earned the distinction of being one of the largest human activities and the Election Commission has earned the distinction of being one of the largest management organisations. The Election Commission is also called upon by the Courts to see and execute elections to various governing bodies of other independent organisations such as the Syndicate of Universities, statutory professional bodies etc. The Chief Election Commissioner and the Election Commissioners are appointed by the President. The term of their office is six years or up to the age of sixty-five whichever is earlier. They enjoy the same status and receive salary and perks as received by the judges of Supreme Court of India. The Chief Election Commissioner can be removed from office only through impeachment by Parliament.

4. Finance Commission:

The definitive and final division of financial resources between the Union and the States in India is not possible owing to its federal structure with unitary features. Therefore, the need for some machinery for periodical adjustments and reallocations in resources by way of transfers in the light of changing conditions.

The Indian Constitution has designed the Finance Commission precisely to serve this purpose. The Indian Constitution is unique in that way as no other federal constitution in the world has provision for any such permanent machinery to serve such a purpose.

Functions of the Finance Commission

Article 280 of the Indian Constitution is related to the appointment, functioning and duties of the Finance Commission.

Article 280(3) states as follows :

"It shall be the duty of the Commission to make recommendations to the President as to –

a) The distribution between the Union and the States of the net proceeds of taxes which are to be, or may be, divided between them under this Chapter and the allocation between the States of the respective shares of said proceeds;

b) The principles which should govern the grants-in-aid of the revenues of the States out of the "Consolidated Fund of India".

Finance Commission's role in allocation of finances to local bodies

Article 280 (3) further states the role of the Finance Commission in allocation of funds to local bodies as follows :

(a) the measures needed to augment the Consolidated Fund of a State to supplement the resources of the Panchayats in the State on the basis of the recommendations made by the Finance Commission of the State;

(b) Nature of the recommendations made by the Finance Commission:
There are four categories of recommendations made by the finance commission:
1. Those to be implemented by an Order of the President (under Art. 270 and Art. 275 of the Constitution)
2. Those to be implemented by law of Parliament (under Art. 272)
3. Those to be implemented by executive orders (grants for relief expenditure, upgradation, debt relief and grant in lieu of tax on railway passenger fares)
4. Those to be examined further.

Composition of the Finance Commission:
The Finance Commission constituted by the President of India pursuant to clause (1) of article 280 of the Constitution is composed of four members, headed by the Chairman.

The Chairman of the Commission shall be selected from among persons who have had experience in public affairs, and the four other members shall be selected from among persons who—
(a) are, or have been, or are qualified to be appointed as Judges of a High Court; or
(b) have special knowledge of the finances and accounts of Government; or
(c) have had wide experience in financial matters and in administration; or
(d) have special knowledge of economics.

5. Official Language Commission-
The official language of the Union of India according to our Constitution is Hindi in Devanagari script. The Constitution authorises the President at the expiration of every ten years since the commencement of the Constitution, to constitute a Commission which shall consist a Chairman and other members. The Official Language Commission makes recommendations to the President as to the :
a) Progressive use of Hindi language for the official purposes of the Union;
b) Restriction in the use of the English language for all or any of the official purposes of the Union;
c) Form of numerals to be used for any one or more specified purposes of the Union;
d) Matter (Any other) referred to the Commission by the President as regards the official language of the Union and the language for communication between the Union and a State or between one State and another and their use. Thus, the Official Language Commission tries to establish linguistic harmony within the Union and between the States.

6. Union Public Service Commission (UPSC): Indianisation of the superior Civil Services became one of the major demands of the political movement compelling the British Indian Government to consider setting up of a Public Service Commission for recruitment to its services in the territory. The first

Public Service Commission was set up on October 1st, 1926. However, its limited advisory functions failed to satisfy the people's aspirations and the continued stress on this aspect by the leaders of our freedom movement resulted in the setting up of the Federal Public Service Commission under the Government of India Act 1935. Under this Act, for the first time, provision was also made for the formation of Public Service Commission at the provincial level.

The Constituent Assembly, after independence, saw the need for giving a secure and autonomous status to Public Service Commissions both at Federal and Provincial levels for ensuring unbiased recruitment to Civil Services as also for protection of service interests. With the promulgation of the new Constitution for independent India on 26th January, 1950, the Federal Public Service Commission was accorded a constitutional status as an autonomous entity and given the title – Union Public Service Commission.

Constitutional Provisions: The Union Public Service Commission has been established under Article 315 of the Constitution of India. The Commission consists of a Chairman and ten Members.

The terms and conditions of service of Chairman and Members of the Commission are governed by the Union Public Service Commission (Members) Regulations, 1969.

The Commission is serviced by a Secretariat headed by a Secretary with two Additional Secretaries, a number of Joint Secretaries, Deputy Secretaries and other supporting staff.

The Union Public Service Commission has been entrusted with the following duties and role under the Constitution:
• Recruitment to services and posts under the Union through conduct of competitive examinations;
• Recruitment to services and posts under the Central Government by Selection through Interviews;
• Advising on the suitability of officers for appointment on promotion as well as transfer-on-deputation;
• Advising the Government on all matters relating to methods of Recruitment to various services and posts;
• Disciplinary cases relating to different civil services; and
• Miscellaneous matters relating to grant of extra ordinary pensions, reimbursement of legal expenses etc.

The major role played by the Commission is to select persons to man the various Central Civil Services and Posts and the Services common to the Union and States (viz. All-India Services).

Recruitment to Various Services and Posts: Under Article 320 of the Constitution of India, the Commission are, inter-alia, required to be consulted on all matters relating to recruitment to civil services and posts.

Recruitment is made by one of the following three methods:

• Direct Recruitment;

• Promotion; and

• Transfer

Direct Recruitment is conducted broadly under the following two methods:

• Recruitment by competitive examination.

• Recruitment by selection through interview.

Recruitment by Competitive Examination: Under the Constitution one of the functions of the Commission is to conduct examinations for appointment to Civil Services or Posts of the Union. In addition, competitive examinations are also held by the Commission under arrangements with the Ministry of Defence for entry to certain Defence Services, through the National Defence Academy, Indian Military Academy, Naval Academy, Air Force Academy and the Officers Training Academy.

The Commission usually conducts over a dozen examinations every year on an all India basis. These include Examinations for recruitment to services or posts in various fields, such as Civil Services, Engineering, Medical and Forest Service, etc.

At present the Union Public Service Commission conduct their examinations at numerous venues spread over 42 regular centers throughout the country.

Recruitment by Selection: Recruitment by Selection is made by the following methods:

• By Interview Only

• By Recruitment test followed by Interview

By Interview: Where the number of applicants is very large, it is not practicable to call for Interview all the applicants who fulfill the minimum eligibility conditions prescribed. The Commission, therefore, shortlist the candidates to be called for the interview on the basis of certain pre-determined criteria related to the job. A large number of recruitment cases is handled by the Commission by the method (1) above.

By Written Test Followed by Interview: In this category, there are two types of procedure followed:

• An objective-type written and/or practical test to test the skill of the candidates followed by Interview, the final selection being decided by Interview, aided by the performance of the candidates in the written test and/or practical test.

• An objective-type written and/or practical test to screen candidates to be called for interview, the final selection being decided by Interview only.

7. National Commission for Scheduled Castes-The 89th Constitution Amendment Act 2003, provided for the creation of National Commission for Scheduled Castes. The commission shall consist of a Chairperson, Vice-chairperson and three other Members. The President determines the condition of service, the tenure of the office of the Chairperson, vice-Chairperson and other Members from time to time. The President will appoint them by warrant and under his hand and seal. The duties of the Commission are as follows:

1) The Commission shall have the power to regulate its own procedure.

2) It shall be the duty of the Commission-

a) to investigate and monitor all matters relating to the safeguards provided for the Scheduled Castes under this Constitution or under any other law for the time being in force or under any order of the Government and to evaluate the working of such safeguards;

b) to inquire into specific complaints with respect to the deprivation of rights and safeguards of the Scheduled Castes;

c) to participate and advise on the planning process of socio-economic development of the Scheduled Castes and to evaluate the progress of their development under the Union and any State;

d) to present to the President, annually and at such other times as the Commission may deem fit, reports upon the working of those safeguards;

e) To make is such reports recommendations as to the measures that should be taken by the Union or any State for the effective implementation of those safeguards and other measures for the protection, welfare and socio-economic development of the Scheduled Castes; and

f) to discharge such other functions in relation to the protection, welfare and development and advancement of the Scheduled Castes as the President may, subject to the provisions of any law made by Parliament, by the rule specify.

3) The President shall cause all such reports to be laid before each House of Parliament along with a memorandum explaining the action taken or proposed to be taken on the recommendations relating to the Union and the reasons for the non-acceptance, if any, of any of such recommendations.

4) Where any such report, of any part thereof, relates to any matter with which any State Government is concerned, a copy of such report shall be forwarded to the governor of the State who shall cause it to be laid before the legislature of the State along with a memorandum explaining the action taken or proposed to be taken on the recommendations relating to the State and the reasons for the non-acceptance, if any, of any of such recommendations.

5) The Commission shall, while investigating any matter referred to in sub-clause (a) or inquiring into any complaint referred to in sub-clause (b) of clause (5), have all the powers of a civil court trying a suit and in particular in respect of the following manners, namely:

a) summoning and enforcing the attendance of any person from any part of India and examining him on oath;

b) requiring the discovery and production of any document;

c) receiving evidence on affidavits;

d) requisitioning any public or copy thereof from any court or office;

e) issuing commissions for the examination of witnesses and documents;

f) any other matter which the President may, by rule, determine.

6) The Union and every State Government shall consult the Commission on all major policy matters affecting Scheduled Castes.

8. National Commission for Scheduled Tribes:

Ans. The 89th Constitution Amendment Act 2003, provided for the creation of National Commission for Scheduled Tribes. The Commission shall consist of a Chairperson, Vice-Chairperson and three other Members. The President determines the condition of service, the tenure of the office of the Chairperson, Vice-Chairperson and other Members from time to time. The President will appoint them by warrant under his hand and seal. The duties of the Commission are as follows:

1. The Commission shall have the power to regulate its own procedure.

2. It shall be the duty of the Commission -

(a) to investigate and monitor all matters relating to the safeguards provided for the Scheduled Tribes under this Constitution or under any other law for the time being in force or under any order of the Government and to evaluate the working of such safeguards;

(b) to inquire into specific complaints with respect to the deprivation of rights and safeguards of the Scheduled Tribes;

(c) to participate and advise on the planning process of socio-economic development of the Scheduled Tribes and to evaluate the progress of their development under the Union and any State;

(d) to present to the President, annually and at such other times as the Commission may deem fit, reports upon the working of those safeguards;

(e) to make in such reports recommendations as to the measures that should be taken by the Union or any State for the effective implementation of those safeguards and other measures for the protection, welfare and socio-economic development of the Scheduled Tribes; and

(f) to discharge such other functions in relation to the protection, welfare and development and advancement of the Scheduled Tribes as the President may, subject to the provisions of any law made by Parliament, by rule specify.

3. The President shall cause all such reports to be laid before each House of Parliament along with a memorandum explaining the action taken or proposed to be taken on the recommendations relating to the Union and the reasons for the non-acceptance, if any, of any of such recommendations.

4. Where any such report, of any part thereof, relates to any matter with which any State Government is concerned, a copy of such report shall be forwarded to the Governor of the State who shall cause it to be laid before the

Legislature of the State along with a memorandum explaining the action taken or proposed to be taken on the recommendations relating to the State and the reasons for the non-acceptance, if any, of any of such recommendations.

5. The Commission shall while investigating any matter referred to in sub-clause (a) or inquiring into any complaint referred to in sub-clause (b) of clause, (5), have all the powers of a civil court trying a suit and in particular in respect of the following matters, namely:

(a) summoning and enforcing the attendance of any person from any part of India and examining him on oath;

(b) requiring the discovery and production of any document;

(c) receiving evidence on affidavits;

(d) requisitioning any public or copy thereof from any court or office;

(e) issuing commissions for the examinations of witnesses and documents;

(f) any other matter which the President may, by rule, determine.

6. The Union and every State Government shall consult the Commission on all major policy matters affecting Scheduled Tribes.

Q5. Explain the meaning, evolution and functions of the Central Secretariat.

Ans. To begin with, the Secretariat in India referred to the office of the Governor General in British India. However, the size of the Central Secretariat and the scope of its activities have undergone considerable change over the last two hundred years of its evolution in keeping with the changes in the aims, objectives and nature of the central government in India.

At the end of the eighteenth century, the central government consisted of a Governor General and three Councillors, and the Secretariat of four departments. Each of them was under a Secretary, and there was a Chief Secretary heading them all. A hundred years later, on the eve of the Montford Reforms in 1919, the Government of India consisted of a Governor General and seven members and there were nine secretariat departments. This number remained the same till the outbreak of the Second World War in 1939.

Prior to 1919, the Central Government, while administering certain subjects directly like the army, posts and telegraphs and railways, had by and large left the task of implementation of other subjects to the local provincial governments. A major change came in the above position with the inauguration of the reforms of 1919 which for the first time, made a division of functions between the Central and provincial governments. Both the Central and provincial governments became responsible for both policy and administration. As a result, the role of the secretariat began to change from a merely policy-formulating, supervising and coordinating agency to that of a executive agency as well. The inauguration of provincial autonomy in 1937 and the outbreak of the Second World War accelerated the above process. In consequence, there was a fourfold increase of the Central Secretariat and its total strength rose to about two hundred.

The Government of India was still struggling with the post-war problems of demobilisation and reconstruction, when Independence came, accompanied by the partition of the country. At its very inception, therefore, the new government found itself faced with tremendous problems like rehabilitation of refugees from Pakistan, external aggression in Jammu and Kashmir, integration of princely states into the Indian Union, internal security, shortage of essential articles, at a time when there occurred serious shortage of personnel due to the British officers returning home and many Muslim officers opting for Pakistan. Soon after, the adoption of the goal of a welfare state made unprecedented demands on the already over burdened administrative machinery. At the same time, the Industrial Policy Resolution of 1948 started the process of a vast expansion of the public sector. The inevitable consequence of such a vast expansion, in the functions and responsibilities of the government was a marked increase in the number of departments, and personnel. Thus, the number of departments in the secretariat, which stood at four in 1858, (9 in 1919, 10 in 1939, 18 in 1947) had risen to 74 by 1994.

Meaning: The Central Secretariat occupies a key position in Indian administration. The Secretariat refers to the conglomeration of various ministries/departments of the Central Government. The Secretariat works as a single unit with collective responsibility as in the case of the Council of Ministers. Under existing rules, each secretariat department is required to consult any other department that may be interested or concerned before disposing of a case. Secretaries, thus, are secretaries to the Government as a whole and not to any particular minister.

Role: The Secretariat assists the ministers in the formulation of governmental policies. Ministers finalise policies on the basis of adequate data, precedents and other relevant information. The Secretariat makes these available to the minister, thus, enabling him to formulate policies. Secondly, the Secretariat assists the ministers in their legislative work too. The Secretariat prepares legislative drafts to be introduced in the legislature. It engages in the collection of relevant information for answering parliamentary questions, and, also, for various parliamentary committees. Fourthly, it carries out a detailed scrutiny of a problem bringing an overall comprehensive viewpoint on it, getting approval, if require, of other lateral agencies like the Ministry of Law and the Ministry of Finance; and also, consulting, other organisations concerned with a particular matter. The Secretariat is the clearing house preliminary to governmental decisions. Fifthly, it functions as the main channel of communication between the Government and other concerned agencies like the Planning Commission, Finance Commission, etc. And lastly, the Secretariat also ensures that field offices execute, with efficiency and economy, the policies and decisions of the Government.

Q6. Describe the structure of secretariat. What are the functions of different grades of officers of the secretariat?   [June-09, Q.7]

Ans. Structure of Secretariat: The Central Secretariat is a collection of various ministries and departments.

A ministry is responsible for the formulation of the policy of government within its sphere of responsibility as well as for the execution and review of that policy. A ministry, for the purpose of internal organisation, is divided into the following sub-groups with an officer in charge of each of them.

Department	-	Secretary/Additional/Special Secretary
Wing	-	Additional/Joint Secretary
Division	-	Deputy Secretary
Branch	-	Under Secretary
Section	-	Section Officer

The lowest of these units is the section in charge of a Section Officer and consists of a number of assistants, clerks, typists and peons. It deals with the work relating to the subject allotted to it. It is also referred to as the office. Two sections constitute the branch which is under the charge of an under secretary, also known as the branch officer. Two branches ordinarily form a division which is normally headed by a deputy secretary. When the volume of work in a ministry exceeds the manageable charge of a secretary, one or more wings are established with a joint secretary in charge of each wing. At the top of the hierarchy comes the department which is headed by the secretary himself or in some cases by an additional/special secretary. In some cases, a department may as autonomous as a ministry and equivalent to it in rank.

Department/Ministry: The distinction between 'department' and 'ministry' may be explained by referring to 'ministry' as the minister's charge and 'department' as the secretary's charge. Although a ministry stands for the minister's charge, its administrative divisions are not uniform. A ministry may not have a department or may have one or more than one department in which it is formally divided.

While a department may be referred to as the secretary's charge, all secretaries, although they get the same salary, are not necessarily of equal 'rank'. A Ministry may have two or more secretaries, each in charge of a specified segment of the Ministry's work, or of a department in it, but there is, in addition, one Secretary who is head of, and represents, the entire ministry. Although all of them are secretaries, the former are subordinate to the latter who, in addition to his own work, coordinates the work of these secretaries of departments/ segments of work within the ministry.

Functions of different Grades of Officers of the Secretariat: At present the grades of officers in the Central Secretariat are as follows:

1) Secretary

2) Additional Secretary

3) Joint Secretary

4) Deputy Secretary

5) Under Secretary

The first three grades constitute what is administrative parlance may be called 'Top Management' while the grades of deputy secretary and under secretary, are referred to as the 'Middle Management'. The Secretary is the administrative head of the ministry/department and the principal adviser to the Minister. He represents his ministry/department before the committees of Parliament.

He is supposed to keep himself fully informed of the work of his ministry/ department by demanding weekly summaries on the nature of cases disposed of by lower levels and the manner of their disposal.

Where the charge of a Secretary is too large, he many be assisted by a joint or additional secretary who formally functions as Secretary in relation to the subject allotted to him in the ministry/department. The function of the latter is to relieve the Secretary of a bloc of work and to deal where necessary direct with the minister. The Secretary, however, is invariably kept informed on all these direct dealings with the minister, for he is not formally relieved of his responsibility as head of the ministry/department.

The deputy secretary is an officer who, as his designation implies, acts on behalf of the Secretary. He should dispose of as many cases as possible on his own. Only on more important cases he should – in fact must – seek the Secretary's instruction either by referring to him in writing or discussing with him orally.

The under secretary should dispose of minor cases on his own. He should submit more important matters to the deputy secretary in such a form that the latter is able to deal with them quickly.

It must be stressed here that the functionaries at these different levels are supposed to perform their functions, keeping in mind the interests of the Government of India as a whole. The Secretary, in other words, is the Secretary to the Government of India, not to his minister alone. This is true of lower levels as well.

Q7. Explain the tenure system in Secretariat. What are its disadvantages?
[Dec-08, Q.13]

Ans. The system of filling senior posts in the Secretariat by officers who come from the States (or from the Central Services) for a particular period and who after serving their tenure, revert back to their parent States or services is known as the tenure system. It has been a principle of Secretariat staffing since 1905 and continued by the Government of India, even after Independence. The reasons for the continuance of the system may be summed up as follows:

1) A joint pool of officers at the reserve of both the centre and the states helps in administrative coordination at the centre and state level and exercises a unifying influence on the functioning of our federal policy.

2) The Central Secretariat benefits from the administrative experience of a number of bureaucrats who have first hand work experience at the district and state levels.

3) A prolonged stay in the Secretariat may get senior bureaucrats out of touch with actual administrative reality at the field level. The tenure system enables them to get a constant feedback from the field and from the general public.

4) The states also benefit from having at their service senior experienced officers with a wide national perspective on all problems.

5) Under the tenure system most officers are promised a chance of work at the Secretariat thus equalising opportunities for all.

6) It strengthens the independence of the civil service. It is a check against the possible dangers of subservience by a few to the political masters for narrow personal gains.

Though the tenure system is still in operation many arguments have been put forth against it. They may be briefly summarised as below:

1) Bureaucratic work in the Secretariats is gradually becoming specialised. The tenure system is essentially based on the myth of the superior efficiency of the generalist civil servants.

2) District experience is really not necessary in many areas of Secretariat work.

3) The tenure system has led to the bureaucrats getting too dependent on the office establishment to get things done. This had led to 'over bureaucratisation' of the Secretariat.

The tenure system, however, was never prevalent in all the departments of the Government of India. Foreign Affairs, Indian Audit and Accounts, Post and Telegraphs, Customs and Income Tax Departments had been the well-known exceptions even during the British period. The creation of the Central Secretariat service has, thrown a new challenge to this practice (even in departments where tenure system officially operates). The specialists whose numbers are increasing in the Secretariat are also not subject to rotation to areas away from the Secretariat. The creation in 1957 of the Central Administrative Pool has also made a significant impact on the system. This 'Pool' was established by the selection of officers from the Indian Administrative Services. There are two categories of posts in it- general purpose and specialised. The 'Pool' system was meant to overcome the uncertainties in the matters of quality and quantity inherent in the tenure system. Finally, despite the tenure system, there are numerous offices in the Secretariat who have never gone back to their parent State. Therefore, the original intention of the tenure system does not necessarily hold well in the changed conditions today.

Q8. Examine the relation between Executive Agencies and the Secretariat.   [Dec-08, Q.7]

Ans. The existence of Secretariat as an entity separate from the executive agencies is based on the belief that the task of policy-making needs to be separated from that of its execution. Development administration must necessarily move towards decentralisation which means that effective power and authority must be possessed by the executive agencies. Though the numbers of executive agencies have steadily risen over the years there has not been an increase in their power corresponding to their responsibilities. It is common knowledge that the Secretariat performs a lot of policy executing tasks of an original nature which could readily be passed on to the executive agencies. However, what need to be noted is that the relations between the Central Secretariat and the executive agencies have been quite strained and tension-ridden instead of gradually becoming cooperative and amiable.

There are six principal patterns of relationship developed at the Central level, between the secretariat and the executive agencies. These may briefly be discussed here:

1) There is complete merger between the ministry and heads of executive departments. The examples are the Railway Board and the Ministry of Railways, the Posts and Telegraphs Board and the Ministry of Communications. This pattern is most suitable for organisation undertaking work of an operational or commercial nature.

2) In the second pattern, a senior officer of the ministry concurrently operates as head of the executive department. In this way he becomes responsible both for formulation of policies and for its implementation with the assistance of the common office located in the Ministry. The Additional Secretary in the Department of Agriculture is the Director General of Food. But the main disadvantage of this pattern is that the system completely blurs the functions of the Secretariat and the head of an executive department.

3) The ministry's Office is merged in the office of the executive department. The common office serves both the Secretariat offices and the officers of the executive office.

The advantages of this arrangement are that any administrative proposal is examined only once, thus, expedition the disposal of cases, and, secondly it

results in sizeable economy – office maintenance becomes more economical.
4) The ministry and the executive department continues to have separate officers but have common files and common file bureau, all located in the organisation of the executive agency. This pattern has significant advantages but it does not do away with the problems of separate offices with duplicate staff and double scrutiny. A good example is the Ministry of Defence and the Air Force Headquarters.

5) The ministry and the executive departments continue to have separate offices and separate files but the head of the executive office is given an ex-officio Secretariat status. Thus, the Textile Commissioner is the ex-officio Joint Secretary in the Ministry of Commerce.

This pattern has the following advantages:

Under this arrangement, there is considerable saving of time as well as the paper work, as every matter does not travel up to the Secretariat for finalisation. Also, the accepted policy is implemented in a more efficient manner, as the head of the office, because of his secretariat status is fully aware of the background in which the policy was framed.

Its major drawback, however, is that it goes against the fundamental principle of secretariat system, namely, policy-making must remain separated from policy implementation.

6) Both the Ministry and the executive agency have separate and distinct offices and files of their own, and consultation between them occurs through self-contained letters. This is the standard pattern both at the Centre and in the States. This pattern is based on the dichotomy between staff and line. The ministry is Staff: the executive office is Line.

An example is the Directorate General of All India Radio in relation to the Ministry of Information and Broadcasting.

In other words, in this pattern, a wider perspective is brought to bear on the examination of a proposal. Secondly, it is always desirable to have a specialist's scheme scrutinised by a layman. Thirdly, this arrangement provides for a division of work between the Secretariat and the executive agencies. The former concentrates on policy-making and the latter on the execution of the policy. The disadvantages of this arrangement is that, this scheme is processed twice in two different offices. This involves duplication of work and cause delay.

Each pattern has thus advantages as well as disadvantage. No hard and fast rules can be laid down regarding the pattern of relationship which could be appropriate to a particular sphere of governmental activity. The pattern has to be so tailored as to suit the nature of activities or the past experience of the organisation. Nevertheless, neither absolute separation nor absolute merger of both is normally desirable.

Q9. Write a short note on the structure of Secretariat.

Ans. The work of the government of India is divided into ministries and departments which together constitute the Central Secretariat.

Administrative machinery at the Central Level: central secretariat may be defined as a common name for all the ministeries and departments of the central government. The political head of the ministry is the minister and administrative head is the Secretary. The department is centre of two or more wings. A wing consists of two or more divisions and a division consists of two or more branches. At the lowest level is the office which may consist of a number of secretariats. A ministry may be composed of one department or more than one department. The main function of the secretariat is to advise the minister concerned in matters of policy and administration. Each minister is aided by the secretariat staff.

The three essential components of the government at the centre are: the minister who decides upon policy, the secretary who provides material and advice to reach such decisions and to oversee the implementation of decisions, and the executive head, who carries the decisions into effect. The secretaries are secretaries to the union government as a whole but not to any particular minister. The secretariat is a policy forming, coordinating and supervising agency of the government. The secretariat's primary responsibility is to assist and advise the ministers in respect to the following matters:

1. Making and modifying policies from time to time.
2. Forming legislation, rules and regulations.
3. Sectoral planning and programme formulation,
4. Budgeting and control of expenditure,
5. Supervision and control over execution of policies and programmes by field agencies and evaluation of results,
6. Coordination and integration of policies and programmes, contact with state governments.
7. Developing greater organisational competence, and
8. Assisting the minister in discharge of his parliamentary responsibilities. Secretariat is to assist and advise the political executive in policy making. However, the secretariat has come to be criticised on various grounds which may be stated as follows: it takes upon itself a number of field functions; it tends to indulge in empire building; over a period of time the secretariat has turned into an over grown institution and over staffing is apparent in many areas; secretaries very often tend to take a superior attitude vis-à-vis the field agencies. With the increase of a number of departments in the secretariat, coordination has become the real problem. Lack of adequate delegation of work to executive agencies, cumbersome procedures of doing work, widespread desire to postpone decisions to over-consult, to over-coordinate,

etc. all lead to delay in the work of the Secretariat. These faults lie not with the concept of the secretariat but with the manner in which it has been functioning.

Q10. Describe the organisation and functions of the Prime Minister's Office.

Ans. The Prime Minister's Office came into existence after India became independent. The Prime Minister's Secretariat, as is was then know, provided the Secretariat assistance needed by the Prime Minister in his public activities and functions as the head of the government. In 1948-49, during the Premiership of Nehru, the office staff included a modest number of 117 members, which steadily increased over a period of time. During Lal Bahadur Shastri era, the Prime Minister's Secretariat emerged as a regular department under a full-fledged Secretary and its influence in top-level policy making increased. It was, however, during Indira Gandhi's Prime Ministership from 1966 to 1977 that the Prime Minister's Secretariat not only swelled in size but in power and authority as well. The Prime Minister's Secretariat had a personnel of about 200 in 1968-69 and during the internal emergency of 1975-77, emerged as a real centre of extra-constitutional power and authority.

During the Janata regime (1977-80), the Prime Minister's Secretariat was cut down to size both in terms of number and authority. In June 1977, the Prime Minister's Secretariat was renamed as the Prime Minister's Office. Though the number of its personnel has again been growing steadily in the last ten years, the office now maintains a low public profile, assisting the Prime Minister in his public activities rather than always attempting to exercise extra-constitutional power and authority.

Organisation: The Prime Minister's Office is headed politically by Prime Minister and administratively by the Principal Secretary. Additionally it consists of one or two Additional Secretaries, three to five Joint Secretaries, a number of Directors/Deputy Secretaries and Under Secretaries. There are also other officers like Officer on Special Duty, Private Secretaries, and so on. These offices are supported by regular office establishment.

The background and experience of the key personnel in the Prime Minister's Office is not stated in a formal manner and the incumbents are appointed in this office to essentially provide 'secretariat help' to the Prime Minister. It has Secretary who may or may not come from the civil service. Other personnel are generally drawn from the civil services and posted for varying periods. The work is shared between the Secretary, the Additional Secretary, Joint Secretaries, the Deputy Secretary and other personnel. Being a small office and because they should interact freely among themselves, no fixed duties are laid down for the members of staff. The division of work is made according to the convenience and experience of the staff in the office.

Functions: The main task of the secretariat is to help the Prime Minister in the performance of his functions as the head of the government. It is responsible for assisting him in maintaining, on the official side, liaison with Union Ministers, the President, Governors, Chief Ministers, Representatives of Foreign Governments in India and others, and, on the public side, in handling various requests or complaints from members of the public addressed to the Prime Minister. In general, the jurisdiction of the Secretariat may be said to extend over all such subjects and activities which are not specially allotted to any individual ministry/department. It also prepares answers for questions raised in parliament on some general subjects which could not, on strict classification, be allotted to any particular ministry. The Prime Minister's Office performs several functions:

(1) Assisting the prime minister in respect of his overall responsibilities as head of the government like maintaining liaison with central ministries/ departments and the state governments.

(2) Helping the prime minister in respect of his responsibilities as chairman of the Planning commission, and the National Development Council.

(3) Looking after the public relations of the prime minister like contact with the press and general public.

(4) Dealing with all references, which under the Rules of Business have to come to the prime minister.

(5) Providing assistance to the prime minister in the examination of cases submitted to him for orders under prescribed rules.

(6) Maintaining liaison with the President, Governors, and Foreign Representatives in the country.

(7) Acting as the 'think-tank' of the prime minister.

However, the Prime Minister's Office is not responsible for functions devolving on the Prime Minister in his capacity as the head of the Cabinet, except to the extent to which matters are handled in personal correspondence between him and individual ministers, or for handling correspondence either relating to party polices or of a domestic nature.

Q11. Examine the changing role of Prime Minister's Office.

Ans. The role of the Prime Minister's office has evolved and varied from Prime Minister to Prime Minister. Under Nehru the size of the office was limited, so was its role. Under his tenure, a greater reliance on the Ministries and their advisers seems to have been a characteristic way of working and the Cabinet Secretary provided a primary link. In subsequent periods, the Prime Minister's Secretariat has been performing some of these functions, though all Cabinet matters must go through the Cabinet Secretariat. Demarcation between the two is not rigid and indeed it cannot be so.

It was Nehru's successor Shastri, who took the first step towards establishment of a powerful Secretariat. He appointed L.K. Jha as the Secretary to the Prime Minister and he became the head of the Secretariat. Jha's powerful and dynamic personality raised the status and stature of the Secretariat and also added to its tasks. Under Jha's stewardship, the Prime Minister's Office started commanding a formidable influence in the making of decisions, a trend which got further strengthened during Indira Gandhi's Prime Ministership. At the time of assuming office she had a very limited experience of administration; hence, her dependency on her Secretariat became greater, especially, on complex economic and foreign policy issues. Mr. L.K. Jha was succeeded by Mr. P.N. Haksar under whom the Prime Minister's Secretariat grew to such an extent that it became an independent executive force. Much of the domestic and foreign policy took shape at the secretariat and a lot of authority came to be concentrated in the Prime Minister's Office. This became all the more marked during the period of the Internal emergency (1975-1977) which ushered in era of authoritarian Prime Ministerial rule. As a consequence the Prime Minister's Secretariat became the focus of all authority and its writs began to be obeyed by all central ministries, departments and other executive agencies. During Indira Gandhi's reign, the Prime Minister's Secretariat virtually became a national policy formulation body and the Cabinet Secretariat its enforcement arm. During the Janata period, an effort was made to diffuse the existing concentration of power in the Prime Minister's Secretariat and reduce it to the status of a mere 'office' whose functions were merely secretariat in nature. As a result the Secretariat was divested of its various policy making cells.

However, in the last eight years there is a noticeable trend towards concentration of policy making power in the Secretariat, once again. There remains a feeling often articulated by the opposition and newspapers from time to time that the Prime Minister's Secretariat is in fact a 'micro-cabinet', since it often attempts to supplant the cabinet in all major policy making functions.

Q12. Describe the role of the cabinet secretary of India.[June-08, Q.2]
Ans. Cabinet Secretary is the administrative head of the cabinet Secretariat. The office of Cabinet Secretary was created in 1950. The Cabinet Secretary functions under the leadership of the Prime Minister who is its minister in charge at the political level. He is drawn from the senior most officers of the Indian Administrative Services. It is expected that he should be a man of rich administrative experience.

Although the chief function of the Cabinet Secretary is to provide assistance to the council of ministers, infact, he deals primarily with cabinet affairs. For this purpose, though, he keeps contact with the various ministers, he keeps a close touch with the secretaries in charge of different ministries / departments.

He is also the head of the civil service and ensures that the moral of the civil servants remain high. He has to act as a buffer between the politicians and the civil servants and protect the interest of the latter in situations of conflict between the two. It is a dream-post for every bureaucrat. Eminent civil servants have occupied this post e.g. Naresh Chandra, B.G. Deshmukh, T.N. Seshan etc. In the meetings of the cabinet, the Cabinet Secretary draws up the minutes which contain the decisions reached. After the Prime Minister's approval these are circulated by him to the ministers and the secretaries concerned. He has to maintain complete secrecy about these matters. The Cabinet Secretary is to ensure that the decisions of the cabinet are implemented properly. He maintains a close proximity with the Prime Minister. He advises the Prime Minister on whatever matter his advice is sought. One important function of the Cabinet Secretary is to preside over the meetings of the Committee of Secretaries on Administration which is set up to resolve inter ministerial disputes. He also presides over the Chief Secretaries conferences.

In relation to the Prime Minister and the country as a whole, the Cabinet Secretary has yet another role to play. Like all civil servants, he provides the element of stability and continuity. When a Prime Minister resigns or dies. A care taker Prime Minister and a Ministry does Exist in the interim period, but it is at this time that the services of the Cabinet Secretary are of immense value. He is the chief coordinator of Central Government.

Q13. Define cabinet committees. What are the roles and functions of cabinet committees?

Ans. Cabinet committees provide the forum for more detailed consideration and discussion of issues before reference to Cabinet. Unlike Cabinet, officials may be invited to attend the meeting to assist Ministers if the committee wishes. Most Cabinet committees are standing committees of Cabinet, and meet regularly. Cabinet also may establish from time to time ad hoc Cabinet committees to undertake particular tasks or to consider proposals on a specific issue. The structure, terms of reference, chair and membership of each Cabinet committee are decided by the Prime Minister, in consultation with the leader of the coalition partner, if there is one. The Cabinet Office issues a circular from time to time setting out the current terms of reference and membership of Cabinet committees. Cabinet committees are chaired by the designated chair, or the next most senior committee member present.

The Cabinet makes use of the committee system to facilitate decision-making in specific areas. The Business Rules provide for the constitution of standing committees of the Cabinet to ensure speedy decisions on vital questions of political and economic significance and other matters of importance as also to ensure coordination in well-defined fields of administration. These committees change according to the requirements of the situation and occasionally ad hoc committees are appointed.

Size: The number of such committees has been changing from time to time and no outsider could tell exactly what the existing committees are at a given time.

However, the membership of the Cabinet Committees normally varies from three to eight. The Chairmanship of them is shared between the Prime Minister and Home Minister. The committees which function on a more or less permanent basis are the Political Affairs Committee, Economic Affairs Committee, Committee on Parliamentary Affairs, Appointments Committee, Committee on Accommodation, Committee on Industry and Trade, and the Committee on Food and Agriculture etc. Of these the most powerful is the Political Affairs Committee. Consisting as it does of the seniormost minister, it functions as a super Cabinet in providing direction to the government.

Function and Role: The Cabinet committees are instruments to organise coordination in clearly defined fields of administration and relieve the Cabinet of their burden of work. The flexibility in membership of these committee enable interested Minister to exchange views, and arrive at agreed solutions without involving the Cabinet, thus, reducing pressure of work upon the latter. Lastly, there is considerable sharing of work, with the result that many matters which could otherwise travel upto the Cabinet for decision-making are settled at the level of Cabinet Committees. This ensures continuous coordination on vital economic and political issues, and speedy decision-making when required. Any matter which calls for a Cabinet decision may come directly to the appropriate committee before the Cabinet takes a decision. The Cabinet may often merely accept the decision already taken by the Cabinet Committees.

However, despite the fact that some Cabinet Committees have often exercised real authority, these committees have not been uniformly or consistently effective. Firstly, they do not cover all important areas of governmental functioning. Secondly, they can take up a matter only when it is referred to by the Minister concerned or by the Cabinet. Lastly, they do not meet regularly, which is absolutely necessary if sustained attention is to be given to complex problems and the progress in implementation of important policies and programmes is to be kept under constant review.

Q14. Throw light on the evolution of the U.P.S.C.
Ans. Since the very beginning of the Indian National Struggle for Freedom from British rule, Indianisation of the superior Civil Services had been one of the foremost demands of nationalist leaders. The demand kept growing as the hold of bureaucracy was increased. The enlightened leaders were able to see the enormous powers centered in the hands of young ICS officers of European

origin. This was found to be detrimental to the general good of the society. It was increasingly being realised that it was absolutely required to have Indians at these key positions to have any kind of hope of ameliorating the wretched conditions of poor, illiterate and rural citizens. The nationalist demands were paid lip service only, till the report of Sir Islington commission appointed in 1912 made some firm recommendations regarding the Indianisation of superior Civil services and formation of a Statutory commission charged with the responsibility of recruiting personnel for these services. The recommendation was repeated by Montague-Chelmsford report which came in the form of Government of India Act, 1919. This led to the creation of the British Indian Government to consider setting up of a Public Service Commission for recruitment to its services in the territory. The first Public Service Commission was set up on October 1st, 1926. However, its limited advisory functions failed to satisfy the people's aspirations and the continued stress on this aspect by the leaders of our freedom movement resulted in the setting up of the Federal Public Service Commission under the Government of India Act 1935. Under this Act, for the first time, provision was also made for the formation of Public Service Commission at the provincial level. After the independence the Federal Public Service Commission was renamed as Union Public Service Commission and its role significantly expanded. UPSC as it stands today is the highest level personnel agency of Government of India. It is a constitutional body created under the provisions of Article 315 of the constitution. It is highly autonomous body of experts chosen for their integrity and long experience in administration at various levels of the hierarchy. It is currently composed of One chairperson and Ten members. Its status is that of an Attached office of Ministry of Personnel, Public Grievances and Pensions. Before coming under the purview of current ministry, UPSC has been under the control Ministry of Home Affairs for significant period of its existence. It was brought under the Ministry of Personnel on the recommendation of the First Administrative Reforms Commission of India.

Lee Commission was formed in 1923 under the chairmanship of Lord Lee taking equal number of Indian and British members with the purpose of studying the racial composition of the superior public service of the government of India. The commission examined the recommendations of the Islington commission report (1912) and reviewed the existing position of two groups of services, the All-India Services and the Central Services. The Provincial Services were not considered as they had already come under the control of the provincial governments.

The commission in its report of 1924 divided the All-India Services into two groups. The first group included services operating in transferred fields, i.e., Higher Education (IES), Agriculture, Veterinary, Engineering (Roads and

Buildings branch) and the Medical Services. These services were provincialised and their recruitment was vested in the provincial governments. This was done in accordance with the spirits of the policy of montagu-chelmsford reforms (1919) that gave special emphasis on the problem of Indianising higher services. The services operating in reserved fields were in the second group. The commission suggested that the secretary of state for India should, for the present, retain his power of appointment and control of these services - the Indian Civil Service, the Indian Police Service, the Indian Services of Engineers (Irrigation Branch) and the Indian Forest Service. These four services were to be retained on All-India basis.

The Montagu-Chelmsford reforms proposed that one-third of total appointments to higher posts should go to Indians and thus the Islington Commission that had recommended only 25 percent posts for Indians became a dead letter. While this situation was developing within the services one of the major grievances of Indians regarding the holding of simultaneous examinations in India was redressed. Simultaneous examinations were instituted in London and New Delhi in 1922. By this time owing to political developments, many uncertainties arose and there was a shortage of British entrants.

In this background the Lee Commission's main recommendation was that 20 percent of the superior posts should be filled by promotions from provincial civil services and of the remaining 80 percent future entrants, 40 percent should be British and 40 percent Indians directly recruited. Owing to increase in the cost of living the civil servants for quite some time was demanding an increase of their salaries and improvements of other conditions of services. In this regard the commission decided neither to reduce the basic pay of the service nor to increase it all round, but it proposed to give substantial benefits to the European officers in the shape of various allowances. The European civil servants, however, considered the commission's recommendations quite unsatisfactory. Some of them viewed that the commission's report was very liberal towards Indianisation of higher administrations. The Indian political circle, on the contrary, felt that the commission's report had been too partial and liberal to the European civil servants. The Indian legislature criticised the proposed increase in the emoluments of the European civil servants in the shape of overseas pay and other allowances.

On the whole, the Indians were not satisfied with the rate of Indianisation of ICS and other superior services. The next important commission that examined the problems on the superior services of India after the Lee Commission was the Indian Statutory Commission of 1930. By 1947 more than 50 percent of about 1000 civil service personnel were Indians, many with long experience and holding high positions.

Q15. Discuss the constitution of the UPSC with reference to its composition, appointments, and terms of members.

Ans. Union Public Service Commission is a Constitutional Body constituted under Article 315 of the Constitution of India. The Commission is housed in the office complex in Dholpur House, at Shahjahan Road (Near India Gate), New Delhi.

Appointment and term of office of members: As laid down in Article 316 of the Constitution, the Chairman and other members of Union Public Service Commission are appointed by the President. However, as nearly as one half of the Members of the Commission are required to be those persons who have held office for at least ten years either under the Central Government or a State Government. The term of Member of Union Public Service Commission is six years from the date of assumption of office or till he attains the age of 65 years, whichever is earlier. Member of the Commission is eligible to continue in office for one term only. Member of the Commission can resign his office by addressing resignation letter to the President.

Removal and suspension of a member of U.P.S.C.: The procedure regarding removal and suspension of Chairman or any other member of the Commission are laid down in Article 317 of the Constitution of India. For the purpose of the higher level civil services of the Union Government, the Constitution provides for the setting up of the Union Public Service Commission (UPSC). The number of members of the Commission and the conditions of their service are left to be determined by the President, which means the government. It has since been decided that there shall be a chairman and six to eight members of the Commission. At present the strength of the Commission is nine including the chairman. The chairman and the members of the Commission are appointed by the President. The Constitution provides that at least half the members have to be persons who have served for at least ten years under the Government of India or a State Government. A member holds office for a term of six years from the date he joins duty or until he attain the age of sixty five years, whichever is earlier. The Chairman is ineligible for any future employment under the government, but other members are entitled to accept the chairmanship of the UPSC or of a State Public Service Commission. The conditions of service of members cannot be changed to their disadvantage after appointment. Their salaries, allowances, etc. are not submitted to the vote of Parliament as they are charged on the Consolidated Fund of India. It is also provided that the chairman or a member of the Commission can be removed from office by the President on the ground of misbehaviour. It is only after an inquiry by Supreme Court, on a reference being made to it by the President. Pending the inquiry by the Court, the President may suspend the member concerned. A member including the chairman would be deemed guilty of misbehaviour if he becomes interested in any monetary benefit in the discharge of duties as a member. It is also provided that the President may remove the chairman or any other member from office, on the ground of insolvency, infirmity of mind or body, or if he is engaged during the term of office in any paid employment outside the duties of his office.

Q16. What are the functions of the UPSC?

[June-09, Q.13][June-08, Q.6]

Ans. As per the Constitution the functions of UPSC are:

1. Recruitment to services and posts under the Union through conduct of competitive examinations;

2. Recruitment to services and posts under the Central Government by Selection through Interviews;

3. Advising on the suitability of officers for appointment on promotion as well as transfer-on-deputation;

4. Advising the Government on all matters relating to methods of recruitment to various services and posts;

5. Disciplinary cases relating to different civil services; and

6. Miscellaneous matters relating to grant of extra ordinary pensions, reimbursement of legal expenses etc.

Besides these constitutionally mandated functions, Commission looks into various matters related to personnel management as referred to it by president from time to time. Under Article 320 of the Constitution of India, the Commission are, inter-alia, required to be consulted on all matters relating to recruitment to civil services and posts. Commission is required to submit a report under Article 323 on its performance and recommendations made on annual basis to the President. This report is caused to be laid by the President in front of the Parliament along with written explanation for the cases in which any of UPSC's advice or recommendation was not accepted by the Union government. This gives a lot of weight to UPSC's recommendations and though advisory in nature these recommendations are generally accepted by government with few exceptions.

To ensure the highest standards in the recruitment process the Commission has been given highest degree of latitude in its operations. In fact, the Constitution itself ensures the independence of the commission from the political pressures coming from the executive. Briefly, these provisions are:

1. All the members of the Commission are appointed by the President under the warrant of his/her hand and seal.

2. They can be removed from their post only after an enquiry to this effect undertaken by a committee headed by the Chief Justice of India recommends for such an action on the grounds of proven misbehavior or incapacity.

3. All the expenses of the UPSC are charged on the Consolidated Fund of India.

4. The Chairperson of the UPSC cannot take any employment under the Government of India or any of the State governments, after his retirement. Other members can be employed only as either Chairperson of the UPSC or any of the State PSCs.

Commission has managed to retain its identity and autonomous character despite the pressures of a democratic polity. It has served its purpose of ensuring highest quality in recruitment and personnel affairs till date. With the changing dynamics of society, the commission is also changing its culture of working and administration. The coming of Right to Information on the scene has considerably changed the character of Indian democracy. UPSC is one of the major recipients of application of information under the RTI Act of 2005. This has not only disturbed the smooth functioning of UPSC till now but has also brought it under the scanner of judiciary. Though it has an impeccable record of integrity in Indian administrative scenario, it has to submit to the diktats of the people who are the ultimate sovereign of this country. The culture of secrecy is not good for democracy and has already done enough harm to the moral fiber of the administration. Under the veil of secrecy, corruption flourishes. The UPSC is also charged with the task of ensuring integrity and discipline in the administration, therefore it becomes the moral responsibility of the Commission to be open towards the demands of openness coming from various quarters of society and lead other departments by its example.

The UPSC is one of the most important institutions of democratic governance and has been instrumental in ensuring the constitutional provision of Equality of Opportunity to all the citizens by adhering to the standards of fairness and honesty in the administration of its competitive exams. It is abundantly obvious by looking at the back ground of the candidates who succeed at this exam. It has always given hope to millions of aspirants who come from poorest to richest of the backgrounds. It won't be wrong to say that UPSC has been a beacon of bright light in the dark sea of failing institutions of governance in India.

Q17. Discuss the advisory role of UPSC.

Ans. Though the Commission has been entrusted with important constitutional duties and functions, it has been assigned only an advisory and consultative role. Under the Government of India Act 1935, the position of the Federal Public Service Commission also was advisory in nature. It was then felt that vesting of excessive authority with the Commission would lead to its interference with the powers of the executive. The functions of the UPSC are just to advice the government and the executive is under no legal obligation to accept its advice.

The basic issue that is raised is whether the Commission can effectively discharge its functions with an advisory role. Therefore, the problem is whether a Commission constituted on the limited advisory basis would command the confidence of the public and of the services to the degree which is necessary, if it is to function effectively. But there is a viewpoint that Public Service Commission's role should be advisory in nature. This question was debated in the Constituent Assembly also and the Constitution makers gave an advisory role to the Commission.

It may be held that under the Constitution, there are certain matters regarding which the government is bound to take the advice of the Commission. Any violation of this provision would be considered unconstitutional. But the government is under no obligation to accept the advice of the Commission. At the same time, a constitutional restraint is imposed on the non-acceptance of the Commission's advice by the introduction of a new Article 323 in the Constitution. In cases where the advice of the Commission is not accepted, the government is required by this article to lay before the parliament a memorandum explaining the reasons for such non-acceptance. Further, in dealing with the Commission's advice, the power of Minister or Department has been deliberately restricted under which the advice cannot be rejected unless it has the approval of the Appointment Committee of the Cabinet. No action can be taken by any administrative department against the advice of the Commission unless it has the concurrence of the Committee. On account of these checks, internal and external, the number of cases of non-acceptance of the Commission's advice has been negligible.

Q18. Define Planning. Explain the needs and types of Planning.

Ans. Planning in organisations and public policy is both the organisational process of creating and maintaining a plan; and the psychological process of thinking about the activities required to create a desired goal on some scale. As such, it is a fundamental property of intelligent behavior. This thought process is essential to the creation and refinement of a plan, or integration of it with other plans, that is, it combines forecasting of developments with the preparation of scenarios of how to react to them.

The term is also used to describe the formal procedures used in such an endeavour, such as the creation of documents diagrams, or meetings to discuss the important issues to be addressed, the objectives to be met, and the strategy to be followed. Beyond this, planning has a different meaning depending on the political or economic context in which it is used.

Two attitudes to planning need to be held in tension: on the one hand we need to be prepared for what may lie ahead, which may mean contingencies and flexible processes. On the other hand, our future is shaped by consequences of our own planning and actions.

As the planning is of continuous process it is impossible to suggest water-tight categories of planning, none of the types of planning are self-contained, they are mere ideal types. Following may be stated as the types of planning:

a) Overall Planning

b) Limited Planning

c) Administrative Planning

a) Overall Planning: The overall planning, commonly called socio-economic planning, is more comprehensive. It is more than laying down a few economic targets here and a few physical targets there. It is an overall effort to achieve an all round development of the country. This type was first adopted by Stalin in USSR and being used in Russia since then. Most of the third world countries are adopting this type. Four years and seven years plans are manifestations of this type.

b) Limited Planning:: Limited planning does not centralise all the socio-economic activities at one focal point. The state opting for this type of planning selects the main objectives which the society as a whole considers fundamental. Through proper planning and regulation of the activities of the individual and group, it directs the life and activity of the society in such a way that those objectives are attained.

c) Administrative Planning:: Government planning is nothing but administrative planning. The administrative planning is mainly concerned with administrative programmes. It seeks to provide a broad framework for action as it defines major objectives, establishes inter-bureau policy and links departmental policy and programmes with the related departments. Its main purpose is to give a detailed shape to the policy plan, to make objectives clearer and more workable.

Administrative planning may be divided into four different phases, viz., policy planning, administrative planning, programme planning and operational planning. A brief explanation of these phases is given below:

i) Policy Planning: Policy planning is concerned with developing broad general outlines of government in power.

ii) Administrative Planning: According to Pfiffner it seeks 'to provide a broad framework for action by defining major objectives, establishing inter-bureau policy and to a lesser extent, lining departmental policy and programmes with those of related departments'. This policy is formulated by the chief executive in consultations with the departmental heads to give effect to the policy planning and to make objective clearer and more workable for the public officials.

iii) Programme Planning: According to Millett, it is 'concerned with the preparation of the specific purposes to be realised and the procedures to be employed by administrative agencies within the framework of existing public policy'. It is an overall review of the proposed programme to determine the volume of service involved, the resources in man and money needed to provide them, the general procedures required and the organisation structure necessary to use these resources to the best advantage. It is a detailed plan for implementing the programmes in a particular department.

iv) Operation Planning: According to Pfiffner, it is 'concerned with the systematic analysis of an authorised programme and determination of the detailed means of carrying it out. After the objectives have been determined and the means and methods of achieving those objectives have been found, then comes operational planning by the divisional and sectional heads who lay down specific procedures and how those have to be used to save time, accelerate production and increase net output. The different units are assigned specific functions and their performance measured in terms of time, quantity and quality of production and overall product. It is, in fact, a 'workshop-stage' of the programme planning.

Besides the above types of planning, several new types of planning have emerged in the recent years known as Perspective Planning, Rolling Plan, Short Rage or Long-Range Planning, and District Planning or Grass Root Planning.

Q19. Discuss the genesis of Planning in India.

Ans. India has attempted to bring about rapid economic and social development of the country through a planned effort. Although an awareness of the importance of planning was manifest in the pre-independence era, realistic and ambitious planning on an all-India basis could not be started effectively until India became free in 1947 and its major problems growing out of the partition of the country and the task of unification of the native Indian States were resolved.

The first effort at introducing social planning in Indian was made by an individual noted for his pioneering seal and breadth of vision, the late Dr. M. Visveswarayya. In 1936, he published an essay underlining the desirability and feasibility of planning for industrialisation of the country. For the formulation, implementation and administration of the plan, he had suggested formation of a 60-member advisory body, with political leaders, economists, businessmen, administrators, etc., and a Planning Commission of five to seven members for discharging day-to-day functions. He also recommended the setting up of a development department at the Centre and Economic Councils in the provinces. Though interesting as an intellectual exercise, this could not directly influence any social action or any governmental move.

In 1937, soon after the assumption of power in the provinces, the Working Committee of the Indian National Congress initiated planning preliminaries by adopting a resolution which recommended to the Congress Ministry the appointment of a committee of experts to consider urgent and vital problems, the solution of which was necessary to any scheme of national re-construction and social planning. Following this resolution, a Planning Committee was constituted by Subhash Chandra Bose, the then President of the Indian National Congress under the Chairmanship of Jawaharlal Nehru. Later in 1944, the government established a Planning and Development Board and published three private development plans – the Bombay Plan, the Gandhi Plan and the People's Plan. A Planning Advisory Board was also constituted in 1946 after the establishment of the interim government headed by Jawaharlal Nehru. These pre-Independence efforts at planning tend to bring out a certain unity of approach to the problems of national reconstruction in as much as each of these plans mooted not only had certain objectives in common but also sought to achieve them through similar means. All the plan proposal explicitly accepted the rapid improvement of the living standards of the people as the central objective of development.

The central theme of public policy and philosophy of national planning in India since Independence has been promotion of balanced economic development so as to provide foundations for sustained economic growth; for increasing opportunities for gainful employment, for promoting greater equality in income and wealth and raising living standards and working conditions for the masses. Even the Directive Principles of State Policy carries the same spirit of balanced economic development. The Constitution of India includes the subject of social and economic planning in the concurrent list. The legal basis for national planning for the country as a whole, therefore, has been provided through a parliamentary statute on the subject. The discussions on the setting up of a planning machinery in 1949 had envisaged the establishment of a Planning Commission and the creation of National Economic Council which would work as an organ of intergovernmental cooperation in the economic and social fields. Following the recommendations of the Advisory Planning Board of 1946, the Planning Commission was established by a Cabinet resolution of March 15, 1950. The National Development Council was later constituted in 1952.

Q20. Write a short note on Planning Commission of India.

Ans. Planning Commission of India: The Planning Commission is an institution in the Government of India, which formulates India's Five-Year Plans, among other functions.

History: Rudimentary economic planning, deriving the sovereign authority of the state, first began in India in 1930s under the British Raj, and the Colonial Government of India formally established a planning board that functioned from 1944 to 1946. Private industrialists and economist formulated at least three development plans in 1944. After India gained independence, a formal model of planning was adopted, and the Planning Commission, reporting directly to the Prime Minister of India was established. Accordingly, the Planning Commission was set up on 15 March 1950, with Prime Minister Jawahar Lal Nehru as the chairman.

Organisation: The composition of the Commission has undergone a lot of change since its inception. With the Prime Minister as the ex-officio Chairman, the committee has a nominated Deputy Chairman, who is given the rank of a full Cabinet Minister. Mr. Montek Singh Ahluwalia is presently the Deputy Chairman of the Commission.

Cabinet Ministers with certain important portfolios act as part-time members of the Commission, while the full-time members as experts of various fields like Economics, Industry, Science and General Administration.

The Commission works through its various divisions, of which there are two kind:

· General Planning Divisions

· Programme Administration Divisions

The majority of experts in the Commission are economists, making the Commission the biggest employer of the Indian Economic Services.

Functions:

1. Assessment of resources of the country

2. Formulation of Five-Year Plans for effective use of these resources

3. Determination of priorities, and allocation of resources for the Plans

4. Determination of requisite machinery for successful implementation of the Plans

5. Periodical appraisal of the progress of the Plan

6. To formulate plans for the most effective and balanced utilisation of country's resources.

7. To indicate the factors which are hampering economic development.

8. To determine the machinery, which will be necessary for the successful implementation of each stage of plan.

Q21. Write a short note on National Development Council (NDC).

Ans. The NDC is headed by the Prime Minister and consists of the Central Ministers, Chief Ministers of the States and Lt. Governors, Administrators of Union Territories and Members of the Planning Commission. It is a nodal body, which considers and approves polices and strategies of development planning. The Secretary of the Planning Commission acts as the Secretary of the Council. From a strictly legal point of view, NDC is essentially an advisory body. Since it comprises the highest political authority in the country, it has assumed an important position. The meetings of NDC are held at least twice a year. The role of the NDC is discussed briefly:

i) it acts as a kind of bridge between the Union Government, the Planning Commission and the State Governments.

ii) NDC prescribes guidelines for the formulation of National Plan including the assessment of resources for the Plan.

iii) NDC considers the National Plan as formulated by the Planning Commission.

iv) NDC considers important questions of social and economic policy affecting national development.

v) It also reviews the work of the Plan from time to time and recommends such measures as are necessary for achieving the aims and targets set out in the national plan including measures to secure the active participation and cooperation of the people, improve the efficiency of the administrative services, ensure the fullest development of the less advance regions and sections of the community and, through sacrifice, borne equally by all the citizens, build up resources for national development.

The NDC gives its advice at various stages of the formulation of the Plan and it is only after its approval has been obtained that a Plan is presented to the Parliament for its consideration. The Council has been largely responsible for giving India plan a national character and for ensuring unanimity in approach and uniformity in working.

Q22. Discuss the problems which arise in the path of centralised planning?

Ans. Ever since 1951, when the First Five Year Plan went into operation, right through the formulation of the Seventh Five Year Plan in recent years, India has been following national policy of central planning for controlled and unified development. This has given rise to a number of problems in administration:

1) Whether planning should come from above or below?

2) To what extent should the society be subject to planning and how the people should be associated in the formulation and execution of plans?

3) What modification should be made in the relationship between the Centre and the States which have distinct powers in a federal constitution so as to make centralised planning effective?

4) Who should constitute the members of the planning body?

5) If the planning body is set up outside the normal executive organisation of the government, as the Planning Commission in this country is, should its advisory services be arranged in the existing organisation or should it have an administration of its own for this purpose?

6) To what extent should the Planning Commission concern itself with the details of the Plan?

7) What should be the Planning Commission's responsibility in reviewing the progress of the Plan and what reports is the Planning Commission entitled to ask from the executive authorities?

8) What is the mechanism for dove-tailing the work of the planning machinery in the states which that of the centre, etc.?

Although some of these problems have been taken care of in the initial establishment of the Planning Commission and its subsequent reorganisations, it must be confessed that the administrative organisation for planning has grown haphazardly without any systematic examination of these problems. The result is that Planning Commission today is a mammoth organisation, almost 'a parallel government' in the words of Pandit Nehru.

It is to be noted that the Planning Commission and the National Development Council are not constitutional bodies. Now we have a constitutionally mandated District Planning Committee every District, for further reading vide the planning process.

Q23. Write a short note on followings:
1. Indian Administrative Services
2. Indian Police Services
3. Indian Forest Services
4. Indian Foreign Services
Ans. 1. Indian Administrative Service (IAS):
· The Indian Administrative Service (IAS) was formed in the year of 1946.
· It is one of the three All India Services. (The other two are Indian Forest Services and Indian Police Services)
· The cadre controlling authority is Ministry of Personnel, Public Grievances and Pension, Department of Personnel and Training.
· Cadre size: 5159 posts.
· The selected candidates' training ground is at Lal Bahadur Shastri National Academy of Administration.
Functions of IAS Officers:
· The IAS handles affairs of government, which involves the framing and implementation of policy in consultation with the concerned Minister.
· Implementation of policies calls for supervision and also travelling to the places where the decisions taken are being implemented.
· Implementation entails disbursement of funds, which calls for personal supervision
· The officers are answerable to the Parliament and State Legislatures for any irregularities that may occur.
· The functions and responsibilities of an IAS officer change at different points of his/her career.

· All the beginning of their career IAS officers join the state administration at the sub-divisional level, as a sub-divisional magistrate, and look after law and order, general administration and development work in the area under their charge.

· The post of the District Officer variously known as District Magistrate, District Collector or Deputy Commissioner is the most prestigious and identifiable post held by the members of the service.

· At the district level, these officers are mainly concerned with district affairs, including implementation of developmental programs.

· During the normal course of a career, the officers also serve in the State Secretariat or as Heads of Departments or in Public Sector Undertakings.

· Officers may move from positions at the State, under deputation, to the Centre and back again.

· At the top of the hierarchy of IAS officers at the Centre is the Cabinet Secretary followed by Secretary/Additional Secretary, Joint Secretary, Director, Deputy Secretary and Under Secretary. These posts are filled according to seniority.

· The main work of IAS officers at the Centre, involves formulation and implementation of policies pertaining to a particular area e.g., finance, Commerce, etc.

· In the process of policy formulation and decision making, officers at various levels like Joint Secretary, Deputy Secretary make their contributions and the final shape to the policy is given or a final decision is taken with the concurrence of the minister concerned or the Cabinet depending upon the gravity of the issue.

2. Indian Police Service (IPS):

· The Indian Police Service (IPS) was formed in the year of 1948.

· It is one of the three All India Services. (The other two are Indian Forest Services and Indian Administrative Services)

· The cadre controlling authority is Ministry of Home Affairs.

· Cadre size: 3549 posts.

The selected candidates' training ground is at Sardar Vallabhbhai Patel National Police Academy.

Kiran bedi- first women IPS officer

Functions of IPS Officers:

· Day-to-day duties, particularly in the areas of maintenance of public peace and order, crime prevention, investigation, and detection, collection of intelligence, VIP security, border policing, railway policing, smuggling, drug trafficking, economic offences, corruption in public life, disaster management, enforcement of socio-economic legislation, bio-diversity and protection of environmental laws etc.

· Leading and commanding the civil and armed police forces in all the states and union territories.

· Leading and commanding the Central Police Organisations like Intelligence Bureau, Central Bureau of Investigation, Border Security Force, Central Reserve Police Force, Indo-Tibetan Border Police, National Security Guard, and Vigilance Organisations etc.

· Serve at managerial/policy making levels in the Ministries and Departments of Central and State Governments and public sector undertakings both at centre and states, and the RAW, Government of India.

· Required to interact and coordinate closely with the members of other All India Services and Central Civil Services and also with the Armed Forces.

· Last but not the least, lead the force with courage, uprightness, dedication and a strong sense of service to the people.

· Endeavour to inculcate in the police forces under their command such values and norms as would help them serve the people better.

· Inculcate integrity of the highest order, sensitivity to aspirations of people in a fast-changing social and economic milieu, respect for human rights, broad liberal perspective of law and justice, high standard of professionalism, physical fitness and mental alertness.

3. Indian Forest Services: India is one of the first countries in the world to have stated scientific management of its forests. During the year 1864 the then British India Government started the Imperial Forest Department and appointed Dr. Dietrich Brandis, a German Forest officer Inspector General of Forests in 1866. Having recognised the need to have a premier forest service to manage the varied natural resources of the vast country and to organise the affairs of the Imperial Forest Department, Imperial Forest Service was constituted in 1867.

Having realised the importance of a multi-tier forest Administration in the federal and provincial Governments for effective management of forest resources. The British India Government also constituted Provincial Forest Service and Executive and Subordinate Services, which were quite similar to the present day forest administrative hierarchy.

The officers appointed to the Imperial Forest Service from 1867 to 1885 were trained in France and Germany. Thereafter, until 1905 they were trained at

Cooper's Hill, London, which had been one of the prestigious professional colleges of Forestry at that time. From 1905 to 1926, the Universities of Oxford, Cambridge and Edinburgh had undertaken the task of training the officers of the Imperial Forest Service. The Imperial Forest Research Institute, Dehradun, presently and popularly known all over the world as FRI was established at Dehradun in the year 1906. The baton to train the IFS officers was passed on to Forest Research Institute, which it did successfully from 1927 to 1932. Subsequently the Indian Forest College (IFC) was established in the year 1938 at Dehradun and the officers recruited to the Superior Forest Service by the provinces/states were trained there.

The subject of "Forestry" which was managed by the Federal Government until then was transferred to the "Provincial List" by the Government of India Act, 1935 and subsequently recruitment to the Imperial Forest Service was discontinued.

The Indian Forest Service, one of the three All India Services, was constituted in the year 1966 under the All India Services Act, 1951 by the Government of India.

The main mandate of the service is the implementation of the National Forest Policy which envisages scientific management of forests and to exploit them on a sustained basis for primary timber products, among other things. Since 1935 the management of the forests remained in the hands of the Provincial Governments and even today the Forest Departments are managing the forests of the country under the respective State governments.

Organisation of the Service: The initial constitution of the Indian Forest Service consisted of the four following categories of the officers

1. Initial Recruits (IR);

2. Emergency Commissioned/Short Service Commissioned (EC/SSC)

3. Direct Recruits also known as Regular Recruits (DR/RRs); and

4. Promotees (appointed from State Forest Service).

Initial Recruits: With the constitution of the Service, the serving members of the State Forest Service borne on various State Governments and Union Territory Administrations were inducted into the Service and they had been accordingly designated as "Initial Recruits" to the Service. All members under the "IR" category have since retired on superannuation.

Emergency Commissioned/Short Service Commissioned : 20% of the permanent vacancies in the Indian Forest Service were filled by Direct Recruitment from the released "Emergency Commissioned" (EC) officers and "Short Service Commissioned" (SSC) officers and they were designated as ECs/SSCs and it continued till 28th January 1971. The last of the EC/SSC officers would superannuate from the service by 2006.

Direct Recruits: 66.33 per cent of the cadre strength of the service is filled by Direct Recruitment done through the Union Public Service Commission (UPSC) by conducting an all India level competitive examination open to graduates with science background. After qualifying the written examination, the candidates have to appear for a personality test, a walking test and a standard medical fitness test.

Promotees: 33.33 per cent of the cadre strength of the service, as per the regulations, is to be filled by appointing eligible officers of the State Forest Service to IFS. Vacancies under promotion quota are determined by calculating 33.33% of the total Senior Duty Posts in the Cadre in addition to Central Deputation Reserve posts, State Deputation Reserve posts and Training Reserve.

Composition: The Indian Forest Service, by virtue of being the youngest of the three All India Services, also happens to be the smallest. The total authorised cadre strength of the Indian Forest Service as on date is 2751 which includes 1917 Direct Recruit and 834 Promotion posts. The total Senior Duty Posts (SDP) in the Indian Forest Service are 1674 and the remaining under various reserves.

4. Indian Foreign Service: The origin of the Indian Foreign Service can be traced back to the British rule when the Foreign Department was created to conduct business with the "Foreign European Powers". In fact it was on September 13, 1783, when the Board of Directors of the East India Company passed a resolution at Fort William, Calcutta (now Kolkata), to create a department, which could help "relieve the pressure" on the Warren Hastings administration in conducting its "secret and political business". Subsequently known as the "Indian Foreign Department", it went ahead with the expansion of diplomatic representation, wherever necessary, to protect British interests. In 1843, Governor General Ellenborough carried out administrative reforms under which the Secretariat of the Government was organised under four departments – Foreign, Home, Finance and Military. Each was headed by a Secretary level officer. The foreign department Secretary was entrusted with the "conduct of all correspondence belonging to the external and internal diplomatic relations of the government".

From the very beginning, a distinction was maintained between the "foreign" and "political" functions of the Foreign Department; relations with all "Asiatic powers" (including native princely states of India during the British Raj) were treated as "political" and with all European powers as "foreign".

Although the Government of India Act, 1935 sought to delineate more clearly functions of the "Foreign" and "Political" wings of the Foreign Department, it was soon realised that it was administratively imperative to completely bifurcate the Foreign department. Consequently, the External Affairs Department was set up separately under the direct charge of the Governor General.

The idea of establishing a separate diplomatic service to handle the external activities of the Government of India originated from a note dated September 30, 1944, recorded by Lt-Gen T. J. Hutton, Secretary, Planning and Development Department of the Government. When this note was referred to the Department of External Affairs for comments, Mr. Olaf Caroe, the Foreign Secretary, recorded his comments in an exhaustive note detailing the scope, composition and functions of the proposed service. Mr Caroe pointed out that as India emerged to a position of autonomy and national consciousness, it was imperative to build up a system of representation abroad that would be in complete harmony with the objectives of the future government.

In September 1946, on the eve of India's independence, the Government of India decided to create a service called the Indian Foreign Service for India's diplomatic, consular and commercial representation overseas.

In 1947, there was a near seamless transformation of the Foreign and Political department of the British India government into what then became the new Ministry of External Affairs and Commonwealth Relations and in 1948 the first batch recruited under the combined Civil service examination system of the Union Public Service Commission joined the service. This system of entry has remained the staple mode of intake into the IFS to this day.

Training: On selection to the Indian Foreign Service through the combined Civil Service examination, the new entrants undergo a multi-faceted and comprehensive training programme intended to give them a thorough grounding in diplomatic knowledge, diplomatic qualities and diplomatic skills. The probationers commence their training, together with their colleagues from the other All India Services, at the Lal Bahadur Shastri National Academy of Administration, Mussourie. Thereafter the probationers join the Foreign Service Institute in New Delhi and undergo focused training in the various disciplines that a career diplomat needs to familiarise himself with. The Foreign Service Institute course involves lectures, attachments with various wings of the Government as well as familiarisation tours both within the country and abroad. The aim of this course is to inculcate in the diplomatic recruit a strong sense of history, knowledge of diplomacy and international relations and a grasp of general economic and political principles.

At the conclusion of the training programme, the officer is assigned his/her compulsory foreign language (CFL). After a brief period of desk attachment in the Ministry of External Affairs the officer is posted to an Indian Mission abroad in a country where his CFL is the native language and enrolled in a language course. The officer is expected to develop proficiency in his CFL and pass the requisite examination before he is confirmed in service.

Career: A Foreign Service Officer begins his career abroad as a Third Secretary and is promoted to Second Secretary as soon as he is confirmed in service. Subsequent promotions are to the levels of First Secretary, Counsellor, Minister and Ambassador/High Commissioner/Permanent Representative. Officers can also be posted to Indian Consulates abroad where the hierarchy (going upwards) is Vice-Consul, Consul and Consul General.

The hierarchy at the Ministry of External Affairs includes 6 stages: Under Secretary, Deputy Secretary, Director, Joint Secretary, Additional Secretary and Secretary.

Functions: As a career diplomat, the Foreign Service Officer is required to project India's interests, both at home and abroad on a wide variety of issues. These include bilateral political and economic cooperation, trade and investment promotion, cultural interaction, press and media liaison as well as a whole host of multilateral issues.

The functions of an Indian diplomat may be summarised as:

· Representing India in its Embassies, High Commissions, Consulates, and Permanent Missions to multilateral organisations like UN;

· Protecting India's national interests in the country of his/her posting;

· Promoting friendly relations with the receiving state as also its people, including NRI / PIOs;

· Reporting accurately on developments in the country of posting which are likely to influence the formulation of India's policies;

· Negotiating agreements on various issues with the authorities of the receiving state; and

· Extending consular facilities to foreigners and Indian nationals abroad.

· At home, Ministry of External Affairs is responsible for all aspects of external relations. Territorial divisions deal with bilateral political and economic work while functional divisions look after policy planning, multilateral organisations, regional groupings, legal matters, disarmament, protocol, consular, Indian Diaspora, press and publicity, administration and other aspects.

Strength: In recent years, the intake into the Indian Foreign Service has averaged between 8-15 persons annually. The present cadre strength of the service stands at approximately 600 officers manning around 162 Indian missions and posts abroad and the various posts in the Ministry at home.

Q24. Briefly describe the method of recruitment in the All India Services.
Ans. The recruitment to the All India Services is made by the Central Government on the basis of a competitive examination annually conducted by the Union Public Service Commission (UPSC). The examination is a combined one – for a number of services like the IFS, IAS, IPS and the Central Services Class I and II. To appear at the examination, a candidate must be between the age of 21 and 30. Only a University graduate (one holding B.A. or B.Sc. or an equivalent degree) can appear at the examination. The examination combines a written test of a high standard with a 'personality test" by the Union Public

Service Commission in the form of a personal interview. The former aims at judging the level of intelligence and academic learning and the latter attempts to make a measure of the qualities of personality and character. The examination system is modeled on the British 'general' type rather than the American 'specialised' type.

There is a provision for relaxation of age upto a maximum of five years for SC/ST candidates and three years for candidates belonging to OBC category. The number of permissible attempts to appear in the examination has been restricted to four, with relaxation for OBC candidates (seven attempts) and SC/ST candidates (no limit).

Prior to 1979 a single competitive examination used to be held. There were three compulsory papers: Essay, General Knowledge and General English – each carrying 150 marks. But of a number of optional papers, three papers of 200 marks each, and two additional subjects (for IAS and IFS only) out of another list of subjects each carrying 200 marks were to be offered. The candidates who qualified in the written examination were called for interview, which carried 300 marks. The candidates who failed to secure a minimum of 33% of qualifying marks in the interview were declared unsuccessful. It was abolished in 1958. The interview marks were added to the marks obtained in the written papers. After this, the Commission recommended the list of selected candidates in order of merit to the government.

The above system of recruitment in the All India Services was criticised from a number of view points, and the UPSC decided to review the system thoroughly. For this purpose a Committee on Recruitment and Selection Methods under the Chairmanship of Prof. D.S. Kothari was appointed by the UPSC in 1974. The Committee submitted its report in 1976 and made the following recommendations:

1) To hold a Preliminary examination to screen the candidates for the Main examination;

2) To hold the Main examination to select candidates for entry to the LBS National Academy for a foundation course of about nine months;

3) To hold a post-training test of 400 marks to be conducted by the UPSC on completion of the foundation course, the purpose being to assess personal qualities and attributes relevant to the civil services;

4) To assign candidates to a particular service on the basis of the total marks obtained in the Main examination and the Post-Training Text at LBS Academy, taking into account the candidate's preferences for the services;

5) To allow the candidates to answer all papers, except the language paper, in any language listed in the Eighth Schedule of the Constitution, or in English.

The Kothari Committee's recommendations regarding the examination scheme (preliminary and main) was accepted by the government, and it was implemented by UPSC in 1979.

Satish Chandra Committee: The UPSC set up another Committee in 1988 under the Chairmanship of the former UGC Chairman Satish Chandra to review and evaluate the system of selection to the higher Civil Services and to make suggestions for further improvement. The Committee submitted its report in 1993 and the government is gradually implementing some of the recommendations with effect from the Civil Service Examination of 1993. The main recommendations as accepted by the government are:

1. The practice of holding a common examination should continue;

2. An essay paper should be introduced from 1993 examination, and the candidates should be allowed to answer this paper in any one of the languages included in the Eighth Schedule or in English;

3. The marks for the personality test should be raised from 250 marks to 300;

4. From the list of optional subjects certain languages like French, German, Arabic, Pali should be excluded;

5. For both Preliminary and Main Examinations, Medical Science should be included as an optional subject;

6. Allotment of services should be on the basis of the candidate's rank and preferences;

7. LBS Academy of Administration should be developed into a high level professional institution;

8. Adequate infrastructural facilities and proper faculty support should be provided to the training institutions;

9. The UGC may review the scheme of conducting coaching classes for students belonging to the minority communities to enable them to complete in various competitive examinations.

Present Pattern of Civil Services Examination: The competitive examination comprises three successive stages;**(a)** Civil Services (Preliminary) Examination, **(b)** Civil Services (Main) Examination, and **(c)** Interview.

(a) The preliminary Examination consists of two papers of objective type (multiple choice questions) and carry a maximum of 450 marks: on paper on general studies having 150 marks, and another paper of 300 marks on one subject to be selected from a list of optional subjects. The question papers are set in English and Hindi. The Preliminary Examination is meant to serve as a screening test only; the marks obtained in this examination by the candidates who are declared qualified for admission to the Main Examination are not counted for determining their final order of merit. The number of candidates to be admitted to the Main Examination is twelve to thirteen times the total number of vacancies in the year.

(b) The Main Examination consists of a written examination and an interview test.

The written examination consists of 9 papers of conventional essay type. The nine papers are:

Paper-I	One of the Indian languages to be selected by the candidate from the languages included in the Eighth Schedule of the constitution	300 marks
Paper-II	English	300 marks
Paper-IV	General Studies	300 marks for each paper
Paper-V		
Paper-VI	Any two subjects to be	300 marks for each paper
Paper-VII& VIII	Selected from the list of optional subjects	
Paper-IX	Each subject will have two papers	

·It is to be noted that the papers on Indian language and English are of Matriculation or equivalent standard and are of a qualifying nature; the marks obtained in the papers will not be counted for ranking. Moreover, the papers on Essay, General Knowledge and optional subjects of only such candidates will be evaluated as attain such minimum standard fixed by the UPSC. The Paper-I on Indian Languages is not, however, compulsory for the candidates hailing from certain North-Eastern States like Manipur, Mizoram.

The question papers for the examination are of conventional (Essay) type, and each paper is of three hours duration. The candidates may answer all the question papers, except the language papers in any one of the languages included in the Eighth Schedule. The question papers other than language papers are, however, set both in Hindi and English.

c) The candidates securing minimum qualifying marks in the civil Services (Main Examination, as stipulated by the UPSC, are called for an interview for personality test. The Candidates are interviewed by a Board and are asked question of general interest. The object of the interview is to assess the personal suitability of the candidate for a career in Public Service. The test is intended to judge the mental caliber of a candidate. The interview carries 250 marks.

The rank order list of candidates is prepared on the basis of total marks secured in the Main Examination and the interview. The allocation of candidates to different services is made on the basis of their rank in the tests and preferences. The rank order list is forwarded by the UPSC to the government for further necessary action.

State Administration

Q1. Discuss the threefold distribution of power between Union and State.
Ans. Legislative powers of the government, that is the power to make laws upon a specific subject, are separated in India by means of the three lists - Union list, State list and Concurrent list. These powers are divided between the Central Government : the Parliament and the State Government, that is the State legislature.
Union list: The union list consists of 97 subjects on which the Central Government or the Parliament can make laws. The subjects in this list include subjects of nation importance like Defense, Foreign Affairs, Atomic Energy, Banking, Post and Telegraph. The Central Government makes laws on these at all times, including in times of emergencies.
State list: The state list contains 66 subjects of local or state importance on which the State Governments can make laws. These subjects include Police, Local Governments, Trade, Commerce and Agriculture. In times of national and state emergency, the power to make laws on these subjects is transferred to the Parliament.
Concurrent list: The concurrent list contains 47 subjects on which both the Parliament and the State legislatures can make laws. It includes Criminal and Civil Procedure, Marriage and Divorce, Education, Economic Planning and Trade Unions. However, in case of conflict between a law made by the Central Government and a law made by the State Legislatures, the law made by the Central government will prevail.
India has borrowed the idea of the Concurrent list from the Constitution of Australia. Education was shifted from the State list to the Concurrent list by the 42nd Amendment Act of 1976.
Distribution of Legislative Subjects between the Union and the States: The division of the powers of the Union and the State can be traced to the distribution of the powers as stated by the three lists laid down by the Indian Constitution. Derived from the Australian Constitution, these lists clearly divide the powers vested on the State and the Union. They are the Union List, the

State List and the Concurrent List.

The Union List: Also referred to as List I, this list contains legislations, on which the Union enjoys exclusive control. Of the total 99 subjects that are included in the Union list, some are enlisted below:

· Defence
· Banking
· Taxes
· Coinage
· Insurance
· Currency
· Union Duties
· Foreign Affairs

The State List: This is the List II of the Indian Legislative. There are a total of 69 subjects in this particular list, all of which are exclusive legislative powers of the State. Some of the subjects enlisted in the State list are as follows:

· Public Order and Police
· State Taxes and Duties
· Agriculture
· Sanitation
· Local governments
· Forests
· Fisheries
· Public Health

The Concurrent List: This list contains 52 items, which are powers vested on the State as well as the Union. Some of the subjects included in the Concurrent List are as follows:

· Economic and Social Planning
· Criminal Law and Procedure
· Civil Procedure
· Torts
· Trusts
· Marriage
· Education
· Welfare and Labor
· Contracts

However, in case there is any repugnance, the Union legislature will prevail over the State legislature. In case a State Law has already been reserved for the consent of the President, or if such an assent has already been granted, then the State Law will hold irrespective of the repugnance. However, the Parliament can override the Law through subsequent legislation.

The Residuary Powers are the legislative powers that fall in none of the above categories. The lists are usually exhaustive enough to include all possible subjects, and it is generally believed that the field of application will be very narrow. These powers are neither under the legislative powers of the State nor the Union, but is under the jurisdiction of the Judiciary.

It should be mentioned in this context, that the legislative powers of the Parliament can be extended under special situations to include certain subjects of the State List. Some of the conditions under which the Parliament may extend its powers include the follows:

· In the National Interest: This is in accordance of the Article 249 of the Indian Constitution.

· Proclamation of Emergency: Based on the Article 250 of the Indian Constitution, the Union takes over the Legislative powers of the State subjects once the President declares emergency in any state.

· Agreement between the States: If two states agree that the Parliament can legally make laws with respect to the two states, then the Parliament can make laws relating to any law or set of laws related to the State Laws. This is an extension of the Parliamentary legislative as laid down by the Article 252 of the Indian Constitution.

· Implementation of Treaties: The Parliament makes laws for the implementation of treaties, even if the subject falls under the legislative power of the State, for the bigger international interest of the country. This power has been given to the Union by the Article 253.

· Failure of Constitutional Machinery in a State: This power of legislative extension follows a proclamation by the President that declares the inefficiency of a State Legislature. The powers of the State Legislature then come directly under the jurisdiction of the Union Legislative. It is guided by the Article 356 (1) (b) of the Indian Constitution.

Distribution of Executive Powers between the Union and the States: The distribution of the executive powers is much more complicated than the distribution of the legislative powers. Article 162 vests the executive powers on the Union and the States largely on the lines of the Legislative Powers. The executive powers related to laws included in the Concurrent list ordinarily remain within the state's power. However, the Union has the right to take up the administration of the Union Laws relating to any Concurrent subject, as and when it thinks fit. The Union also has the right to mediate during any dispute between the States. Generally, it can be thus concluded that the exercise of the Concurrent list remains with the State, except in the following situations:

· Whenever the Parliament vests some functions exclusively on the Union.

· Where the provisions of the Constitution itself vests some executive functions exclusively on the Union like international agreement, irrespective whether the subject falls in the Concurrent, Union or State List.

Q2. Briefly discuss the role of the Governor in State administration.

[June-08, Q.3][June-07, Q.3]

Ans. Role of the Governor:

· There shall be a Governor for each state (Article 153 of the Constitution of India).

· The executive power of the State shall be vested in the Governor and shall be exercised by him either directly or through officers subordinate to him in accordance with the Constitution of India (Article 154).

· The Governor of a State shall be appointed by the President by warrant under his hand and seal (Article 155).

· A person to be eligible for appointment as Governor should be citizen of India and has completed age of 35 years (Article 157).

· The Governor shall not be a member of the Legislature or Parliament; shall not hold any office of profit, shall be entitled to emoluments and allowances. (Article 158).

· Every Governor and every person discharging the function of the Governor shall make a subscribe, an oath or Affirmation(Article 159).

· The President may make such a provision as he thinks fit for the discharge of the functions of the Governor of a State in any contingency not provided for in Chapter II of the Constitution.(Article 160).

· The Governor shall have the power to grant pardons, reprieves, etc. (Article 161).

· There shall be Council of Ministers with the Chief Minister at the head to aid and advise the Governor in the exercise of his functions except in so far as he is by or under the Constitution required to exercise his functions or any of them in his discretion (Article 163).

· The Governor appoints Chief Minister and other Ministers. (Article 164).

· The Governor appoints the Advocate General for the State. (Article 165).

· All executive actions ,of the Governor of a State shall be expressed to be taken in the name of Governor. (Article 166).

· The Governor shall from time to time summon and prorogue the House and dissolve the Legislative Assembly. (Article 174).

· The Governor may address the Legislative Assembly....; The Governor may send messages to the House. (Article 175).

· Special Address to the House by the Governor. (Article 176).

· The Governor assents, withholds assent or reserves for the consideration of the Bill passed by the Legislative Assembly. (Article 200).

· The Governor shall in respect of every financial year cause to be laid before the House.... a statement of the estimated receipts and expenditure.(Article 202).

· No demand for a grant shall be made except on the recommendation of the

Governor. (Article 203(3)).

· The Governor shall ....cause to be laid before the House another statement showing estimated amount of expenditure. (Article 205).

· The Governor may promulgate the ordinances under certain circumstances. (Article 213).

· The Governor is consulted for appointment of Judges of High Court. (Article 217).

Q3. What are the various ways through which the Legislature exercise it's control over the administration?

Or

Comment over the legislature control over administration.

Ans. Apart from providing necessary legislative support to the executive, the Legislature also acts as an instrument of popular control over administration. In a Parliamentary democracy like ours, this control is exercised in following forms:

Assembly Questions: The members of the Assembly have a right to ask questions from the government. They can also ask supplementary questions. This device keeps the government on its toes. Whenever weaknesses are notice, the government is compelled to promise and take corrective action.

Discussions: Apart from asking questions, the members may ask for discussions over important matters. They may also bring forward Call Attention Motions and Adjournment Motions on important public matters. Even if such motions are not allowed, a lot of information has to be supplied by the government is kept on a tight leash and has to answer the representatives of the people.

Financial Control by Budget

No money can be raised and no expenditure can be incurred without a vote by the Legislature. By controlling the purse strings, the Legislature controls the programmes and activities of the government. It is true that by virtue of its majority in the Legislature, the government may ultimately get the money it wants voted, but during the process, a lot of discussion takes place. This keeps the government in touch with the needs of the people. The discussion also highlights the weaknesses of the administration in the implementation of the voted programmes.

Post-expenditure Control: The State Legislature also scrutinises the expenditure incurred by the government through the device of audit. Indian Constitution provides for an integrated accounts and audit system. The Comptroller and Auditor General of India (CAG) gets the accounts of the state government audited and sends his report to the Assembly through the Governor. The Public Accounts Committee of the State Legislature goes through this report, examines and finally reports to the Legislature. Any instances of unauthorised, improper, or imprudent expenditure are thus discussed in detail and brought to the notice of the Legislature, which can then keep a vigilant eye on the government.

Control through Legislative Committees: Apart from the Public Accounts Committee mentioned earlier, there are several other committees, viz., Estimates Committee, Committee on Public Undertakings, Committee on Assurances, etc. These committees examine the various aspects of the working of the government and make useful suggestions. They also criticise the government for its failures and bring these failures to the notice of the Legislature and the people. This is a good device of exercising control over the government, as the Assembly is too unwieldy a body to examine the working of the government in detail.

Ministerial Responsibility: The most potent function of the Legislature is to enforce the ministerial responsibility. In a Parliamentary form of government, the political executive is a part of the Legislature and is responsible to it all the time. The government can be thrown out at any time by a vote of no-confidence or even on being rejected on its budget or any of the substantive legislative measures. As the political executive is always responsible to the Legislature, the administrators become indirectly responsible to it through the ministers. In spite of these controls, it is often felt that the administration is not responsive enough. On the other hand, it is argued that the legislative control, especially the one through audit is too tight and takes away the initiative of the administrators.

Q4. Examine the power and functions of the State Council of Ministers.
Ans. As already mentioned, the executive power of the State is exercised in the name of the Governor, who is the Constitutional head of the state. But, the Governor has to have a Council of Ministers with the Chief Minister as its head to aid and advise him. But for a few discretionary functions, the Governor has to act on the advice of the Council of Ministers. It means that the real executive power is exercised by the Council of Ministers.

The Council of Ministers are appointed by the Governor on the advice of the Chief Minister and hold Office during his pleasure. It means that a minister can also be dismissed by the Governor on the advice of the Chief Minister.

On the pattern of the Union government, ministers in the State governments are of the following categories:
i) Cabinet Ministers
ii) Ministers of State
iii) Deputy Ministers
iv) Parliamentary Secretaries

In Government of India, only Cabinet Ministers attend the meetings of the Cabinet. In the State Government, however, all the ministers attend Cabinet meetings, making discussion on serious matters rather difficult. For conditions and efficient transaction of business, some states have adopted the device of forming Cabinet Committees. Some of these committees are Standing Committees, while some are Ad-Hoc committees that are constituted to deal with some specific problems. The system of Cabinet Committees is not so popular in the State governments as in the Central government. Most of the important matters in the states are placed before the Cabinet, which meets quite frequently.

As per the recent Ninety First Constitutional Amendment Act 2003, the total number of Ministers including the Chief Minister, in the Council of Ministers in a State shall not exceed fifteen per cent of the total number of members of the Legislative Assembly of the State, provided that number of Ministers, including the Chief Minister in a State shall not be less than twelve. This is the first time that such an Amendment providing for the total strength of Ministers has been enacted.

Powers and Functions of the Council of Ministers: The Council of Ministers is the highest policy-making body of the State government. It lays down policy in respect to all matters within the legislative and administrative competence of the State government. The Council also reviews the implementations of the policy laid down by it and can revise any policy in view of the feedback received during implementation. Since the Governor has to exercise his executive powers on the advice of the Council of Ministers and all the executive power is exercised in the name of the Governor, there is no limitation on the powers of the Council except the following:

i) The limits imposed by the Constitution and laws passed by the Union and State Legislature.

ii) Self-imposed limits to exclude consideration of less important matters.

Division of Work into Departments at the State Level : According to the doctrine of Ministerial Responsibility, the Council of Ministers is collectively responsible to the State Assembly. It is, however, impossible for the Council to take all the decisions collectively. During the early British period, the administration of the state was carried on the Governor-in-Council. At that time, most of the decisions were taken collectively, because the number of decisions to be taken was not very large. With the passage of time, the scope of governmental activity increased and the matters that came up for the decision of the Council also proliferated. This led to the development of 'portfolio system' in which the Councillors were placed in before the whole Council. The same system has continued after Independence. Under our Constitution, the Governor has to make rules for the efficient conduct of business [Article 166(3)]. The state governments have framed 'Allocation of Business Rules', according to which the work is divided among different minister. This division of work can be done on the basis of functions, or on the basis of clientele, or on geographical basis or on the basis of the combination of these factors. Very often, the division of work is decided on personal considerations rather than rational criteria. Most of the work in respect of subjects allotted to a minister is disposed of by the minister. However, according to the rules or business, some matters have to be reserved by the minister for:

Consideration of the Chief Minister: These are called coordination cases. In these cases, the minister in charge of a portfolio, records his recommendations and submits the file to the Chief Minister for his orders. Rules of business give a list of such cases. The Chief Minister may also reserve some cases or classes of cases for his orders.

Presentation before the Cabinet: These are important policy matters, which have wide repercussions. Important cases of disagreement between two or more ministers are also brought before the Cabinet for its decision. A list of such cases is given in the rules of business. In addition, the Chief Minister may require any particular case of any department to be placed before the Cabinet. A few of the typical Cabinet cases are given below:

i) Annual Financial Statement to be laid before the Legislature and demands for supplementary grants

ii) Proposals affecting state finance not approved by the Finance Minister

iii) Exemption of important matters from the purview of State Public Service Commission

iv) Proposals for imposition of new taxes, etc.

Q5. Discuss the functions of Chief Minister.

Ans. Chief Minister is the head of the government in the State. The Council of Ministers with the Chief Minister as its head exercises real authority at the State level. Each State has a Council of Ministers to aid and advise the Governor in the exercise of his functions. Governor has discretionary powers also. When the Governor sends a report to the President for proclamation of constitutional emergency in the State, he acts within his own discretion.

Chief Minister is appointed by the Governor. The person who commands the majority support in the State Legislative Assembly (Vidhan Sabha) is appointed as the Chief Minister by the Governor. The other Ministers are appointed by the Governor on the advice of the Chief Minister. The Ministers included in the Council of Ministers must belong to either House of the State Legislature. A person who is not a member of the State Legislature may be appointed a minister, but he ceases to hold office if he is not elected to the State Legislature within six months of his appointment. The portfolios are allocated by the Governor on the advice of the Chief Minister.

Functions of the Chief Minister: Chief Minister is the head of the State Council of Minister. The constitutional position of the Chief Minister is more or less similar to that of the Prime Minister. The Chief Minister plays an important role in the administration of the State. We can discuss his functions as follows:

1. Chief Minister is the real head of the State government. Ministers are appointed by the Governor on the advice of the Chief Minister. The Governor allocates portfolios to the Ministers on the advice of the Chief Minister.

2. Chief Minister presides over the Cabinet meetings. He coordinates the functioning of different Ministries. He guides the functioning of the Cabinet.

3. Chief Minister plays a key role in framing the laws and policies of the State Government. Bills are introduced by the Ministers in the State Legislature with his approval. He is the Chief spokesman of the policies of his government both inside and outside the State Legislature.

4. The Constitution provides that the Chief Minister shall communicate to the Governor all decisions of the Council of Ministers relating to the administration of the affairs of the State and proposals for legislation.

5. The Chief Minister shall furnish such information relating to the administration of the affairs of the State and proposals for legislation as the Governor may call for.

6. If the Governor so requires, the Chief Minister submits for consideration of the Council of Ministers any matter on which a decision has been taken by a Minister but which has not been considered by the Cabinet.

7. The Chief Minister is the sole link of communication between the Cabinet and the Governor. The Governor has the right to be informed by the Chief Minister about the decision taken by the Council of Ministers.

The above functions show that the real authority is vested with the Council of Ministers headed by the Chief Ministers. The Council of Ministers is the real executive in the State. The position of the State Council of Ministers largely depends upon the strength of the ruling party in the State Assembly and the personality of the Chief Minister. The position of the Chief Minister is stronger when his party is in power at the Centre as well. As long as the Chief Minister and his Council of Ministers enjoy the confidence of majority in the Legislative Assembly, he exercises the real executive power in the State.

Q6. What are the role and powers of the Chief Minister in State administration?   **[June-09, Q.8][Dec-08, Q.8]**

Ans. Role of the Chief Minister: The Chief Minister performs the same functions in respect of the State Government as the Prime Minister does in respect of the Union Government. Although the real executive power of the State Government vests in the Council of Ministers, the Chief Minister has acquired a very special role in the exercise of this executive power. He is not the first among equals, but is the prime mover of the executive government of the State.

The Chief Minister is appointed by the Governor and holds Office during his pleasure. However, when a single political party has an absolute majority in the Assembly, the Governor has only a ceremonial role in these matters. He has to invite the leader of the majority party to form the government and cannot dismiss him so long as he enjoys the confidence of the Assembly. The only exception probable may occur when the majority party changes its leader in the Assembly. Of course, the Governor does have some discretion in these matters during periods of instability when no single party can claim an absolute majority in the Assembly.

Powers of the Chief Minister in Relation to the Council of Ministers: The Chief Minister is the leader of the Council of Ministers. With the passage of time, the position of Chief Minister has strengthened vis-à-vis his Council of Ministers. He has to assign portfolios among his ministers and can change such portfolios when he likes. He plays a coordinating role in the functioning of his Council of Ministers. He has to see that the decisions of the various departments are coherent. He has to lead and defend his Council of Ministers in the Assembly. In short, he has to ensure the collective responsibility of the Council of Ministers to the State Assembly. The Chief Minister sets the agenda for the Cabinet and greatly influence its decisions. He takes decisions on important matters of coordination even though these are allotted to individual ministers. Moreover, the Governor appoints the Council of Ministers on the advice of the Chief Minister and the ministers hold Office during the pleasure of the Governor. As a result of these provisions, the Minister, in fact, holds office during the pleasure of the Chief Minister. This power of dismissing the ministers at will and the power to change their portfolios has greatly strengthened the power of the Chief Minister in relation to his ministers and ultimately the Council of Ministers.

It must also be realised that the power of the Chief Minister in relation to his Council of Ministers also depends on political conditions prevailing in the state. If a cohesive party has an absolute majority in the Assembly, the Chief Minister becomes very powerful and the ministers are afraid of him. His power is further enhanced in case of a statewide regional party for, in that case he is not subject to the discipline of the national leadership. The position of a Chief Minister gets weakened if he heads a coalition government or a faction-ridden party. In either case, he or she has to effect compromises to keep a balance among the coalition partners or various factions within the party.

Powers of the Chief Minister in Relation to the Governor: The powers of Chief Minister in relation to the Governor have not been mentioned anywhere in the Constitution. A convention was sought to be established whereby the Chief Minister could be consulted regarding the appointment of the Governor in his state. Even this has not been followed by the Union government in many cases. The only other power, which can be indirectly inferred from the Constitution is the power to exercise executive power of the State in the name of the Governor. All the public appearances of the Governor and the speeches delivered by him on such occasions have to be in accordance with policy laid down by the Council of Ministers headed by the Chief Minister. Similarly, the speeches of the Governor on ceremonial occasions and the annual speech before the Assembly have to be approved by the Cabinet.

Powers of the Chief Minister in Relation to the Legislature: The Chief Minister is also the leader of the House. Apart from this formal position, the Chief Minister provides real legislative leadership to the House in the sense that he sets the legislative agenda. The legislative measures are brought before the Assembly after the approval of the Council of Minister headed by the Chief Minister. It is true that private members may also bring a Bill before the Assembly. But, that has a limited chance of success. Apart from the fact that it has no backing of the majority party, the private members do not have the wealth of information that is available to the government. Apart from setting up the legislative agenda, the Chief Minister has to keep the Assembly informed about the various activities of the government by answering questions, making statements, intervening in the debates etc.

Powers of the Chief Minister in Relation to the Executive: By virtue of being the head of the political executive, the Chief Minister controls the entire bureaucracy of the state. In this function, he is assisted by the Secretariat headed by the Chief Secretary. He approves all senior appointments like those of Secretaries, Additional/Joint/Deputy Secretaries, Heads of the Departments, Chairpersons and controls their service conditions and disciplinary matters. He provides them leadership to ensure good performance and good morale. At the same time, he has to keep a watch on their performance through administrative channels as well as through his own sources like party workers, complaints from aggrieved persons and actual observation during tours etc.

Q7. Discuss the position and role of State Secretariat.

Ans. Position and role of State Secretariat: The following extract from the Administrative Reforms Commission's Report on State Administration gives a succinct expression to the position and role of the State Secretariat:

The State Secretariat, as the top layer of the state administration, is primarily meant to assist the State government in policy making and in discharging its legislative functions. It also acts "as a memory and a clearing house, preparatory to certain types of decisions and as a general supervisor of executive action". The main functions of the State Secretariat are broadly as follows:

i) Assisting the ministers in policy making, in modifying policies from time to time and in discharging their legislative responsibilities

ii) Framing draft legislation, and rules and regulations

iii) Coordinating policies and programmes, supervising and controlling their execution, and reviewing of the results

iv) Budgeting and control of expenditure

v) Maintaining contact with the Government of India and other state governments; and

vi) Overseeing the smooth and efficient running of the administrative machinery and initiating measures to develop greater personnel and organisational competence.

The administrative philosophy to which the Secretariat system owes its existence is that policy-making must be kept separate from policy-execution. Several advantages are claimed in favour of such an arrangement:

i) Freedom from operational involvement makes the policy making apparatus forward looking and allows it to think in terms of overall goals of government rather than narrow, sectional interests of individual departments.

ii) Policy-making receives the time and attention it deserves, it's different set of persona are charged with the functions of policy making as well as its execution. This is because, policy-making, is a serious exercise in drawing up what would be a future course of action. It should not be treated as less urgent than policy execution, which involves routine, day-to-day administration.

iii) Secretariat serves as a disinterested adviser to the minister. It is important to remember that the Secretary is the Secretary to the government and not to the minister concerned, which ensures objective examination of the proposals coming from the executive departments. It enables a more balanced scrutiny of proposals.

iv) Policy-making must be separated from current administration and day-to-day implementation should be left to a different agency with executive freedom, which ensures delegation of authority.

It should be in order at this stage to portray the broad dimensions of the Secretariat's role in some detail. The foremost of these is the Secretariat's role in policy-making. It assists the ministers in the formulation of governmental policies.

This has many aspects. First, the Secretary supplies to the minister all the data and information needed for policy formulation. Second, the secretaries sometimes provide the programmes, with content by working out their details, on whose strength ministers are voted to power. Third, the Secretariat assists ministers in their legislative work. Drafts of legislations to be introduced in the legislature by ministers are prepared by the secretaries. Besides, to answer questions in the Legislature, the minister needs relevant information; the secretary supplies this in formations to the Minister. Secretary also collects information required with respect to the legislative committees.

Fourth, the Secretariat functions as an institutionalised memory. This means that the emerging problems require an examination in the light of precedents. Records and files maintained in the Secretariat serve as an institutional memory and ensure continuity and consistency in the disposal of cases. Fifth, the Secretariat is a channel of communication between one government and another, and between the government and such agencies as the Planning Commission and Finance Commission. Finally, the Secretariat evaluates and keeps track of execution of policies by the field agencies.

Q8. What is the typical pattern of departmentalisation in the State secretariat? [June-08, Q.14]

Ans. Each secretary is normally in charge of more than one department. The number of secretariat departments would therefore be large than the number of secretaries. The number of secretariat departments, quite naturally, varies from state to state. Their number broadly ranges between 10 and 40 in different states. The number of departments in a particular state is not necessarily related to its size in terms of population. For instance, a small state like Mizoram had as many as 36 secretariat departments in 1987, the corresponding figure for Andhra Pradesh (which is a much larger state), was 19 in 1982. Following is a typical example of the pattern of departmentalisation at the Secretariat Level:

· General Administration Department
· Home Department
· Revenue Department
· Food and Agriculture Department
· Finance and Planning Department (Planning Wing)
· Finance and Planning Department (Finance Wing)
· Law Department
· Irrigation and Power Department
· Medical and Health Department
· Education Department
· Industries Department
· Legislature Department
· Panchayati Raj Department
· Command Area Development Department
· Transport, Roads and Buildings Department
· Housing and Municipal Administration and Urban Development Department
· Labour, Employment and Technical Education Department
· Social Welfare Department
· Rural Development Department
· Forest Department

· Environment Department
· Women and Child Welfare Department

Large number of departments, in particular states, would result from restricting the scope of the functions and charges of those which may be created. Partly, such increase in the number of departments may arise from the peculiar problems a particular state may face. There is a lot of criticism about the work allocation existing in the secretariat departments, which is: First, work allocation is lop-sided in that some departments are burdened with more work than others. Second, allocation is far from rational even in terms of homogeneity of work. Not only are the subjects handled by a particular department too numerous and therefore unmanageable but these are also too heterogeneous, causing problems of coordination. These are further aggravated when charges of particular departments are incomplete in scope.

Q9. Bring out the main functions and position of the chief secretary.
[June-08, Q.7]

Ans. Position of Chief Secretary: Every state has a Chief Secretary. This functionary is the kingpin of the State Secretariat, his control extending to all secretariat departments. He is not simply first among equals, he is, in fact, the chief of the secretaries. The Chief Secretary's pre-eminent position is clearly reflected in the varied roles the chief secretary assumes in the state administrative set-up.

The Chief Secretary is the Chief advisor to the Chief Minister and Secretary to the State Cabinet. He is the head of he General Administration Department whose political head is the Chief Minister himself. Chief Secretary is also the head of the civil services in the state. He is the main channel of communication between the state government and the Central and other state governments. Chief Secretary is the chief spokesman and public relations officer of the state government and is looked upon to provide leadership to the state's administrative system.

The office of the chief Secretary is an institution unique to the states; it is without a parallel in the administrative landscape of the entire country. The Chief Secretary's office has, for instance, no parallel in the Central government. The work he performs in relation to the state government is, at the Union level, shared by three high-ranking functionaries of more or less an equal status, i.e., Cabinet Secretary, Home Secretary, and Finance Secretary. This is a vivid reflection on the wide scope of the duties and powers of the Chief Secretary.

Yet another significant reflection on the position of the Chief Secretary's office is the fact that it has been excluded from the operation of the tenure system. Chief Secretary would normally retire as the Chief Secretary or else he would, from this position, move to the Union government to take up a more important position. In considering the position of the Chief Secretary, another fact needs to be taken note of. The incumbent of this office is not necessarily the senior most civil servant of the state. This was at any rate the situation till 1973 when, for instance, in U.P., the chief Secretary was junior in rank and seniority to the members of the Board of Revenue. Same was the case in Punjab, where he was junior to the Financial Commissioner. Since 1973, however, the office of the Chief Secretary has been standardised; its incumbent since then has begun to hold the rank of the Secretary to government of India and receives emoluments admissible to the latter.

How does the clamping of the Presidents' rule on a state affect the Chief Secretary's Office? Where the Centre does not appoint advisers during the President's rule, the chief Secretary becomes clothed with the powers belonging to the Chief Minister. When, however, central advisers are appointed, it tends to inhibit the Chief Secretary in his administrative capacity because the former are drawn from the ranks of senior civil servants (senior to the state's Chief Secretary) as a result of which a hierarchical relationship becomes operative.

The principal functions of the Chief Secretary are listed below:

1. He is the principal adviser to the Chief Minister in which capacity he, inter alia, works out the detailed administrative implications of the proposal made by ministers and coordinates them into a cohesive plan of action.

2. The Chief Secretary is the secretary to the Cabinet. He prepares the agenda for cabinet meetings, arranges them, maintains records of these meetings, ensures follow-up action on Cabinet decision, and provides assistance to Cabinet committees.

3. The Chief Secretary is the head of the civil services of the state. In that capacity, he decides on the postings and transfers of civil servants.

4. By virtue of the unique position he holds as the head of the official machinery and adviser to the Council of Ministers, the Chief Secretary is the coordinator-in-chief of the Secretariat departments. He takes steps to secure inter-departmental cooperation and coordination. For this purpose, he convenes and attends a large number of meetings at the secretariat and other levels. Meetings serve as a powerful tool of effecting coordination and securing cooperation of different agencies.

5. As the chief of the secretaries, the Chief Secretary also presides over a large number of committees and holds membership of many others. Besides, he looks after all matters not falling within the jurisdiction of other secretaries. In this sense, the Chief Secretary is a residual legatee.

6. The Chief Secretary is the secretary, by rotation, of the Zonal Council of which the particular state is a member.

7. He exercises administrative control over the secretariat buildings, including matters connected with space allocation. He also controls the Central Record Branch, the secretariat library, and the conservancy and watch and Ward staff. The Chief Secretary also controls the staff attached to the ministers.

8. In situations of crisis, Chief Secretary acts as the nerve centre of the state, providing lead and guidance to the concerned agencies in order to expedite relief operations. It would be no exaggeration to say that in times of drought, flood, communal disturbances, etc., he virtually represents the government for all the functionaries and agencies concerned to provide relief.

In conclusion, it may be noted that a host of personnel matters and many other minute and unimportant administrative details consume a sizeable chunk of the Chief Secretary's time. The Administrative Reforms Commission (ARC) is constrained to agree with the following observations of the Maharashtra Reorganisation Commission (1962-68) on the manner in which the Chief Secretary has become burdened with trivial details: "… it seems unfortunate that the highest official in the state has to sign gazette notifications of appointments, promotions, transfers, leave, etc., that he has to spend time on minutiae of protocol, passports, etc." To rectify this situation, the ARC has recommended that this functionary be relieved of the work of routine nature as well as be provided with appropriate staff assistance. That alone will ensure speedy implementation of decisions and effective coordination of policies and programmes of the state government.

Q10. What is the meaning of Directorates? Throw light on the organisation of Directorates at the state and sub-state level.

Ans. Directorates: Directorates are the executive arm of the State government; they translate into action, the polices that are framed by the State Secretariat. Even though the terms 'Directorates' and 'Executive Agencies' are often used interchangeably, Directorates are but one type of executive agency. This point is pursued later in the Unit. Directorates, as we shall see, are classified into two categories- Attached Offices and Subordinate Offices. This classification facilitates academic comprehension of the roles, which the two types perform in policy execution.

Meaning and Nomenclature: The Secretariat is concerned with the setting of the broader policies and goals of the State government while the responsibility for achieving those goals and executing those polices rests with the heads of the executive departments. The executive agencies are as a rule located outside the Secretariat and constitute distinct organisational entities. A popular label to identify an executive agency is 'Directorate'. In a large number of this could be cited; director of agriculture, director of animal husbandry, director of education, director of social welfare, director of transport, director of public health, director of town planning, and so on.

However, other nomenclatures are also used to refer to the heads of the executive departments. This, the executive head of the department of police is known as the Inspector/Director General of Police; that of the jail department, the Inspector General of jails; that of the forest department, the chief conservator of forests; that of the cooperative department, the registrar of cooperative societies; that of the sales tax department, the commissioner of sales tax; that of the irrigation department, the chief engineer (irrigation); that of he printing and stationery department, the controller and so forth. In other words, although in a large number of cases, the heads of the executive departments are called Directors, they are also known by other names.

Organisation of Directorates at the State and Sub-state Levels: Apart from the state level, the executive agencies also function at the sub-state levels. This is quite natural. Because, while the policy must be formulated at one centre (the stare headquarters: presently, the state headquarters is signified by Secretariat and Directorates), its execution must necessarily take place in the field. Therefore, the Directorates must make a conscious effort at achieving a vertical penetration down to the grassroots level. When this is done, lesser Directorates emerge at the regional level. When this is done, lesser Directorates emerge at the regional level: the state level executive department established offices in the regions; a region is simply a territorial unit below the state but above the district level. When this process progresses further down the line, the district, block and village level field agencies of a Directorate emerge.

To illustrate the organisational structure of the Directorate at the state and sub-state levels, we present below the Organisation chart of the Directorate of Food and Agriculture of the Government at the state level.

The Organisation of Directorate of Food and Agriculture at the State Headquarters Level: The Head of the Department

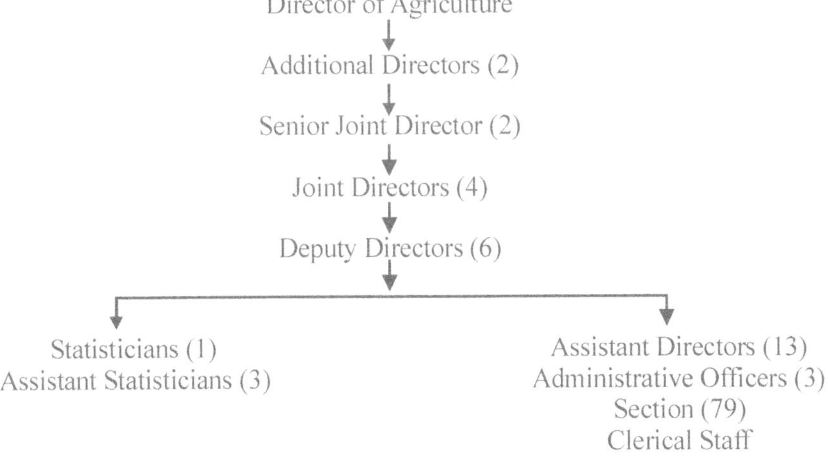

At the state level, as is shown in the Organisation Chart, the headship would normally be with a 'full' director who would be assisted by a group of lesser directors: additional directors, senor joint directors, deputy directors, assistant directors, and other functionaries. Of course, as would be understood, depending upon the workload of a department, the number of levels of hierarchy at the headquarters could be larger or smaller. The regional level set up of an executive department, would usually be headed by an officer of a lower rank, a senor joint director in this case. It could indeed even be a person of simply a joint director or even lower level; that would again depend on the workload and other factors. The district level organisation of the Food and Agriculture Department has as its head a joint director. This is, again, not a typical situation. Many district level offices of the executive departments are headed by deputy or even assistant directors. Again, many factors will combine to determine the rank of the officer who may head the district level set up.

At the level immediately below the district (block level), each development department is represented by an extension officer who is a part of the extension team functioning under the block development officer. Thus, to take an example, there would be an agriculture extension officer in each block, representing the state level directorate of agriculture. At the village level, as is well-known, there exist the multi-purpose extension functionaries known as village level workers (VLWs).

Q11. Highlight the composition and functions of the board of revenue.
Ans. Status and Position: The Board of Revenue, as the name itself suggests, is an agency, at the state level, is concerned with revenue administration. Although, it exists at the state level, it is not a part and parcel of the state government machinery. The preceding statement is intended to underline and emphasis the fact that unlike the government departments—which are definitionally a part and parcel of the governmental machinery—the Board of Revenue is an autonomous agency created under a statute. By virtue of this fact, the Board has an existence, distinct and separate from the government.

The Board as a Supra-district Level Agency: The principal justification for the creation of Board of Revenue lies in that it relieves the state government of the detailed work in the field of revenue administration. It also has a large supervisory and coordination role vis-à-vis the district level revenue functionaries (Collectors/Deputy Commissioners). The fact that it exists at the state headquarters level should not be allowed to blur the truth that the Board of Revenue is an agency, separate from the Central or state government as such. (Since it is a statutory body, it is endowed with a distinct legal identity of its own). This, coupled with the fact that it discharges supervisory functions in relation t the District Collector's lends justification to its classifications as a supra-district level agency.

The pattern of Revenue Administration at the Supra-district Level: There is no uniformity in the pattern of revenue administration at the supra-district level in the country. In this connection, two points need to be particularly remembered. First, there are some states in which there are two administrative agencies (one at the state headquarters level and another at the regional level) between the district and the state government and there are others in which there is only one administrative agency. Second, all states do not have a Board of Revenue; some have, in place of the Board, a Financial Commissioner or Revenue Tribunal. In these terms, five distinct patterns of revenue administration at the supra-district level can be identified. These are:

Pattern One: Under this, there is only one intermediate level, i.e., the Board of Revenue, with no regional/divisional level revenue set up (known as the Divisional Commissioner). Under this pattern fall the states of Tamil Nadu, Kerala and Rajasthan.

Pattern Two: Under this pattern, there are two intermediate agencies, viz, Board of Revenue and Divisional Commissioners. This Pattern is prevailing in the states of U.P, M.P., Bihar, West Bengal, Orissa and Assam.

Pattern Three: Under this pattern also, there are two intermediate agencies. But here there is no Board of Revenue; the Board's equivalent under this pattern is Financial Commissioner. So, under this pattern, there is a Financial Commissioner at the headquarters level and Divisional Commissioner at the regional level. This situation prevails in Punjab and Jammu and Kashmir.

Pattern Four: Under this pattern, again, there are two intermediate agencies. But, as is the case with the Pattern three, here also there is no Board of Revenue. The Board's equivalent, under this pattern, is the Revenue Tribunal. The two intermediate links here, therefore, consist of (i) Revenue Tribunal, and (ii) Divisional Commissioner. This pattern is prevailing in Maharashtra and Gujarat. The difference between the two states is that whereas Commissioners in Maharashtra and regionally located, in Gujarat they are located at the state headquarters and their duties are functionally distributed.

Pattern Five: This pattern is prevalent in Andhra Pradesh, where the Board of Revenue was abolished in 1977 and since then its functions are being discharged by independent Heads of Departments called Commissioners. There are no Divisional Commissioners at the regional level. At present, there are five Commissioners each looking after **(i)** Land Revenue; **(ii)** Survey, Settlement and Land Records; **(iii)** Commercial Taxes; **(iv)** Excise, and **(v)** Civil Supplies, respectively.

Composition and functions of the Board of Revenue:

Composition: The number of the members of the Board varies from state to state. The U.P. Board, for instance, has six members, whereas the Bihar and

Orissa Boards have one full-time member each. The practice everywhere is to appoint only the senior officers as members of the Board. The work among members is functionally divided. Decisions on important policy matters are taken by the full Board. The Board has a Secretariat of its own.

Functions: The functions of Boards of Revenue vary a little from state to state. Generally speaking, the Boards perform the following functions:

(i) The Boards advises the government on all matters of revenue policy.

(ii) It is the highest body in the revenue hierarchy of the state. Being the highest revenue court, it hears appeals and is empowered to revise decisions in revenue cases.

(iii) It exercises general superintendence over the revenue of the state, from whichever source they may arise.

(iv) Board is the final authority under the Sales Tax Act, Excise Act, Prohibition Act and Agricultural Income Tax Act.

(v) The Board undertakes the settlement operation in the state under its jurisdiction. This is a function, which holds the key to peace and stability in the rural India.

(vi) The Board exercises large inspectorial duties. It inspects revenue department in Collectorates and Divisional Commissioners' offices.

(vii) In some states, the Chairman, Board of revenue, writes annual confidential reports of the Divisional Commissioners and District Collectors.

(viii) In states, which do not have Divisional Commissioners, the Board comes in direct contact with district administration. This, *inter alia*, means that it assumes a more pervasive supervisory role in respect of them.

(ix) In general, the Board relieves the state government of a great deal of detailed work in the sphere of revenue administration and functions as an institutional adviser to government on a wide variety of matters.

Q12. Discuss the factors responsible for the expansion in the secretariat.
Ans. The principle of legislative accountability – under which the minister is, *inter alia*, supposed to answer questions, concerning his department, on the floor of the house—has brought about centralisation of functions in the Secretariat. Also, easy access of ministers to their constituents generates pressures on ministers in regard to matters such as appointments, promotions, transfers, and so forth. Now, clearly, these are matters of executive nature. The ministerial desire to nurture his constituency (and therefore, respond to demands for appointments, etc.) results in the minister's involvement in executive matters. This is how the Secretariat, a policy making body, becomes involved in the matters of policy execution.

The second factor, which has been responsible for a steady and substantial increase in the volume of work in the Secretariat is the governmental policy to develop the economy through planning and state intervention and a whole host of welfare functions with the government in recent years has assumed. Every effort at directing and administering the economy leads to increased volume of work in the government. Secretariat, in particular, has gained in stature and influence from this situation. The reason for this is that more important work as well as decisions commanding wide impact have devolved on the Secretariat. Two factors account for this. First, the generalist secretaries are thought to possess a breadth of vision and a well-rounded experience, which comes from the varied job placements that an IAS officer is typically exposed to in the course of his career. In contrast, the head of the department is considered narrow in vision and too theoretical in approach. Secondly, the ministerial staff in the Secretariat is considered to be off a higher caliber as compared to that in the Attached Offices. The result is that the Secretariat attracts more business. Thirdly, as noted above, not an insignificant portion of growth in the Secretariat is due to its taking over numerous executive functions and multifarious unimportant tasks, which do not properly belong to it. Finally, some expansion is also due to the tendency of the bureaucracy to proliferate in any situation. The Secretariat is, thus, today encumbered with non-essential work and has become unwieldy and overstaffed.

Q13. Enumerate important argument in favour of secretariat and directorates.

Ans. Arguments in Favour of Secretariat:

• The Secretariat is an essential administrative institution. The Secretariat System of work, with all its deficiencies, has lent balance, consistency and continuity to the administration and has served as a nucleus of the total machinery of a Ministry. It has facilitated inter-ministry coordination and accountability to the Parliament at the ministerial level.

• The Secretariat System helps to separate policy—making from policy execution. This is a welcome thing to happen with the Secretariat concentrating on the long-term policy issues and the executive agencies being given the freedom to implement policies. It has encouraged division of work, specialisation, and above all delegation of authority.

• Since the Secretariat is required to concentrate on policy-making alone, it is able to achieve freedom from involvement in matters of detailed, day-to-day administration. This helps the Secretariat to remain forward-looking and plan in terms of the overall, aggregative national objectives.

• The generalist secretary, who is the kingpin of the system, is uniquely suited to advise the minister, who is a layperson. The secretary is, on the one hand, able to keep the exalted fervour of the specialist head of the department in check, and on the other, tender objective advice to the minister, examining proposals submitted by the head from a large viewpoint of the government as a whole.

• The existence of Secretariat ensures objective evaluation of programme implementation in the field. This task cannot be left to the executive agencies, which actually implement policies, for they should not be asked to judge their own performance. The Secretariat is best suited to do this job.

• Overall, the Secretariat is an institution of proven merit. It has stood the test of time and successfully delivered goods; the combination of 'tenure system' and a permanent 'office', which has been evolved as a part of the system has given it strength, vitality and dynamism. There is no viable substitute in sight for the Secretariat System.

Arguments in Favour of Directorates

• Unlike the Secretariat, the Directorates are staffed by specialist who have achieved excellence in their respective specialisations. These specialists have, moreover, over the years, been able to gather an intimate knowledge of the field conditions. By virtue of these facts, the director or the head of the department, it is argued, is comfortably placed to discharger the role of tendering policy advice to the Minister. This will permit fuller projection of the Director's experience in the policy-making process.

• As the specialists rise in the functional hierarchy, they are able to acquire a valuable administrative experience. This coupled with the fact that they are, by virtue of their training, well-versed in the technical aspects of the policy issues and could provide the head of the departments a superior equipment— as compared with the generalist secretaries—to tender advice on policy matters. The argument, in other words, is that the heads combine with administrative experience the valuable technical know-how, which the secretaries lack.

• As science and technology makes rapid advances, the volume and complexity of governmental activity of a technical and scientific character has been on the increase. And, with this, specialised areas of administrative activity have emerged in the government. The specialist heads of departments are uniquely suited to respond to this situation.

• The specialist heads of departments alone, rather than the generalist secretaries, are in tune with the modern trend of specialisation and professionalism in the government. There is virtually no professional area, it is argued, which is not represented in the government today. Pure sciences, medicine, veterinary science, engineering, agricultural science, architecture, and accountancy are some of the examples of this trend.

Q14. Write a short note on followings: **[Dec-08, Q.2]**
1. Status-quo approach
2. Bridging gulf approach   **[June-08, Q.12]**
3. De-amalgamation approach

Ans. 1. Status-quo approach

The Status-quo Approach favours the traditional split system and holds that the Secretariat and the directorates have well-defined roles in our administrative setup to which they would continue to stick. The approach is based on the traditional concepts of staff-line dichotomy where the secretariat performs the role of a Staff Agency and the Attached Office that of the Line Agency. The Status-quo Approach also accepts the traditional policy-administration dichotomy. The advocates of this approach believe that the relationship between the Secretariat and Directorates should be based on the following principles:

(i) Policy-making should be the responsibility of the Secretariat and Policy implementation that of the Directorates.

(ii) Subject to the rules governing the conditions of service, the Head of Department should have fullest control over the personnel under him.

(iii) The Secretariat Department should provide common services and undertake domestic housekeeping in respect of the Directorate(s) attached to it (for instance, the allocation of office accommodation).

Arguments For: The advocates of Status-quo Approach justify the existence of separate agencies for policy formulation and policy implementation on the following grounds.

(i) personal responsible for the execution of policy must not be entrusted with the responsibility for the assessment of its achievement and failures.

(ii) Agency concerned with execution of policy remains so much engrossed in details that it may lack a broad outlook necessary for the framing of a policy.

(iii) When schemes framed by specialist are scrutinised by the generalists, it gives these schemes a broader orientation and greater objectivity.

(iv) Separation encourages delegation and decentralisation. It also provides for division of work between the Secretariat and Directorate.

(v) Split system has the important merit of being a familiar arrangement. Besides, it is a system of proven effectiveness; it has, till now, delivered the goods. It has stood the test of time. Its scrapping will break continuity with the past.

Arguments Against:

Arguments against the traditional split system are too well-known to need any detailed cataloguing. Briefly, these are as follows:

(i) Schemes are processed twice in two different offices, which causes avoidable delays.

(ii) Scrutiny of schemes in Secretariat begins at the assistant's level; who is hardly qualified to scrutinise the schemes framed by heads. The assistant's notings tend to confuse the issues and lead to unnecessary quires. In the process, the original intentions underlying the schemes get distorted and obscured.

(iii) More fundamentally, the critics of the split system point out, it is doubtful if generalist secretaries have the necessary know-how to undertake examination of the schemes prepared by qualified specialist; whether they may, in fact, be expected to make a worthwhile contribution to this exercise.

(iv) Split system is also criticised on the ground that it is inegalitarian in outlook. That it makes the Attached Office feel like an inferior entity far removed from the charmed circle. One result of this could be a low sense of participation among the personnel of Attached Offices.

2. Bridging gulf approach

As against the School advocating Status-quo Approach there is another, which advocates measures for bridging-the-gulf between the Secretariat and Non-secretariat organisations. Its protagonists suggest various devices for bridging-the-gulf. These include **(i)** the conferment of **ex-officio secretariat status** on the heads of Executive Departments; **(ii)** the system under which a Secretary concurrently holds the office of the head of the Executive Department; **(iii)** the merger or amalgamation device under which an Executive Department is placed in a corresponding Secretariat Department; and **(iv)** a device which is a variant of (point iii), involving, once again, merger or amalgamation, but under this device, the Secretariat Department is placed with the corresponding Head of the Department, rather than the other way around. Each of these methods is in turn discussed below;

Ex-Officio Secretariat Status:

Meaning: This device consists the conferment of a suitable ex-officio secretariat status on the heads of Executive Departments. The result is that by virtue of holding office as a head, the incumbent of the (head's) position holds a suitable rank in the Secretariat. The clear advantage is that the two offices (those of the Director and Secretary) are now combined in a single individual. The director, by virtue of being an ex-officio secretary, can sign on behalf of the government. The need or scrutiny of schemes in two offices is done away with. The same individual, in his capacity as Director, proposes the scheme and, in his capacity as Secretary, scrutinises it. This is, of course, an over-simplified description of the ex-officio system but this is how, in essence, it functions. Thus, to take an example, in some states, the Chief Conservation of Forests is an ex-officio Secretary to the state government in the Department of Forest and Environment. To take an example from the Central Government, the Director General of the Indian Council of Agricultural Research is an ex-officio Additional Secretary to the Government of India.

Advocacy by State Level Administrative Reforms Committees: The Administrative Reforms Committees appointed by certain state governments have from time to time recommended conferment of ex-officio secretariat status on the heads of the Executive Department. It would be helpful to pause at this stage to take a brief look at their recommendations; the exercise will inter alia assist us in analysing the advantages or the merits, which particular state governments ascribe to the ex-officio system.

The Andhra Pradesh Administrative Reforms Committee (ARC) (1964-65) recommended conferment of the ex-officio status as a method of achieving psychological closeness between the Secretariat and Directorates. The device, the Committee felt, would make the head of department feel a part and parcel of the broad-based (governmental) team – comprising its tow major organisational components; the Secretariat and the Directorate – which is entrusted with a common task. It would remove the feeling of 'separateness' on the part of the head and ensure his fuller association in the Secretariat's policy formulation work. The Committee recommended conferment of the secretariat status on 23 heads but opined that, to start with, the secretariat status be given "only to those who are doing important work an spending large amounts' particularly on work connected with development activities."

The Punjab ARC (1964-66) recommended conferment of secretariat status as a method of ensuring adequate financial and administrative powers to the heads of the executive departments. The Kerala Administrative Reorganisation and Economy Committee (1965-67) recommended conferment of appropriate secretariat status on the heads of departments to achieve "better quality of work and the *esprit de corps* that follow from the psychological satisfaction that such status would give to the Heads of Departments". The Committee recommended the grant of the ex-officio secretariat status to 55 officials of the Executive Departments.

The Rajasthan ARC (1962-63) had recommended the adoption of the ex-officio system on an experimental basis. It proposed that the government may, to begin with, make the Chief Engineer, Public Works Department (Buildings and Roads), and the Director of Industries and Supplies, ex-officio Additional Secretaries to the government. And that it may, later, extend the system to other departments.

Arguments For:

(i) When the Head of Department has an ex-officio secretariat status, he can make decisions, and sign, on behalf of the government. This permits much economy of time since the matter does not have to move up the secretariat for finalisation. The twin roles of Secretariat and Directorate are now performed by a single functionary; the making of the proposal (a Head of Department function) and its scrutiny consideration, and sanction (a Secretariat Function), both the roles are performed by the same functionary.

(ii) The Head of Department is more closely involved in the policy-making process. This means that his experience is more adequately projected in policy formulation. Also, more desirable policy implementation is possible since the Head of Department, under this arrangement, develops fuller awareness of the considerations, which underlay a policy.

(iii) Overall, the Head of Department gains in status and weight. He achieves a particular facility of the governmental system to deliver goods is enhanced. Bureaucratic procedures become de-emphasised; a programmatic bias and a performance orientation is achieved.

Arguments Against:

(i) Integration is apt to blur the line of demarcation between the functions of policy-making and policy-implementation. As a result, the task of long-term policy making is liable to be neglected because the day-to-day operational problems are likely to induce a sense of urgency about them.

(ii) Not only the policy formulation work per se will suffer, but also the short-term considerations may overwhelm the strategic ones and deprive policy making of the long-term content.

(iii) Integration may also affect the programme implementation adversely. This is because the executive officers have, as such, plenty to do in the fields; their involvement in the secretariat work will overburden them.

(iv) Government will be deprived of the advantage of a broad and balanced scrutiny of the policy proposals when a technocrat takes over the Secretariat functions.

(v) Integration violates the fundamental principle of the Secretariat System, namely policy-making that must remain separated from policy implementation.

(vi) Indiscriminate conferment of the secretariat status will debase the value of the secretariat designations and, at the same time, undermine the authority of such functionaries of the Executive Agencies that do not have the secretariat status.

3. De-amalgamation approach:

How has merger or amalgamation worked in practice? Has it produced the desired results? Bihar is one state in the country where amalgamation was effected as far back as 1951. Empirical results are available from the Bihar experiment on amalgamation. There is a sharp division of opinion among the functionaries who have had the opportunity to work under amalgamated setup. A number of officials report that the scheme has been successful and has yielded good results. At the same time, a large number of officials have criticised the scheme and opined that it should be done away with. In other words, they feel that amalgamation has failed and the process of de-amalgamation should now be started.

Arguments for continued Amalgamation: Those who report favourably on the experience of amalgamation argue as follows:

(i) Amalgamation has obviated the need for examination of proposal independently by the Directorate and Secretariat.

(ii) It has cut down delays and ensured expeditions disposal of cases.

(iii) It has effected economy in establishment expenditure

Arguments for De-amalgamation: The officials who recommend de-amalgamation give the following arguments:

(i) Although amalgamation permits much economy of time in that it does away with two parallel scrutinises of proposal, the experience has shown that, under the amalgamated set up, the quality of final proposals/schemes has declined, which frequently involves reconsideration. This, they point out, was not so when Directorate and Secretariat functioned separately.

(ii) Amalgamation has resulted in gradual removal of distinction between the functions of the Heads of Departments and those of the Secretariat.

(iii) Amalgamation has rendered objective examination of proposals and schemes at the Secretariat level difficult. The secretaries have to write their notes on files in a guarded manner so as to avoid causing offence to the head of department. This extra caution often prevents a frank examination of the cases by the secretariat officers.

(iv) Under the amalgamation schemes, the Head of Department remains stuck up in the Secretariat. He is not able to go on tours and inspections, which are his main obligations.

What is involved in effecting De-amalgamation? In 1979, Bihar decided to scrap the amalgamation or, in other words, to return to the traditional split system. However, Bihar has experienced difficulties in implementing the de-amalgamation plan. Difficulties have been mainly two-fold. First, during the three decades of amalgamation, there has been a unified cadre of the subordinate staff, i.e., for the Secretariat and the Heads of Departments. De-amalgamation involves separation of this unified cadre. Second, because of the amalgamation of the Secretariat and Executive Department, no separate files had been maintained for the two sets of departments. De-amalgamation necessitated duplicating many files and documents.

In view of these difficulties, it was decided to enforce de-amalgamation in two stages. In the first stage, the heads were to confine themselves to field work alone, meaning they would curtail their involvement in the Secretariat duties. And, in the second stage, separation of cadres and files were planned. For these reasons, the process of de-amalgamation in Bihar could not be completed until 1982 although the decision to de-amalgamate was reached in the year 1979.

Q15. How the Civil Services are classified at the state level?

Or

Discuss the classification of State Public Services.						[June-08, Q.8]

Ans. A two-fold system of classification of the State Services is in vogue:

Under the first system, the Services are classified into Class I, Class II, Class III and Class IV. The criteria of this classification are: **(i)** admissible pay scales; **(ii)** the degree of responsibility of the work performed; and **(iii)** the corresponding qualifications required. All State Services are constituted department-wise.

Under the second system, the posts in the services are classified into the gazetted and non-gazetted categories.

(i) Classification Based on Pay Scales, etc.: Class I and Class II services constitute the officers' class of the state-level services, whereas Class III and Class IV consist of the clerical employees and manual workers, respectively.

Class I Services: Class I Services include a number of posts on a common time-scale of pay and some posts carrying salaries above the ordinary time-scale. Each departmental service ordinarily has a Class I cadre.

Recruitment to Class I posts is made on the basis of promotions from Class II services as well as by direct recruitment by State Public Service Commission. Direct recruitment takes place on the basis of an open competitive examination. Generally, this would include written examination and personality test; sometimes, however, direct recruitment may also take place on the basis of an interview.

It may be noted that there is no uniform practice as to the number of posts, which may be filled up by promotion or direct recruitment. In fact, there are wide variations on this account from state to state.

Class II Services: Class II services are generally of a specialised nature, although there are some generalists services as well in this category. These are subordinate civil service, subordinate police service, and the like. Class II services are lower in status and responsibility than those in Class I. These are, however, considered important enough to require that the authority for making appointments to them be vested in the state government itself.

The most important among the Class II services is the subordinate civil service (also classed the subordinate executive/administrative service). Some states have even instituted a higher salary scale for this service vis-à-vis other Class II services; this signifies the special place, which this service enjoys in the overall range of Class II services.

It may be noted that, as in Class I service, there is no common pay-scale for Class II services among different states.

Recruitment to Class II posts in made partly by promotion and partly by open competition (direct recruitment). In case of specialised services, direct recruitment is done on the basis of interviews held by the state PSCs. For civil, police, and judicial services (Class II), however, a more comprehensive selection procedure is employed. This includes the written examination and interview.

Unlike in the case of Class I services, no uniform practice prevails with regard to the Class II services also as to the number of posts to be filled by promotion or by open competition. The practices very over a wide range from state to state.

Class III and Class IV Services: Class III services are divided into two categories: **(i)** subordinate executive services (including, for instance, naib tehsildars, sub-inspectors of police, deputy inspectors of education, and so on), and **(ii)** clerical services. Recruitment to these posts is made partly at the level of their Public Service Commissions and partly at the departmental or district heads' level.

Class IV services include persons performing manual work, skilled or unskilled. Posts falling under this category are those of peons, watchmen, drivers, carpenters, fitters, cooks, laboratory servants, and the like. Until recently, these posts were classified as inferior services with their holders enjoying less favourable terms of service with regard to leave, pension, etc. Lately, however, their conditions of service have improved.

(ii) Gazetted and Non-gazetted Classification: As stated above, the second system of classification employed for the state services places them under the familiar categories of gazetted and non-gazetted.

A gazetted government servant is one whose appointment, transfer, promotion, retirement, etc., are announced in the Official Gazette in a notification issued by order of the Governor. A gazetted officer holds charge of an office and his duties are of a supervisory or directorial nature. Gazetted posts include All India Services and Class I and Class II State Services. Non-gazetted posts are those in Class III and Class IV Services.

Recently, there has been a little change in the classification grading system. The gazetted post at the Centre and at the state levels are now categorised as Group A and Group B. The non-gazetted posts are categorised as Group C and Group D.

Q16. Write a brief note on Public Services Commission at State level.
Ans. Constitutional provisions governing the Public Service Commissions (PSCs) at the state level are given below:
• Article 315 of the Constitution provides for the establishment of PSCs. It stipulates that there shall be a PSC for the Union as well as a PSC for each state.
• Article 316 prescribes the composition of such Commissions. It also deliberates on the method of appointment of the Chairperson and members as well as their terms of office. While Article 316 stipulates what the normal tenure of a Chairperson or member shall be, Article 317 prescribes grounds and procedure for early termination of such tenure.

• We have already explained that with a view to ensuring objectivity and impartiality in recruitment, this task has been entrusted to a Commission and it has been accorded a Constitutional status. In the context, the question of ensuring independence of the Commission assumes particular significance. Articles 318, 319 and 322 provide measures for safeguarding and fostering the independence of the Commission.

• What will be the scope of duties and functions of the PSCs? What will be the overall sweep of their role as recruiting agencies? These matters are dealt with under Articles 320, 321 and 323 of the Constitution.

• Commissions, as previously stated, are advisory bodies. How to ensure that this situation does not work to their disadvantage and render them ineffective? Under Article 323, there is a provision for submission by Commission of annual reports in which *inter alia* the cases where government rejects its advice are recorded and reasons for non-acceptance stated. There is a further requirement that these reports shall be placed before the appropriate legislature.

Composition and Functions of the Commission: The number of members, which a state PSC may have is not fixed. The Constitution stipulates that this shall be determined by the Governor of the concerned state. At least, half of the members of a Commission are persons with a minimum of ten years of experience under the Central or a state government. Members are appointed for a term of six years or until the age of sixty years. Governor is the appointing authority, but it must be carefully noted that members are removable only by the President and not by the Governor. Conditions of service of the members are determined by the Governor but very importantly, the Constitution stipulates that these shall not be revised to their disadvantage. Implicit in the foregoing are certain safeguards to ensure the Commission's independence. Later we shall dwell on this aspect.

Functions of the Commission: As recruiting agencies, the principal function of the state PSCs is to conduct examination for appointment to civil services. However, certain other duties arise from this and Commission is enjoined to discharge them. These include: **(i)** to tender advice to the state government on a matter so referred to it by the Governor. **(ii)** to exercise such additional functions as may be provided for by and act of the Legislature. These may be with respect to the State Civil Service, or the services of a local authority or other corporate bodies. **(iii)** to present annually to the Governor, a report with regard to the work done by it.

Besides, the Constitution stipulates that a PSC shall be consulted on the following matters:

(i) On all matters relating to the methods of recruitment to civil services and civil posts.

(ii) On the principles to be followed in making appointments to civil services and posts and making promotions and transfers from one service to another, and on the suitability of candidates for such appointments, promotions or transfers.

(iii) On all disciplinary matters affecting a person serving under the government of a state in a civil capacity.

Advisory role of the Commission: The importance of the Commission's role lies in that its decisions are in the nature of advice to the government and the latter has no obligation to act upon the reason for according an advisory status to the Commission is clear enough. Under the Parliamentary system of government, the responsibility for the proper administration of the country is vested in the Cabinet and or this it is accountable to the Legislature. Therefore, the Cabinet cannot adjure this ultimate responsibility by binding itself to the opinion of any other agency. If the Commission's decision were made mandatory, it would amount to setting up of two governments. But, at the same time, there is scarcely any doubt that in matters relating to recruitment to civil services, and the like, it would be profitable for the ministers to take the advice of a body of experts.

This underlines the need for necessary safeguards against a flagrant disregard of the advice of the Commission by the government. The Constitution does where its advice has been rejected must be placed before the State Legislature through the Governor. And the government is under obligation, when such report is presented, to give reason as to why in any particular case the recommendation of the Commission has been overridden by it. But the number of such cases have tended to remain very low, almost negligible.

Independence of the Commission: In the introduction, we have explained the significance of maintaining the independence of the recruiting agency vis-à-vis the executive government. The Constitution also incorporates well-designed safeguards to foster the Commission's independence. These are:

(i) As a check against a possible abuse of power, the appointing and removing authority is vested in different functionaries. The power to appoint the Chairperson and members of a Commission vests with the Governor, but the power of removal is vested in the President.

(ii) Removal can be effected only in the meaner and on the grounds prescribed in the Constitution.

iii) Salaries and other conditions of service of a member cannot be revised to his disadvantage after his appointment.

(iv) The expenses of the Commission are charged on the Consolidated Fund of the State.

(v) Certain disabilities have been imposed on the Chairperson and members of the Commission with respect to future employment under the government. On ceasing to hold office they are not eligible to hold office under government outside the Union and/or state PSCs.

The purpose of the above provisions is to place the Commission and its members well beyond any possibility of being influenced either by a lure of office or by a threat of insecurity or for any other reason.

Commission's Working: We have so far considered the formal framework within which a state PSC functions. We shall now discuss the actual working. Our comments on the actual working centre around two aspects. One, exercise of patronage in civil appointments by the government in spite of the Commission's existence. Two, the question of the Commission's membership. Notwithstanding the Constitutional safeguard against the non-acceptance of the Commission's advice, there is criticism that the government is able to have its way in making appointments.

(i) Making ad hoc appointments without prior consultation with the Commission: Commission is not consulted for making ad hoc appointments. Through repeated renewals, such persons pick up necessary experience of the job, which puts them at an advantage vis-à-vis the fresh applicant. In such cases, the Commission is faced with a *fait accompli.*

(ii) Exclusion of certain categories of posts from the purview of PSC: In theory, recruitment to all civil posts in a state is done by the PSC. However, the Constitution provides that the executive may exclude certain categories of posts form the purview of the PSC. Under this dispensation, Class III and Class IV appointments are made without the PSC's intervention. This is understandable in view of the large volume of work, which these matters would devolve on the Central recruitment agency. However, there are some higher appointments, which have also been excluded. This, the critics point out, is an encroachment on the Commission's jurisdiction. Moreover, it is alleged that such exclusions are made by state governments without consulting the state PSCs.

(iii) Drafting of advertisements by the concerned department: Advertisements for filling up vacancies are drafted by the concerned departments. And these are sometimes drafted to suit particular candidates, which the departments may have in view. The Commission cannot vary the terms of advertisements.

(iv) Revision of terms of appointment and merit lists: Occasional cases have been reported where the terms offered to the selected candidate were revised to his disadvantage without consulting the Commission. There are also occasional instances where the order in the merit list prepared by the Commission is changed by the government for reasons which are unknown.

(v) Delay in issuing appointment letters: Occasionally, there are inordinate delays on the part of the government in issuing appointment letters to the selected candidates. This results in the best qualified candidates being lost to other professions. Besides, it gives rise to a suspicion that such delays may be motivated.

The above situations affect the operation of the merit system and undermine the Commission's role. The Commission's membership has also drawn flak due to many other reasons:

Membership to persons with insufficient credentials: The matter of membership of the state PSCs has attracted adverse notice. The criticism has been that membership in some states have gone to persons with insufficient credentials: that; in fact, some appointments have been made on grounds of party and political affiliations and not on consideration of merit. Such persons naturally feel beholden to their political masters and could not be expected to stand up to their patrons to uphold merit and professionalism in civil services. This creates apprehensions on the ability of the PSCs to work with objectivity and independence.

Predominance of the members of the official category: The narrow base of the Commission's membership has also attracted adverse attention. The point at issue has been the predominance of the members of the official category. In terms of Article 316, the expectation was that the official and the non-official components of the Commissions' membership would be roughly equal to each other. This has in practice not been realised. Non-official have far outnumbered the officials in some PSCs, while in others, are no non-officials at all. Professions like teaching, law, engineering, science, technology and medicine have remained unrepresented or inadequately represented on the Commissions. It is necessary that professionals receive adequate representation on the PSCs. This would not only help in meeting the Constitutional requirement by evenly balancing the official and non-official components of the Commission's membership, but one would also expect from this a qualitative improvement in their deliberations.

Field and Local Administration

Q1. Define Regional administration. What is the role of a regional administration?

Ans. As the Directorates are concerned with policy execution, and execution, and execution of policy takes place in he field (district, block and village level), therefore the need arises for them (Directorates) to create intermediate level administrative agencies to coordinate and supervise the field operations. This intermediate level administrative set-up between the State Headquarters (the Directorate) and the District is referred as 'Regional Administration'. Each region is comprised of a number of districts; thus a region is a real unit below the State and above the District level.

Significance: The Regional Administration permits more delegation and speedier disposal of business. It lightens the workload of the Head of Department; permits him to concentrate on general policy issues affecting the State, and allows a detailed examination of the problems, which are of particular relevance to specific region. It also facilitates better coordination and supervision of the programmes being executed at the district level.

ARC Study Team Report on District Administration (1967) explains the significance of the regional administrative set-up for a State. "Most States in India are comparatively large, both in area and population. The six largest States together cover approximately 61 per cent of the area of the country. In such large States, there are wide variations in the socio-economic and geographical charismatic of each region. This underlines the need for a regional level in the administrative set-up. On the one hand, policy formulation and coordination can be better achieved at a level intermediate between the District and the State Government; on the other, the State Government between the District and the State Government; on the other , the State Government being comparatively remote form the locale of policy implementation, cannot assess local problems in their proper perspective. It is in these circumstances that the services of senior and experienced administrators are needed at an intermediate level, between the policy formulation level at the State Headquarters and the implementing level in the district".

Meaning and Patterns: The phrase 'Regional Administration' thus refers to the network of organisations that function below the State level but above the district. Most Departments in a State maintain Regional Headquarters in these intermediate geographical territories. These territories do not bear a common name, and are not geographically coterminous in respect of the various Departments at the State level. They often crisscross each other for different purposes (revenue collection, law and order maintenance, forest management and so on). Each Department creates its sub-state formations to suit its particular requirement.

Majority of States are divided, (for purposes of revenue and general administration) into real units called 'divisions'. A Divisional Commissioner who coordinates and supervises the work of the District Collectors under his jurisdiction Heads each division. Similarly, the Police Department at the State Headquarters has Deputy Inspector General at the intermediate level. These territorial divisions in respect of the Police Department are called 'ranges'. This 'range' may be conterminous with the Commissioner's Division. Where he workload of a Department does not warrant this; the intermediate territorial unit may not be conterminous with the Commissioner's Division. Thus, the Forest Department divides the State into intermediate geographical territories (also) called 'ranges' in deciding the geographical area of range. To take one more example, the State level Irrigation Department has Superintending Engineer at the regional level, who is in charge of the Executive Engineers of his region. Briefly, whether a particular Department will have a Regional Administrative set-up or not will depend on (i) size of the State, and (ii) volume and nature of work handled by it. Obviously, the particular historical circumstances in which a Department was created and grew, and the personalities involved in its evolution will also affect such a decision.

Role: The foremost function of the regional level officer is supervision and coordination of the work of district level functionaries of the Department. The important functions of the Regional Officer are mentioned below:

• The Regional Officer also performs the important function of setting norms and standards for the comparatively young district level officers and ensuring that these norms and standards are kept through an elaborate system of inspections, report and returns, directives and periodic meetings with the district level functionaries.

• The Regional Officer keeps himself and the State Headquarters informed about difficulties or problems, which the functionaries at the lower geographical formation may face through on the spot inspection. He also initiates measure for their rectification. Also, he is responsible to ensure that the targets are achieved.

• He maintains an active touch with the Panchayati Raj Institutions under his jurisdiction.

Assessment: The existence of the intermediate administrative set-up between the State Headquarters (policy formulation level) and the districts (policy implementation level) has been criticised on the basis that it has no substantive role to perform. In fact, it is redundant level of administration, which only contributes delay in the administrative process.

Q2. Examine the role and function of Divisional commissioner. Give argument in favour and against of Divisional Commissionership.

Or

Discuss the role of the divisional commissioner.   **[Dec-07, Q.4]**

Ans. Divisional Commissioner: **The most important of the regional level functionaries is the Divisional Commissioner.**

(i) Position and Scope of the Office: The Divisional Commissioner supervises the work of the District Collectors under his charge. He is the coordinator at the divisional level of a wide range of activities such as law and order administration, development administration, rural development as well as revenue administration. Therefore, the Divisional Commissioner occupies a place of special significance in the intermediate (regional) level administrative set-up.

Chequered career of the Institution: The office of Divisional Commissioner in the country has had a chequered career. It has seen a succession of abolitions and revivals in various States since independence. Madhya Pradesh and (old) Mumbai States had abolished it in 1948 and 1950 respectively. However, both revived the commissionership—Madhya Pradesh in 1956 and Mumbai in 1958. Rajasthan abolished the institution in 1961. Utter Pradesh went halfway, it reduced the number of Commissioners and enlarged their geographic jurisdiction. Soon thereafter, however, it restored the status quo. Likewise, the commissionership was abolished in Maharashtra, but was subsequently revived.

(ii) Functions of Divisional Commissioner:

• The Divisional Commissioner is the overall regional officer giving guidance to district-level officers and providing feedback and advice to the State Headquarters.

• Mainly, he remains involved in coordination, supervision, inspection, and appellate work.

• In the sphere of revenue administration, the Commissioner's duties are many folds. He has well-defined power in land revenue matters and hears appeals against the revenue decisions of the District Collectors. He inspects revenue offices within his division. All correspondence to State Government, in regard to revenue matters, is channeled through him. He has responsibilities in regard to land reform also.

• The Commissioner has also responsibilities in the sphere of rural development.
• In the sphere of local self-government, both rural and urban, the Commissioner has been given certain power.
• The Commissioner shoulders direct responsibility in regard to law and order in his division. He is the Head of the law and order administration in the territory under his command.

(iii) Divisional Commissionership: The office of the Commissioner has aroused much controversy. Two distinct schools of thought appear to have emerged, one in its defence and the other against it. Those who support its cause argue that creation of a strong intermediate tier of administration would encourage decentralisation and bring State administration physically and psychologically closer to people at the grassroots level. Besides, improved coordination and supervision of the field establishment would be achieved. Those who argue against it and recommended its abolition maintain that the creation of an intermediate level of administration curbs the initiative and responsibility of the district functionaries. The State where the institution of Divisional Commissioners exists has not achieved any marked improvement in efficiency, or sped in disposal. Even 'coordination' does not appear to have achieved any worthwhile results. Besides, as the Ministers nowadays tour the districts frequently, as a result the problems of coordination are easily notice. The Collector can easily get in touch with the Headquarters, in case of need, due to facilities for speedy communication. Thus, there is no need for referring matters to an intermediate authority.

We may now summarise arguments for and against the institution of Divisional Commissioners.

Arguments For: The ARC Study Team in its Report on district Administration argues in favour of the office of the Divisional Commissioner on following grounds:

i) The Divisional Commissioner's presence will facilitate coordination of the regional level officers of the various development departments. Such coordination cannot be achieved at the State Headquarters because it is too distant for the purpose. Only an officer who has an intimate awareness of the problems of the region can do this effectively.

ii) In large States like Uttar Pradesh and Madhya Pradesh, it is not possible to exercise effective supervision over Collectors unless a regionally based officer undertakes it.

iii) The Commissioner's presence at the intermediate level will encourage delegation from the State level. This will make speedy disposal or cases possible as well as make administration more accessible to the public.

iv) The Commissioner's presence can be used to provide more adequate guidance to the Panchayati Raj Institutions. He can also be utilised to facilitate coordination between the Panchayati Raj bodies, Regional and State Level Agencies.

v) A regionally based officer of an adequate administrative experience will act as a catalyst for regional planning and implementation.

vi) An administrator of the Commissioner's seniority and experience could perform a useful training role in respect of the young IAS and State civil service officers of this division.

Arguments Against: Arguments against the post of Divisional Commissioner as mentioned in the Bengal Administration Enquiry Committee are:

i) The activities of Government have grown too large and complex at the district level. As a result of which a division is no longer a suitable area unit for purpose of supervision. It is too large an area to be an effective unit of administration.

ii) As authorities of supervision over districts and as an appellate revenue bodies, commissioners are disproportionately expensive.

iii) It is doubtful, as an intermediate level of administration, the Commissioners have much useful role to perform or any specific contribution to make in the disposal of work. The post has been reduced to the position of a mere post office and contributes only delay in the dispatch of public business.

iv) Commissioners are officers of wide and mature experience and as such their availability at the State Headquarters would mean a fuller use of their valuable experience. Divisional administration fails to create a much useful preoccupation for officers of the Commissioner's seniority and experience.

Q3. Describe the role of District collector in district administration.

Ans. District Collector, who is also called as the Deputy Commissioner in State like Haryana and Punjab, Heads district administration. Even since the creation of the post in 1772, the District Collector continues to be the administrative Head of district administration. Though created as an agent of the then British Government to establish its hegemony throughout the length and breadth of the country, he plays a significant role both in development and regulatory areas. Basically, he has three major functions namely revenue, magisterial and developmental. Apart from these major functions, the State and Central Government also entrusted a large number of miscellaneous functions to him.

Collector has been the Head of the revenue administration. Though there has been considerable change in the nature of the State form policy to development and welfare, revenue functions continue to claim considerable time and attention. The Collector is also in charge of law and order administration in the district.

He has control and supervisory role over the Police Administration. He advises the Government on various aspects of law and order. However, several controversies have arisen with regard to his role in the maintenance of law and order and his relations with Superintendent of Police, even then law order continues to be one of his important functions.

After Independence and with the adoption of planning strategy, the Collector has become a pivotal figure in implementing the development programmes. He continues to play a significant role in the development administration. There are several other areas like conduct of elections, dealing with calamities, supervising local Government institutions, etc. wherein the Collector has an important role to play. Details of his role in the District Administration would be discussed elaborately later. Suffice it to say that in District Administration there is no area where he is not associated.

Q4. What are the areas of problems in field administration?

[Dec-09, Q.15]

Ans. The broad framework of field administration remained more or less the same except a few reorganisations and addition of developmental functions. This has resulted in several problems for the administration as well as for the community.

Firstly, there are wide variations in the size of the districts both in terms of area and population. The reorganisation that has taken place after Independence is mostly on political considerations than on administrative requirements and efficiency. These variations are creating serious problems for the administration. This is mainly in terms of access of District Administration to the people.

With the increase in the number of functions and role of development departments there has been a considerable decline in the importance of the revenue officials. But their stranglehold over land records and their linkages with local power groups has become a disturbing factor. In spite of the commitment of the Central and State Governments, there have been several difficulties in implementing land reforms in the country. This is another problem area.

Rural and Urban local institutions are an important part of field administration. These local institutions have considerable role to play both in civic and developmental areas. There has been a tendency to entrust more developmental functions to the Panchayati Raj bodies. But there are several complaints of partisan outlook of the elected functionaries leading to favouritism and nepotism. As a result, there is political disharmony, intensified factionalism and increased crime rate.

Similarly, the municipal local institutions also face several problems. Shrinking resource base, inadequate technical capacity, increasing pressure due to growing population coupled with high expectations of the community for more and better services are creating several problems not only to the Municipal institutions but even to the district administration.

One of the well-known features of bureaucracy is its emphasis on rules and regulations. Increase in workload over the decades is leading to delays, red tapism, and consequently corruption. Status-quo conscious officials, in some cases are becoming insensitive to development demands, thereby creating atrophy in administration.

The reforms that have been effected over the years could not tackle the major problems like deterioration in law and order and problems of inter-agency coordination of field administration in the country. Structural reorganisation by itself may not, and probably will not help to improve the efficiency of the district administration. There is a need for attitudinal change among the officials. Unfortunately, the reform committees and commissions have not dealt with this important aspects of the official as well as the expectations of the community in tune with the democratic traditions.

Q5. Discuss the function/role of the Collector.   **[Dec-08, Q.9]**

Ans. The office of the Collector is an important institution transmitted by the British rulers to the Indian administrative system. He performs traditional revenue functions as well as development functions. Throughout the country, the power and functions of the Collector, more or less, remain the same. Broadly, the Collector performs the following functions:

• Head of Revenue Administration;
• Head of Police Administration,
• Head of District Administration, and
• An agent of the Government

Revenue: The Collector started as a revenue functionary and he continues to be the principal Revenue Officer and Head of the Revenue Administration in the district. After independence, the importance of revenue administration has become secondary. The emphasis has shifted to Development Administration, though the revenue functions still remain with the District Collector. Besides collection of revenue, the Collectors are responsible for the collection of all other duties like takkavi loans and dues belonging to other Departments. Maintenance of land records and collection of statistics at the village level are some other functions of the Collector. He exercises appellate jurisdiction in revenue cases. The recovery of arrears of land revenue in respect of all Departments is the responsibility of the Collector. In the discharge of his revenue functions, many officers like the Revenue Divisional Officers, Tahsildars, Revenue Inspectors and Village Officers assist the Collector.

As the Head of the Revenue Administrations, he is the kingpin of relief operations in the district. In emergency situation like floods and famines the Collector plays a very crucial role in relief operations. The Government takes decision regarding the quantum of relief and the manner of distribution mostly on the basis of assessment made by the Collector.

Law and Order: District Collector also functions as District Magistrate and is responsible for the maintenance of law and order in the district. After the separation of judiciary from the executive, the Collector is concerned with the preventive sections of the criminal procedure code. As District Magistrate, he is Head of the Police Administration of the district. In this functions, Superintendent of Police who is the Head of police force in the district helps the Collector in discharge of his police functions. In all important matters, the Superintendent of Police takes orders from the Collector. There have been many instances of strained relations between the Collector and the Superintendent of Police. In certain situations, lack of understanding between the two affect the entire District Administration.

Head of District Administration: The Collector continues to be the Head of the District Administration. As District Magistrate, he is responsible for the maintenance of law and order. As chief revenue officer, he is responsible for the collection of revenues. He is also closely associated with several other Departments like Education, Industries, Cooperatives, Public Works, etc. In respect of Panchayati Raj, in several States, he has a very important relationship with the Panchayati Raj bodies. As a Head of the district administration, he plays a coordinating role between different Departments like Revenue, Police and other Departments. The Collector supervises the working of municipalities. He has power to suspend the resolutions of local bodies, if they constitute a threat to public peace. He also Heads a number of official and non-official bodies in the district like the Road Transport Authority, District Employment Committee, Welfare Committees, Red Cross Society, etc. The amount of time he spends on these activities depends on his personal interest.

An Agent of the Government: He is looked upon as an agent of the Government at the district level. He hoists the national flag on Independence and Republic days. He has several protocol functions like meeting the Ministers and other important dignitaries. In emergencies like floods and famines, he can call upon any branch of the District Administration to undertake any specific work to provide assistance. Census operations and conduct of elections to various democratic bodies from the Parliament to the Gram Panchayat is another important function. The Collector is also an agent of the Governor in respect of scheduled tribes' areas in some of the districts. There are other functions also with which the Collector is intimately associated like social security, pensions, excise, grant of licenses for arms, etc. The scarcity and rising prices due to public distribution system has become an important part of district administration. He is directly responsible for the distribution and control of all essential commodities and goods. He issues licenses for trading in foodgrains and other commodities. As Head of the distribution system, he is expected to ensure timely and equitable distribution of scarce commodities.

The Collector presides over a large number of meetings like meetings of Coordination Committee, Development Committee, and Irrigation Committee etc. These are excellent forums for the Collector to know the way polices are translated into action and to come into contact with the local people and understand their problems.

Q6. Discuss the role of the collector in panchayati raj institutions.

Ans. After independence, the Collector has become responsible for the implementation of the development programmes in the district. As an administrator, he is expected to coordinate all the development programmes being implemented in the district. The Collector's role in development administration is more visible in case of Panchayati Raj Institutions. He is closely associated with these institutions ether from within or outside. The advent of Panchayati Raj Institutions in India has brought about several changes in the set up of the district administration. This is particularly so in case of the role and functions of the District Collector should be the Chairman of Zilla Parishad. At the time of establishment of Panchayati Raj, critics argued that Collectors should not Head the democratic bodies, this would not be in consonance with the spirit of decentralisation. It would curb the democratic spirit. In practice, different types of linkages were established between the Collector and the Panchayati Raj Institutions in different States. In Rajasthan, for example, the Collector was made an associate member of Zilla Parishad without the right to vote. In Andhra Pradesh, he was made a full member of Zilla Parishad and chairman of all the standing committees. Later, however in Andhra Pradesh, the Collector was disassociated from Zilla Parishad. In Maharashtra, the Collector was kept out of Zilla Parishad. But, generally it is felt that the Collectors should have a large share of responsibility in facilitating the success of Panchayati Raj Institutions. Over the years, four patterns of the role of Collector, vis-à-vis Zilla Parishad have emerged. Firstly, the Collector is the chairman of Zilla Prishad giving necessary fillip to the entire development effort. Secondly, the Collector has been kept out of Zilla Parishad completely because of a feeling that it would burden the Collector, who is already over burdened. In some States, the Collector is made Chairman of the standing committees vested with power and decision-making. Finally, in some States, the Collector is a member of Zilla Prishad without right to vote.

The relationship between Collector and Panchayati Raj Institutions can be studied under different heads namely control over staff, power to suspend resolutions, power to remover officers, and power to suspend and dissolve Panchayati Raj Institutions. In these areas, the role of Collector varies from state to state. The Collector has power to write confidential report and has authority to inflict various punishments, such power vary from state to state. Similarly, the Collector can suspend the resolutions of Panchayats. An association with these bodies will bring the Collector in intimate relationship with the people's representatives. This provides him an opportunity to understand the dynamics of Development Administration at the district level. In practice, the role assigned to him varies from state to state as mentioned below:

• In Tamil Nadu he is the Chairman of district Development Council.
• In the States of Utter Pradesh and Bihar he is entitled to attend the meetings of the Panchayat Samiti and its standing committees but without a right to vote.
• In Maharashtra and West Bengal he is kept out of the Zilla Prishad.
• In Andhra Pradesh, he is not only the member of the Zilla Prishad but also the Chairman of all the standing committees in whom executive authority is vested.
• In the States of Assam, Punjab and Rajasthan, the Collector is a non-voting member of the Zilla Parishad and he is associated in a purely advisory capacity. It shows that there is an unconcealed reluctance to have his involvement in the decision-making processes of rural democracy.

After 73rd Constitution Amendment, the relationship of District Collector with Panchayati Raj Institutions (PRIs) has changed immensely. The Constitutional amendment and the enactment of Panchayati Raj laws by various States in 1993 has reduced the burden of the District Collector on development activities. This Act has given scope to the State Government to set forth the yardstick of the relationship of the PRIs and the Collector. In this context, some States have created the post of Chief Executive Officer and some States have opted for District Development Officer or Deputy District Commissioner. In the States like Rajasthan, the Collector is a nominated member of the District Planning Committee (DPC). Whereas, in some other States like Madhya Pradesh the Collector is the Member and Secretary of the DPC. Before these changes, District Collector in Madhya Pradesh had access to Rs. 10 lakh for development works, which has now been hiked to Rs. 1 crore, making him more powerful. However, in Andhra Pradesh the Collector as the Head of the District Administration continues to co-ordinate the development activities. In the capacity of an ex-officio member, he attends the meetings of Zilla Parishad and its standing committees, and participate in their discussions. He participates and attends the meetings but without the right to vote on the resolutions. The District Collector has the authority to suspend or cancel any resolution passed by these bodies; initiate action in the event of default; suspend the Chairman (ZP), the President (MP) and the Sarpanch (GP) and dissolve the Zila Parishad / Mandal Parishad / Gram Panchayat and any of the Standing Committees. It has been observed from the study on Maharshtra that District Collector has limited role to play in the PRIs. He has an important role in elections or reporting regarding resolutions, such as no confidence against office bearers.

The unique feature about the controlling authority assigned to the Collector in Tamil Nadu is that the District Collector has the overall controlling authority as the Inspectors of Panchayats in the district. The Project Officer / Additional Collector (Development) of the District Rural Development Agency (DRDA) assists him in implementing development programmes. The study conducted by the Task Force on Panchayati Raj reveals that except a few States like Karnataka, Kerala and West Bengal, bureaucracy is a dominant partner in decentralised governance.

The Administrative Reforms Commission recommended that all the development functions should be entrusted to the Zilla Parishad. The Collector should only be responsible for regulatory functions. In the context of transfer of development functions, the Committee felt, it would enable the Collector to devote more time and attention to his regulatory functions. This will help to improve the general administrative climate in the district. The Committee on Panchayati Raj Headed by Asoka Mehta also recommended the separation of development functions and entrusting them to the Chief Executive Officer. Thus, even after implementation of 73rd Constitutional Amendment Act, there is no uniform pattern with regard to the position of the District Collector in relation to the Panchayati Raj Institutions.

Q7. Write a short note on Lakhina Experiment.

Ans. Need for administrative efficiency and also responsiveness to the community led Mr. Anil Kumar Lakhina, a District Collector, to undertake an exercise to reform district administration. The exercise was in the Collectorate of Ahmednagar in Satara district of Maharashtra. Some of the changes brought about in the District Administration includes regulation of visitors to the Collectorate; designing the office as per task sequence, making documents available to those who handle them; preparation of desk manuals, weeding out documents which had outlived their usefulness, provision of dust proof and fire fighting equipment; motivation and training etc. This experiment revolved around the assumption that attitudinal changes in the administrator can result in effective administration. It sought to link attitudinal changes with physical work environment. The experiment was undertaken in only one district and possibility of its adoption elsewhere is yet to be proved. But the Lakhina experiment is a pointer that structural changes coupled with attitudinal changes and the 'will' to adopt reforms can bring efficiency in district administration. What is true of the Collectorate is equally true of other administrative organs at the district level.

Q8. Discuss the role and functions of the police.

Ans. Prevention of crime and maintenance of public order are the major functions of the police. According to 1861 Act, Police functions are to prevent commission of offences and public nuisances; bring offenders to justice; collect information affecting public peace; and keep order in all public places, keeping in view the changing political and social scenario. U.N. congress prevention of crime, held in 1970 identified urbanisation, industrialisation, population growth, internal migration, social mobility, technological changes etc. as the crimogenetic factors. Communal tension and other social tensions are also the causes of crime due to which public order gets disturbed and violence breaks out.

The main task of police is to enforce law and order, protect the citizens and safeguard their property. The police have to play a positive role in the scheme of social defence. It can no longer take a restrictive view of their role. In a democratic society the role of police is linked to social service. It is an important area where police has been assigned a positive role in relation of social legislation. These legislations touch upon the lives of the people at countless number of places. This provides various opportunities to serve the people and proves to be a challenge as well. In the changing political context, the police have to function as officers of law rather than officers of the Government or Party in power.

According to the National Police Commission set up by the Government of India in 1977, the duties and responsibilities of the police are to:

(i) Promote and preserve public order;

(ii) Investigate crime;

(iii) Identify problems and situations that are likely to result in commission of crimes;

(iv) Reduce the opportunities for the commission of crimes through preventive patrol and other appropriate police measures;

(v) Aid and co-operate with other relevant agencies in implementing: appropriate measures for prevention of crimes;

(vi) Aid individuals who are in danger of physical harm;

(vii) Create and maintain a feeling of security in the community;

(viii) Facilitate orderly movement of people and vehicles;

(ix) Counsel and resolve conflicts and promote amity;

(x) Provide other appropriate services and afford relief to people in distress situations; and

(xi) Collect intelligence relating to matters affecting public peace and crime including social and economic offences, and national integrity and security.

As civilisation advances, and democracy takes roots, the laws of the land also change. Instead of individual fancies, the people or their chosen representatives base law making on participation. Personalised laws are replaced by public laws. It's inter-dependence with other wings of criminal justice system such as judiciary and prosecution, and its interface with various sections and groups in the society have far reaching implication for its functionary.

Q9. Describe the organisation and functions of a range.

Ans. Many States are too big to be administered effectively and efficiently from a central point. It is not possible for the Head of the police that is the police chief or the DGP/IGP to keep in touch with the functioning of the entire organisation. Therefore, the police organisation in a State is divided into ranges for operational convenience. This is above the district and below the State level. This broadly corresponds to the divisional set up. Deputy Inspector General of Police Heads each range. Each police range comprises a few districts. The number of districts in each range varies from 2 to 8 depending upon the size of the district, population, and importance of the district.

The DIG functions as a staff officer to the State police chief and as a line officer to the district police. His functions include periodic inspections, receiving and processing reports and returns from districts, and issuing instructions to the district police functionaries. A major function of the range DIG is to coordinate the activities of district police and also take measures for inter-district co-operation. He is personally responsible for the enforcement of discipline among the police personnel under his charge. He exercises power of transfer and discipline over certain categories of personnel. He keeps a watch on the crime situation in the district particularly over grave offences like dacoity, murder etc. He also exercises control over police funds. The range of DIG's functions, thus, includes personnel management, budgetary control and coordination. He is responsible for the maintenance of efficiency and discipline of his staff. He ensures uniformity of procedure and securing co-operation between the police functioning in the districts within his range. He has to ensure harmonious relations between the police and the executive magistracy. There are some criticisms about a range becoming a mere post office. It is criticised to be functionally superfluous. Some feel that in spite of range offices the workload of the State level offices has not been reduced and in fact it has been on the increase. The National Police Commission recommended that DIG of the range should play a positive role in functioning of the districts under his control. He should act as coordinating authority between districts in his range and with those of the adjacent ranges. It also recommended that he/

she should be a sensitive judge of public opinion and play an important role in planning and modernisation of the force. The commission felt that to be effective, the range of DIG should not have more than five districts under his control. It also recommended that for adequate supervision, territorial Inspector General of Police should be appointed in large States. They should not have more than 15 to 20 districts or 4-5 ranges under his charge. The Armed Battalions of the range should also be placed under the operational charge of the territorial IGP. They should be delegated administrative, financial, disciplinary and other power. This will reduce the workload on the DGP and enable him to concentrate on higher matters of policy and administration.

Q10. Examine the organisation of police at district and sub-district level.
Ans. District is an important unit of the public administrative structure in the county. Almost all the State Government offices are located in the district. In Police Administration also district plays a pivotal role. All the laws and rules passed by the police are transformed into action at this level. District Police Organisation is responsible for the effective maintenance of law and order and control of crime. Police Administration at the district level is carried out by the chief of the district police, called Superintendent of Police, who is responsible for the maintenance of law and order, and other law enforcement activities. Technically, Superintendent of Police functions under the overall control of the Collector. He and his subordinate officers, in practice, enjoy operational autonomy in the discharge of their functions. The Collector as a District Magistrate in broadly responsible for preventive aspects; and the police is responsible for the control of crime, maintenance of law and order, etc. Police Administration below the district level is organised into divisions; divisions into circles; and circle into Police Stations. The organisation and working of Police Stations, marginally, varies between urban and rural areas.

District Police work under the Superintendent of Police. He is always a member of the Indian Police Service and wields a great amount of power and prestige in the district. He is accountable to the Head of the range police that is Deputy Inspector General of Police for the maintenance of law and order in his district. He is also responsible to the Director General of Police at the State Headquarters. The Superintendent of Police (S.P) is responsible for the efficiency, morale and discipline of the police force in the district. He collects information about various aspects from the entire district and communicates the same to the State Government along with his own assessment.

The Superintendent of Police is primarily responsible for the maintenance of law and order, and prevention of crime. He is empowered to take preventive measures to ensure peace in the district. He has to make adequate police arrangements during fairs and festival as well as elections and agitations. If he apprehends untoward situations, he can advise the Collector to promulgate prohibitory orders and even to clamp curfew. He controls crime by patrolling, investigating and taking preventive measures. He also supervises the operations of crime and special branches working under him. He has many personnel and organisational responsibilities like adequate supply of arms, vehicles, uniform etc. He also has responsibilities regarding matters of training, promotion and discipline of the staff, maintaining financial property etc. He is the link between police organisation and people's representatives at the district level. He maintains cordial and friendly relations with people. In the district where important urban centers are located, he has responsibilities of regulating traffic and receiving VIPs. Thus, the SP occupies a pivotal and a powerful position not only in the district police organisation but also in the District Administration itself. The Additional Superintendent of Police assists him. The later helps him in his day-to-day general administration. Deputy Superintendents of Police, Circle Inspectors of Police, Sub-Inspectors of Police, Head Constables and Police Constable assist him in the enforcement of law and order at various levels. To assist him in undertaking his functions, professional and technical units are also placed at his disposal.

The organisation at the district level broadly consists of two wings namely the District Police Office (DPO) and the Field Organisation. The general administration of the entire police in the district is carried by the DPO. It works under the SP or ASP, who is in-charge of the office administration and also exercises general control and supervision. The office administration is carried out by several sections like crime and statistics, crime bureau, audit and accounts, equipment and stores, etc. The DPO can be considered as the secretariat of the police and the nerve centre of the Police Administration in the district. Generally, the accommodation and facilities at the DPO are not adequate. One find ill-equipped and overstaffed office; insufficient accommodation; and inadequate lighting and ventilation in these offices.

To provide special assistance to the police, a number of field units function at the district level. The district armed reserve, the home guards, the women police, crime bureau, special branch finger print unit, dog squad, transport unit are some of the field units supporting the district Police Administration.

Sub-division: For operational convenience, the district police organisation is divided into a number of sub-divisions. Police sub-division is a unit where police work is coordinated and controlled. It is an intermediary link between police circles. Police Stations and the district police office. The police sub-division is under the charge of a Deputy Superintendent of Police or Additional Superintendent of Police. They are generally called Sub-Divisional Police Officers. The main work of the sub-division is to look into law and order matters, and discipline among the police force and other related matters at the sub-divisional level. A number of reports and registers relating to crime, security and other administrative aspects are maintained in the sub-divisional office. The Sub-Divisional Officers are responsible primarily for the maintenance of law and order and crime control; collection and communication of intelligence; submission of periodic reports to the Superintendent of Police, Inspection of Police Stations and Circle Offices. They also have an important public relations role to perform. They act as a link between the Superintendent of Police and the Sub-Inspectors and Inspectors.

Circles: Sub-Divisions are further divided into police circles, which is a link between Police Stations and sub-division. This is the third tier in the district police organisation. Sometimes, the police circles are coterminous with taluka; sometimes with blocks; and sometimes they may not be in conformity with either of them. As there are no rules governing the formation of police circles, they vary in size from State to State and even in the State from circle to circle. The number of Police Stations in each police circle is determined on the basis of crime, population, area, topography, etc. Each circle may have 3 to 10 Police Stations. The Circle office facilitates smooth administration at the field level.

Inspector of Police is the Head of police circle. He is responsible for the maintenance of law and order, and control of crime. He has to promote discipline among the policemen. He guides, advises, and supervises the work of Police Stations and the men working there. He also investigates grave crimes with the assistance of supporting staff. As is the case with the divisional office, several registers and records are maintained at the circle level. They include communication register, case diary, circle information book, annual review of crime, crime charts, criminal intelligence file, etc.

The Police Station is the lowest tier in the police organisation. It is here that the actual work of the police is undertaken. It is the basic and primary unit, which is responsible for the maintenance of law and order, prevention and control of crime and protection of life and property of the community.

Q11. Discuss the critical issues in police administration.   [Dec-09, Q.3]

Ans. The Police Administration in its present form was established long back. Through the decades the system has not undergone any significant change. The Indian Police Act of 1861 continues to be the basis for police system in India. There are several suggestions for its replacement by new legislation. But they have remained only suggestions. There are several issues, which affect the organisation and working of the police in the country.

In recent years one finds a proliferation of the posts of Inspector General of Police, and Deputy Inspector General of Police. Though expansion of any organisation including police is inevitable. The Police Administration is accused of being a top-heavy administration. Similarly frequent changes of the DGPs whenever there is a change of political leadership has created a serious credibility gap in this police leadership. This problem has been aggravated with emergence of regional parties in some States. The police coming in for criticism and praise by different political parties has led to the politicisation of the police.

Constitutionally, law and order is a State subject. But over the years the central police organisations like Central Reserve Police Force and Border Security Force have increased. Deployment of the police force in the States on occasions without informing them has created tensions in Centre-State relations. Similar is the case with the use of Central Bureau of Investigation. A few States even barred investigations by the CBI in their States leading to acrimony between the Centre and the States.

Several studies on the image of police have revealed that the public has greater dissatisfaction and disenchantment with the working of the police. Apathy of the police, inefficiency and incapacity of the police has given a poor image to it. As long as police image does not improve, it is difficult for the police to create confidence among the public. In such situation, it is not possible for the public to approach the Police Stations confidently and expect justice from them.

Another issue is the accountability of police. The National Police Commission has suggested constitution of State Security Boards to make them more accountable and responsible. These institutions unfortunately have not been constituted and wherever they exist, their working is not up to the mark.

Facilities at the Police Station level are important to make them effective. Accommodation, facilities and modernisation are important areas, which need critical evaluation as well as reform. In all these areas the facilities are inadequate. As a result some Police Stations are not in a position to establish regular contacts with the community. Similarly they are not in a position to take prompt action.

The relation between Superintendent of Police and Collector is an important area of concern. There appears to be a tendency on the part of Superintendents of Police to ignore or undermine the Collector and his authority. This has its implications not only on the police but also on the entire district administration. In recent years terrorism and violence in different parts of the country are on the increase. The community expects the police to take steps to control the problem.

Their failure to do this is not only leading to worsening law and order situation but is also giving a bad name to the police. This has also shattered the confidence of the people in the police.

Recruitment and training are important in any organisation; police organisation is no exception to this. Unfortunately several criticisms are leveled against the practices and methods of recruitment of police personnel. People feel that the best and meritorious are not recruited in the police. There are allegations of partisanship in selections. The recruiting authorities are alleged to be corrupt. Training, that is imparted, is also considered to be inadequate. Training is not able to motivate the police. The committee on Police Training, which was set up by the Government of India in 1973 made several recommendations to improve the training of police officials. Though efforts are being made to rationalise the recruitment and training practices of the personnel.

Police Commissions at the National and State levels have made several suggestions to make the police efficient, responsive and responsible. But unfortunately on one consideration or the other they have not been seriously considered. This indicates that police reform is a low priority area in the country. Whatever reforms were implemented they were done half-heartedly without understanding the socio-political milieu within which the police has to operate. Because of the adhoc and piecemeal nature of the reforms they did not have the intended effect. The reforms are required not only in organisation, personnel, procedures but also in the attitudes of the people and the police officials. Still colonial attitude pervades the minds of the police personnel. Reform should be continuous because no adhoc approach will give the intended results.

The police behaviour like rudeness, non-registration of FIR, maltreatment in lock-ups and so on, are forbidden in the Police Regulations. Mohit Bhattacharya explained the problem areas in the field of human rights. In his words "**(a)** General feeling that the ground realities—how crime and criminals have actually to be dealt with—are not appreciated by "human rights" protagonists, **(b)** the balance seems to be tilting towards criminals, leading to police discomfiture; **(c)** human rights are, no doubt, of great value; at the same time, police discretion is necessary to deal with the ground situation". The major problems faced by police functionaries and Police Stations are intra-organisational issues related to human resource like insufficient manpower, low motivation, lack of promotion opportunities, lack of proper training etc. Infrastructure related problems such as shortage of vehicles and fuel, poor maintenance and limited space to work and lack of communication facilities affect the efficiency. In addition, ill lighted unhealthy place; difficulties in the supply of food for lock-up inmates, short supply of stationary items; lack of elementary investigation kit, inordinately long time in post mortem reports; pending cases and low priority to investigation also affect the services. In the context of finance, Police Station has no system of keeping fund, travelling allowance bills are hard to get and remain pending for months. Strict discipline becomes an artificial barrier to genuine remain pending for months. There is also barrier to genuine inter-personal understanding of work, which affect inter-personal relations as well as dealing with public. In certain cases, police extorts money, nothing moves without greasing palms. In rural areas, payments are generally made in kind.

Human Rights are promised on two important aspects, that is dignity and equality for a human being. The incorporation of the rights on the paper or in the Constitution does not ensure their fulfillment. Constitutional guarantees and legal stipulations are of no use unless these are put into practice by the enforcement agencies. Since police is the first step on the ladder of the criminal justice system as an agency that investigates and detects crime. Human rights can be imperative and effective if the functional level is fair, just and reasonable in its dealings with suspects and others. It largely depends upon the law enforcement officers. Hence, the contribution of police is crucial for the successful implementation of law and order; and in building up of an institution for justice. For this, senior leader must internalise the concept of human rights. He has to undergo a change in his style of thinking and functioning with the conviction that human rights are inevitable and a technique for better governance.

The above mentioned issues need to be examined critically. There is no dearth of suggestions but what is important is the political will. One has to examine the police reforms in the total context of social change, and political dynamics. Reform in the police cannot be viewed in isolation. Structural and institutional changes can only bring marginal improvements in the working of the police system. What is important is attitudinal change, both on the part of the police personnel and also the community. Neither police can take law into its hand and curtail the liberties of the people nor people can expect peace and order unless they themselves co-operate with the police in discharge of its functions.

Q12. What do you understand by Local Self Government?

Ans. Local Government or Local Self-Government is the Government of a locality. It is not the area of the State Government. It is an autonomous unit like the State or Central Government. It is the local will, not the will of the Centre or State, which is reflected through the Local Government. National Government is for the whole nation; hence it is big Government. By contrast, Local Government looks after the 'local' functions like water supply, local streets, garbage collection and disposal and similar other local needs. It is small but important Government for a local area, which can be a town or a group of villages.

The adjective 'local' stands for a small geographical area. Also, it means intimate social relations of the people in a limited geographical space. The other word, 'Government' stands for a public authority. In a democracy, Government may be at national level, state level and the Regional Government at the regional level. Below the regional level, there is the 'local' level where 'Government' can be legally constituted. This means, there are many Local Government units below the National and Regional Governments, which exercise authority and discharge a number of important local functions on the basis of statutory decentralisation.

Local Self-Government has three important features:

i) it is elected by the people of the local area;

ii) it has the power to levy taxes and other fees, like any other Government; and

iii) its functions and activities are clearly laid down in law so that within the scheme of legislation Local Self-Government enjoys a degree of autonomy.

Thus, the Local Self-Government is a statutorily constituted democratic Government with a degree of autonomy exercising jurisdiction over a limited geographical area. The Local Self-Government in a liberal democracy marks for decentralisation of power. So, it is considered as a means of enriching and deepening democracy by extending freedom of actions to many localities. It was the view of John Stuart Mill that Local Government creates conditions for popular participation in governance, and in this process the system has great educative value for good citizenship in a country.

Q13. Write a short note on followings:
1. Trend of urbanisation in India
2. Municipal corporation
3. 74th constitutional amendment   **[June-09, Q.9]**
Ans. 1. Trend of Urbanisation in India:

An urban area is one, which is formally so declared through the statutory establishment in that area of a municipal body, a notified area or a cantonment by a definite legislation. Thus, there are Municipal Acts in different States under which municipal bodies are set-up by the State Governments in specific areas. Cantonment areas are governed by the Central legislation. There can be other areas also that can be declared as 'urban' by the census authorities.

The urban population, which was around 3 per cent at the beginning of the 19th century rose to about 10 per cent by the beginning of the 20th century. Between 1901 and 1921 urban population grew very slowly that is, it rose from 25.6 million to 27.6 million and between 1921 and 1941 population rose 43.5 million. But after 1941 the growth rate gained greater momentum adding to its urban population. From 1961 onwards there has been a dramatic increase in the urban population of the country. In 1961 the urban population stood at 77.5 millions and by 1981 it had more than doubled to make it 109.6 million constituting about 23.7 per cent of India's total population. On the basis of census calculation it can be said that India's urban population has been rising steadily. In 1971 total urban population in India stood at 109.11 million, which rose to 159.46 million in 1918, and 218 million in 1991. During 1971-81 decade India's urban population increased approximately 5 million per annual, or at an average annual growth rate of 3.87 per cent compared to the growth rate of 1.78 per cent for the rural population. In 1991 census, country's total urban population stood at 21.18 million and the average annual growth rate between 1981-91 was 3.09 per cent. Between 1988 and 2001 the projections estimate India's urban population to become almost double and from 2001 to 2021 it is expected to double again taking the urban population to more then 600 millions. India recorded a population of 1,027,015,247 on 1st March 2001. The data indicates that 72.2 per cent persons were recorded in rural areas and remaining 27.8 per cent in urban areas. Urban population growth is supposed to be an indicator of general economic development. Delhi is the most urbanised State in India with over 93 per cent of its population being Urban. Amongst the other major States, the most urbanised is Tamil Nadu with 43.86 per cent urban population. Maharashtra has the maximum urban population but is the second most urbanised State with 42.40 per cent Urban Population. Uttar Pradesh contributing nearly 21 per cent to the State's total population, but in terms of urbanisation it ranks twenty fifth in the list. Gujarat is third most urbanised State having 37.35 per cent urban population. The Himachal Pradesh is least urbanised (most Rural) State having 9.79 per cent followed by Bihar 10.47 per cent and Sikkim 11.1 per cent.

In India, lack of employment opportunities in the rural areas has led to city-ward migration of large rural population, which is commonly known as the 'push' factor of urbanisation. The migrants generally choose to settle in large cities where, as a consequence, population increase is not matched by sewerage, transportation, facilities—all suffer from short supply in the face of mounting population pressure. Our large cities like Kolkata, Mumbai, Chennai, Delhi etc. are all having large slum population and there is chronic shortage of essential civic services and facilities in these cities.

There has been a notion that India is an over-urbanized State, because of their substantial increase in population over the years. This thesis is advanced on the ground that there is a mismatch between the levels of industrialisation and urbanisation. The process of urbanisation is costly and impinges upon the economic growth. The State of infrastructure is poor and is not in a position to take the growing urban pressure.

2. Municipal Corporation:

The administration of civic affairs in a city is challenge. The distinct characteristic of a city is the huge concentration of population within a limited area. The management of civil services therefore, requires an effective organisational structure adequate finance and efficient personnel. The Municipal Corporation as a form of city Government occupies the top position among the local authorities in India. Normally, the Corporation form of urban

Government is found in major cities like Mumbai, Delhi, Kolkata, Chennai, Hyderabad, Bangalore, etc.

Municipal Corporation is established through a special statue, which is passed by the State legislature. In case of Union Territories, they are established through Acts passed by the Parliament. Such legislation may be enacted specially for a particular corporation or for all Corporations in a State, for example the Mumbai and Kolkata Corporations were established through separate legislation. Whereas in Uttar Pradesh and Madhya Pradesh, the State level legislation governs the constitution and working of the Corporation. The Municipal Corporation generally enjoys a greater measure of autonomy than other forms of local Government. In almost all the States, the Municipal Corporations have been assigned numerous functions such as supply of drinking water, electricity, road transport services, public health, education, registration of births and deaths, drainage, construction of public parks, gardens, libraries, etc. These functions are normally divided as obligatory and discretionary.

In Haryana, there is only one Municipal Corporation (MC) that is in Faridabad with more than 5 lakhs population. MC is constituted for governing the area. It has both elected and nominated (ex-officio) members. MC, Faridabad has at present 24 elected Councilors. Under the amended municipal law of the State, election to the municipal bodies must take place every five years, unless a municipal body is dissolved earlier. The Mayor elected by the members of the Corporation from amongst themselves is the first citizen of the city and presides over the meetings of the city Corporation.

3. 74th Constitutional Amendment:

Far reaching changes have been brought about for both Municipal Government and Panchayati Raj Institutions through the two Constitutional Amendments: the Seventy-third (73rd) Constitutional Amendment Act, 1992 for Panchayati Raj, and the Seventy-fourth (74th) Constitutional Amendment Act, 1992 for Municipal Bodies.

The Constitution of India now provides for the constitution of three types of institutions of Urban Local Self-Government. These are Municipal Corporations in larger urban areas, Municipal Councils in urban settlements, and Nagar Panchayats in 'transitional' areas, which are neither fully urban nor fully rural. In addition, it provides for decentralisation of municipal administration by constituting Ward Committees in territorial areas of such municipalities, which have more than three-lakhs population.

Composition

The Municipal authorities are to be constituted of:

• the elected representatives who are to be elected from the different electoral wards;

• the Members of the House of the People and the Legislative Assembly of the State representing constituencies, which are wholly or partly under the municipal area;

• chairpersons of the Committees of the municipal authorities; and

• persons having special knowledge or experience in municipal administration (without right to vote).

The Ward Committees are to be composed of members of the Municipal Council representing the wards within the jurisdiction and one of the elected representatives from within the wards is to be appointed as its Chairperson. But the constitution gives discretion to the State Government to decide the composition.

Another important provision of the Constitution Amendment pertains to the municipal authorities. It gives a term of five years, to the municipalities and if at all they have to be dissolved, they must be given an opportunity of being heard. Even if they have to be dissolved because of any irregularity, fresh elections are to be held within six months. This prevents the phenomenon of prolonged supersession or years together.

Empowerment of weaker sections of society and women is one of the substantive provisions of the Constitution Amendment. With a view to empowering the scheduled castes and tribes as well as women, it provides for the reservation of seats in the Council. Besides such reservations, the most important provision of the Constitution Amendment is empowerment of women for which one-third of the total seats are to be reserved.

To keep the municipal elections out of the direct control of the State Government, and the ensure free and fair elections to the municipal bodies, the Constitution Amendment has provided for an independent State Election Commission (also for Panchayat elections), consisting of an Election Commissioner to be appointed by the Governor.

The most important feature of the Seventy-Fourth Constitutional Amendment, in financial sphere, is the mandatory constitution of Finance Commission by the State Government once in every five years. The State Finance Commission is to make recommendations regarding the principles to govern sharing of the State taxes, fees etc. between the State Government and the Municipalities; and also its distribution among the Municipalities. The commission has also to suggest the principles for the determination of taxes and fees to be assigned to them and the grants-in-aid to be given to the municipal authorities out of the consolidated fund to the State. It also has the mandate to suggest ways and means of improving the financial position of the municipal authorities.

Moreover, the need for non-plan funds of the Municipalities is now to be looked by the Union Finance Commission as well. Federal transfers will now be available also for the municipal authorities. This is an amendment of far reaching importance.

The Constitution Amendment provides for setting up of the District Planning Committees to consolidate the plans prepared by the Municipalities and the Panchayats within the district; and to prepare a draft development plan for the district as a whole. The Municipalities are to be represented on it. Plans so prepared are to be forwarded by the Chairperson of the Planning Committee to the State Government. Similarly, Metropolitan Planning Committees are to be up in the metropolitan areas on which the municipal authorities are to be represented.

The 74th Constitution Amendment is a landmark legislation that, for the first time, accords constitutional status to Municipal Government and provides for broader social participation in local councils people's involvement in civic development, enlargement of functional domain by inserting the Twelfth Schedule, continuity through regular elections and regular funds flow from the higher level Governments. The other important dimension is constitutional recognition of micro-level planning coordinated by the District Planning Committee. These are the brighter aspects of the Amendment.

There are, however, the grayer areas as well. It has missed a valuable opportunity to specify the functions and also the sources of local revenues. This would have prevented the State encroachment into these spheres.

Q14. Discuss the role of urban development authorities.

Ans. Urban Development is very complex and accordingly the strategies for developing urban areas are multi-faced. One of the problems of urban areas today is to prevent haphazard and unplanned physical growth in and around them. When the municipal areas at many places cross their boundaries due to unplanned development of per-urban area, the improvement of living conditions in these areas and their vicinity becomes imperative. But the municipal agencies are unable to solve this problem due to jurisdictional, legal and financial limitations. There are only two ways of controlling it, either to extend the municipal boundaries and strengthen them administratively and financially, or to have a separate agency with more power and finances. The Estimates Committees of the Fifth Lok Sabha recommended the setting up of development authorities for the rapidly growing cities and major towns to achieve a planned development. The planning commission also indicated the desirability of structural innovations in urban local Governments during the Fifth Plan. This led to the constitution of urban development authorities for various metropolitan and other cities. The Delhi Development Authority was the first to be set up in 1964. The urban development authorities are expected to plan, control, and coordinate development programmes in and around metropolitan and other big cities. The following are the major objectives of the authorities:

• To prepare and implement plans for development of the area.

• To prepare zonal development plans for the zones into which the development area may be divided.

• To control the use of land for various purposes.

• To carry out development work and provide infrastructural facilities.

Broadly speaking, the urban development authorities have regulatory, planning and promotional functions. They have to regulate and check the unplanned growth of cities and towns. They have to ensure orderly and planned utilisation of land in accordance with the master and zonal plans. They supplement the development activities of the Municipalities and Corporations. These urban development authorities face several bottlenecks in the discharge of their functions. These include problems of coordinating between the development authority and the Corporation or Municipality, inadequate resources and lack of sufficient and competent technical staff.

Q15. Describe the sources of finance of the urban local self government bodies.   **[June-08, Q.15]**

Ans. Urban local bodies require adequate resources to undertake their obligatory and discretionary functions stipulated in the Act. The Municipal Authorities get their income primarily from their own sources, that is, the tax and non-tax sources, which have been assigned by the State Government and are mentioned in the Municipal States.

A municipal council can statutorily impose the taxes, as follows:

• Tax on building and land, which besides a general tax also includes rates on water, lighting, fire service, etc.;

• Tax on buildings payable along with the application for sanction of the building plan;

• Tax on professions, trades etc.

• Tax on vehicles (other than motor vehicles);

• Tax on animals;

• Tolls on roads and ferries; and

• Octroi.

Not-tax sources include:

• Rents on land and houses;

• Sale proceeds of land another products of land;

• Fees from educational institutions;

• License fees;

• Fines or violating municipal bye-laws and other fines and fees, and

• Receipts from slaughter houses.

In additions, there are provisions for shared revenues, grants-in-aid and loans from the Government and financial institutions, besides tax and non-tax sources.

The resources of local bodies come from both internal and external sources. Receipt of Municipalities in Chennai highlight that the income from taxable sources constitutes 29 per cent and from non-taxable source 43 per cent. Internal receipts include sources from others also that is total 57 per cent. Grants and loans form River Actions Programme etc. constitute 5 per cent. This indicates that internal sources constitute more than half of the total resource base of the urban local bodies. They also receive financial assistance from the Government in terms of devolution (13 per cent), entertainment tax (5 per cent), surcharge on stamp duty (9 per cent) and grants, loans and receipt from others (12 per cent). There are variations from State to State. The expenditure pattern of Municipalities in Chennai (Department of Economics and Statistics, Chennai) reflects that out of the total expenditure 40 per cent is spent on salaries and pension; 32 per cent on maintenance of street lights, water supply, roads, conservancy and others from the revenue account and 28 per cent from the capital account. The data highlights that sound resource base is one of the major requirements of urban local bodies for development works. The committees and commission, both at the National and State level have recommended both short-term and long-term measures. Unfortunately, no serious efforts are being made to correct this imbalance between functions and finances in the urban local bodies. The 74th Constitution Amendment is a hold step in this regard.

Q16. Discuss relationship between the state government and local self-government.

Ans. Urban local bodies are institutions of decentralisation created by the State Government through the Municipal Acts. The provisions of the Act govern the relations between the two. There are several criticisms about State control over local bodies, which are theoretically autonomous. There are four reasons as to why State should exercise control. Firstly, the State Government creates local bodies. Secondly, as part of the State there is a need for homogeneous development of all the areas, which can be ensured by the State. Thirdly, personnel with technical skills and experience required in nation building activities have to be provided by the State. And finally the State Government provides financial assistance to local bodies, which implies control to ensure that the money is properly utilised. Whatever be the rationale, the major objective of control and supervision by the State Government is to ensure efficiency in the performance of functions by the units of Local Self-Government. But what is important is that guidance and control should not be negative. It should strengthen their confidence and enable them to assume more responsibilities. Therefore, there is a need for high degree of cooperation and coordination between them rather than acrimony.

There is a feeling in the country that the stronghold of the State Government over the local bodies is too extensive, which cuts at the roots of the local autonomy. Two arguments are advanced in these connections. Firstly, the resource base of the local bodies is shrinking and State Governments have been doing precious little. Secondly, the power of supersession and dissolution are being indiscriminately used against local bodies. For example, in 1989, out of 73 Municipal Corporations in the country 39 were superseded at different points of time. This is indicative of the extent of control exercised in the States over the local bodies. Most committees have recommended measures to strengthen the resource base and also the capacity of these institutions. Acceptance and implementation of these recommendations would go a long way in ensuring cooperative relations between the State Government and urban local bodies.

It is to be noted that the 74th constitution Amendment gives a term of five years to the Municipalities. The Government may dissolve the bodies but fresh elections are to be held within a period of six months. Moreover, to augment the resources of the Municipalities a Finance Commission has been constituted in every State.

Q17. Write a short note on three-tier Panchayati Raj Institution.
[Dec-09, Q.9][June-09, Q.14]

Ans. After the 73rd Constitutional Amendment, we have in every State a three-tier Panchayati Raj structure at the village, block and district level.

Gram Sabha: An important feature of the structure of panchayats at the village level is Gram Sabha. It is the supreme village assembly and sole of PRIs, having a legal status under the law. It consists of all the adult persons registered as voters in the electoral roll of a village comprised within the area of Gram Panchayat. It has been made obligatory for the Gram Sabha to hold two general meetings in each year. A Gram Sabha may exercise such power and perform such functions as the Legislature of a State may by law provides. In most of the States, Gram Sabhas are constituted as an instrument of popular participation at the cutting edge level. They are vested with the power to consider the accounts and administration of the panchayat, and approve proposals for taxation and plans for development and identifying beneficiaries under various schemes.

Gram Panchayat: Throughout the country village panchayat is the basic unit in the structure of Panchayati Raj. As Village Panchayats have been in existence in the country since ancient times, almost all States have recognised their importance. It is also felt that as panchayats are nearer to the community, they would ensure more direct participation of the people in the implementation of development programmes. All the seats in a Gram Panchayat (GP) are filled by persons chosen by direct elections form the territorial constituencies in the Panchayat area. Seats have been reserved or scheduled castes and tribes as well as women.

Panchayat Samiti: Panchayat Samiti (PS) is the next important body in the structure of panchayati Raj. In almost all the States Samitis have been given important role. The voters in the area directly elect their representatives in a Samiti. The State may provide representation of the Chairperson of the Village Panchayats, MPs, MLAs and MLCs. Thus, the structure of the Panchayat Samitis varies from State to State. The seats are, however, reserved for scheduled castes, tribes and women.

Zilla Parishad: Zilla Parishad (ZP) as the third tier has been established at the district level in all the States. The structural pattern of the Zilla Parishad is the same as in the Panchayat Samiti. The voters directly elect their representatives from their constituencies. These seats have also been reserved for scheduled castes, tribes and women. The State Legislature may provide by law representation of the Chairpersons of the Panchayat Samitis MPs, MLAs, and MLCs.

Q18. What are the different sources of finance of Panchayati raj?

Ans. The financial resources of Panchayati Raj Institutions can broadly be divided into four categories, viz. taxes, grants and public contributions income through productive enterprises, and loans. Taxes levied by Panchayat are both compulsory and discretionary. The Panchayats in some States, collect vehicle tax, profession tax, etc. Unfortunately there has been a general reluctance on the part of Panchayats to levy and collect the taxes. Government grant is another source of income to Panchayat. In most of the States, Panchyats survive only on Government grants. There is, however, no uniformity in the nature and quantum of grants. Panchayats derive income from productive enterprises like cinema halls, flour mills, etc.

The Panchayat Samitis, in many States, also have power of taxation. They can levy house tax, irrigation tax, education tax, etc. But rarely this power of taxation is exercised. These Samitis also receive grants from the Government and there are variations between State to State in the nature and quantum of grants. In some states where functions like education have been transferred to Samitis, they are given grants to undertake these functions. The Zilla Parishads undertake coordinating functions. Therefore, their finances mostly, consist of grants received from the State Government and the assigned revenues. The funds of the Parishad come mainly from the share of the land revenue and other taxes assigned to them by the Government.

A serious problem with Panchayati Raj Institutions is that they have always been starved of finances. Inadequacy of finances is one of the basic reasons for their inability to undertake the development functions. Though, they are considered as principal agencies of rural development, they are not given adequate resources. In almost all the States, there has been heavy dependence of the Panchayati Raj Institutions on the State Grants. The quantum of grants is mostly determined by the State Government based on its own resource base rather than on the functions and needs of Panchayati Raj Institutions.

The taxes, duties, tolls and fees to be levied by the Panchayats are assigned to them and the grants-in-aid to be given to them have been left to the discretion of the State Governments. But after the 73rd Constitution Amendment we have a Finance Commission in every States, and it is constituted once in every five years. The Finance Commission is to make recommendations regarding the principles to govern the distribution of the taxes, duties, tolls and fees between the States and the Panchayats, and also its distribution between the Panchayats at all levels. The Commission also suggests the principles for determination of the taxes, duties, tolls and fees to be assigned to them; and the grants-in-aid to be given from the consolidated fund of the State. It also has the mandate to suggest ways and means of improving the financial positions of the Panchayati Raj Institution. The Union Finance Commission now looks into the need for non-plan funds of the Panchayats. Federal transfers are also available for the Municipalities from the Union Finance Commission.

Citizen and Administration

Q1. Explain the main features of social structure of India and their impact on administration. [June-09, Q.10][June-07, Q.6]

Ans. A **society** is a population of humans characterised by patterns of relationships between individuals that share a distinctive culture and/or institutions. More broadly, a society is an economic, social and industrial infrastructure, in which a varied multitude of people are a part of. Members of a society may be from different ethnic groups. A society may be a particular people, such as the Saxons, a nation state, such as Bhutan, or a broader cultural group, such as a Western society.

A society is a collection of people who are sufficiently organised to create conditions necessary to live together with a common identification. It is an organised network of social interactions and patterned behaviour. Every society has its own identity based on the nature of its social institutions. India has a rich cultural heritage and is a land of diversities. The diversity in social life is reflected in multi-social, multilingual, multi-religious and multi-caste nature of the society. The important features of the India social structure are: predominate rural habitation in small villages; multi-religious and multi-caste social identities and important role of family in the social life. We shall have a detailed discussion on these institutions and their impact on administration in the following sections.

Rural habitation: India is a land of villages. A great majority of villages are small with only around five hundred populations each. Mahatma Gandhi's view that India lives in villages still holds good, at least from the demographic point of view.

The village social life has its own peculiar characteristics. Stanley J. Heginbotham, in his book, Cultures in Conflict (1975), discusses in detail the nature of village life and its influence on the nature of bureaucracy. The village social life norms strengthen the authoritarian and hierarchical norms in administration. The village social life, which is based on the hierarchical exchange relations greatly influence the behaviour of civil servants in public organisation. The differences in the social background of majority of citizens who are poor, illiterate, rural based, and tradition bound and that of majority of civil servants, who are urban, middle class and well educated results in conflicts and contradiction in the interests and values of citizens and civil servants.

The rural base of Indian society has many implications for the development administration and rural people. For administration to be effective, it must appreciate and respond to the socio-cultural ethos of the rural population.

Religion: Historically, Indian has been hospitable to numerous groups of immigrants from different parts of Asia and Europe. People of all religions have been living in India for many centuries. The constitution declares Indian to be a secular state. The State is expected to treat all the religions equally. The Constitution also gives protection to minorities. The Constitution recognises religion as a fundamental right and a citizen can pursue the religion of his choice.

However, in reality, communalism is one of the major threats to the unity and the integrity of the country. In recent years, the communal organisations have become very active in social life resulting in communal clashes in different parts of the country. Some vested interests are using religion for their selfish purposes and are fanning hatred among the communities. The communal disharmony tests the strength of the administration in maintaining law and order and social harmony among the religious groups. Administration has to check disruptive communal activities and maintain social and political stability. Unfortunately, in recent years we also hear the allegations of divisions in the civil services on communal factors. The role played by some state police during the communal disturbances in some parts of the country brings no credit for the state police administration. The political necessity of appeasing each religious section may result in sacrificing rationality in administration.

Caste: The Hindu society is known for its varna and caste system. The society is broadly divided into four orders or varnas on 'functional' basis, namely, Brahmana (traditional priest and scholar), Kshtriya (ruler and soldier), Vaisya (merchant) and Shudra (peasant, labourer and servant). The scheduled castes are outside the varna scheme. Each varna may be divided into different horizontal strata, and each strata is known as caste. The caste system creates:- **(a)** segmental division of society **(b)** hierarchy **(c)** restrictions on social interactions, **(d)** civic and religious disparities and privileges of different sections **(e)** restriction on choice of occupation, and **(f)** restriction on marriage. Though caste is essentially a Hindu institution, some elements of caste are found in every religious group in India. The caste system based on birth created divisions in the society and contributed to the social and economic inequalities. A section of people were treated as untouchables and they were exploited by upper castes in the society.

In recent years, we find some change in the nature and role of the caste system. The role of the caste is changing. We find that the influence of caste in interpersonal and social relationships is decreasing but paradoxically its role in political process is increasing. The caste is being increasingly used or political mobilisation. This has an adverse effect on the working of political and administrative institutions. Formation of informal groups on caste lines among the public services is another developing phenomena. This affects the homogeneity of the public services.

Realising the existence of inegalitarian social system, the Constitution has provided for preferential treatment to scheduled castes, scheduled tribes and other backward classes in public services. In recent years, we find many agitations for any against the reservations in public services. Paradoxically, it is found that the preferential treatment system designed to bring equality is a cause of the internal tensions in the pubic organisations. In a social situation of primordial loyalties, the administrative institutions based on universalistic principles are subjected to a lot of stress and strain. The administrator must understand the dynamics of caste loyalties and caste sensibilities to play the role of an effective change agent.

Family: The joint family was considered as one of the three pillars of Indian social structure, the other two being the caste and the village community. Family is an important social unit and in country like India, the family loyalties are very strong. Traditionally, in India the joint family system played an important role as a social and economic institution. The social norms expect the subordination of individual interests to that of family. However, in recent years the joint family system is giving way to the nuclear family system. Still the emotional ties of extended family continue to play an important role in the social life. Patriarchy dominates the family life. The head of he family is usually the father or the eldest male member. Women generally occupy a subordinate position.

The structure and operation of family has many implications on administrative system. The paternalistic and operation of family has many implications on administrative system. The paternalistic and authoritarian structure of the family life is partly responsible for the paternalistic and authoritarian behavioural orientations of the administrators. The socialisation process in the family influences the attitude formation of the administrators. The family loyalties may also result in sacrifice of values like impartiality, integrity and universality in administration. Many administrators may feel it natural to help their family members by using

Q2. Discuss the relationship between culture and administration.
[Dec-09, Q.10]
Ans. Culture refers to a way of life. It includes the entire gamut of modes of expression and communication as well as the system of values and beliefs

governing the society. Values refer to preferences what is desirable conduct and behaviour for the members of the society.

The culture of a society is a result of a long process of evolution and is reflected in its social, economic and political institutions. The administrative behaviour in the society is influenced to a greater extent by the values cherished by the society.

Riggs states that every culture offers both support and obstacles to change of development. There are values that support change and development. Likewise, there are values, which obstruct the change and development. These values are termed by David Apter as 'instrumental' and 'consummatory', respectively. A society having instrumental values becomes modernised. If the civil servants have instrumental values, they will definitely work towards the development of the society.

V. Subramanyam writing on 'Hindu Values and Administrative Behaviour' emphasised the importance of study of values developed by the administrative structures vis-à-vis the values of surrounding society. He talks about Hindu values since majority of the IAS recruits are Hindus. Subramanyam identified three elements in the Hindu traditions, which work against the rational decision-making. To put in his own words: In the first place, a decision is basically choosing between a number or mutually exclusive alternatives and the basic Hindu approach is to deny the existence of such alternatives. Secondly, a decision means a choice of a course of action with a view to taking that course of action immediately. It is also implied in the western meaning of decision that the difficulties in that particular course of action have all been taken into account in making a decision in favour of it. The average Hindu idea of a decision is, however, more akin to the English phrase 'pious resolution'. The continuous and undignified waiting we hear in India from planners, politician and administrators alike about policies being good and their execution being bad is essentially a product of a particular Indian meaning attached to the term decision. Indeed, the average Hindu mind is so thoroughly reconciled to an (1impossible distance between precept and practice and between ideal and reality that it naturally imports this distance to separate decision and execution, a distance which does not exist in western interpretations of the term. Thirdly, a decision or choice means listing the various alternatives in a particular order of preference and if possible covering this ordinal list of preferences into a cardinal list of quantified values for each. The Hindu mind always indulges in talking of very large number, such as yugas. By using such large numbers casually the small differences that are most important in day-to-day decisions are made to look meaningless.

Many studies were undertaken to identify the cultural moorings of Indians, which result in a particular way of behaviour of administrators. Administrators perceive reality on the basis of their experience. Much of what they see depends upon how they see, which in turn depends on their socio-economic origins. They are insensitive to the problems of the common man and have a sense of superiority, which emanate from their upper class background.

Richard Taub found in his study as how the typical tendencies like 'the tendency for any group of people to divide into smaller groups on the basis of particularistic ties, the lack of trust and reluctance to delegate authority, the ideology of the caste system to think of human relations in hierarchical terms and traditions of reference towards authority" etc. have caused a particular pattern of behaviour among the bureaucrats.

The cultural factors have various implications for the administrative processes like motivation, communication and authority.

(1) Motivation: Many studies on human motivation identified culture as one of the determining factors in motivation. Me Lelland has convincingly argued that due to culture, religious beliefs and class structure, the general population, in may countries tend to have a fairly low achievement drive, whereas in other countries it may be the other way round. In India the 'karma' philosophy with its emphasis on other world may be considered as one of the inhibiting factors in the achievement orientation of bureaucracy. In the words of G.P. Chattopadhyaya, 'The Indian personality, by and large, is incapable of behaving in a mature and mutually dependent way. He fantasises omnipotence if he is in a position of perceived power, which reduces others to dependent positions, or he feels impotent when he faces people who have greater power and believes that he is utterly dependent on them. Fatalism blunts achievement orientation among Indian managers, makes them feel helpless in shaping their environment and makes them highly dependent on authority figures'.

(2) Communication: Communication may be described as the process of transferring concepts ideas, thoughts and feelings among people. Communication process is culture. The one-way process of communication, mostly from top to bottom in our organisations is also a reflection of social culture. In universalistic cultures, people low in status may have no inhibition in speaking against or mentioning unpleasant things to their superiors whereas in particularistic cultures it may be treated impolite and silence may be preferred.

(3) Authority: Attitude to authority is also a reflection of cultural variables. In a feudal society, authority attains the status of divinity. Authority figures are treated as sacred objects. Their conduct and behaviour are above scrutiny. This attitude not only legitimises the authority structure but also ensures personal loyalties of the lower levels of organisation in total disregard of abilities and actions of persons in authority. In public organisations it may lead to certain dysfunctions like growth of personality cult or personal goals of authorities may gain priority over the organisational goals. In this cultural situation, benevolent paternalistic management style may pay rich dividends more than participative leadership style, which may be appreciated only in egalitarian and an open society. Indian culture demands that people higher in status should be addressed with reverence and unpleasant things should not be mentioned before them. It becomes very difficult for the people at lower levels in organisation to give correct information or opinion if they feel that it may be unpalatable to those in authority. The public organisations are considered merely as an extension of the personalities of their chief executives. This may also sometimes result in practice of sycophancy in public organisations.

Q3. Write a short note on followings: [June-08, Q.4]
1. Central Vigilance Commission   [June-09, Q.15]
2. Lokpal and lokayukt

Ans. 1. The Central Vigilance Commission: Being alarmed at increasing corruption; a high-power committee was set up by Government of India in 1962 under the Chairmanship of K Santhanam. The Santhanam Committee recommended; setting up of Vigilance Commissions at the Centre and in the various States. Vigilance Cells have since been created in several government departments and public sector undertakings. At the highest level is the Central Vigilance Commission (CVC).

The CVC is beaded by the Central Vigilance Commissioner, appointed by the President of India, for a period of six years or until he attains the age of 65 years, whichever is earlier. The Commission is located in the Ministry of Home Affairs having an autonomous status. In addition to the Commissioner, it consists of a Secretary, one Officer on Special Duty, one Chief Technical Commissioner, 3 commissioners for departmental enquires, 2 Under-Secretaries and 6 Technical Commissioners. Its jurisdiction extends to all employees of the central government and the employees in the public undertakings, corporate bodies and other organisations dealing with matters falling within the executive powers of the central government. However, it cannot probe cases of corruption against ministers and members of parliament.

The CVC receives complaints directly from the aggrieved persons. It also gathers information about corruption and malpractices or misconduct from other sources such as press reports, audit objections. Information through parliamentary debates and other forms etc. The complaints about Central Government employees received by the State Vigilance Commissions are forwarded by them to the CVC. On receiving complaints, the Commission may ask:

(i) the concerned ministry/department to inquire into them;

(ii) the Central Bureau of Investigation (CBI) to make an inquiry; and register a case and conduct and investigation. Prosecution, however, depends on the approval by the appropriate sanctioning authority.

The CVC has laid down procedures to be followed by the administrative ministries/departments in the case of complaints received by them. These complaints are to be dealt with by the ministries/departments concerned. The CVC may advise the ministries/departments in respect of all matters relating to integrity in administration. It may also call for reports, returns or statements from all ministries/department so as to enable it, to exercise a general check and supervision over vigilance and anti-corruption work in the ministries/departments. It can also take over under its direct control any complaint or case for further action.

Besides these, the CVC has the role to play in the case of the appointment of Chief Vigilance Officer of each ministry /department. The CVC is to be consulted before giving such an appointment. Moreover, the CVC has been empowered to assess the work of the Chief Vigilance Officer. This assessment is recorded in the character rolls of the officers. Finally, all proposals for re-organising or strengthening the Vigilance Organisation by the Chief Vigilance Officers are to be referred to the CVC for scrutiny.

The role of CVC is, however, limited because it is not a statutory commission and has only advisory role. Further, the procedure of investigation is so vexatious that people do not desire to be involved in long and unpleasant proceedings. Thus, it has been commented that the Central Vigilance Commission is not at all a substitute for an Ombudsman. As it is constituted, the Commission is virtually an extension of the bureaucratic apparatus of the Central Government and its operations are very much hedged in by the overpowering ministries/departments and the political forces at the Centre.

2. Lokpal and Lokayukta: The machineries and procedures for handling public grievances, as mentioned above, have been found to be too distant or expensive and time-consuming. They have not been very successful to provide effective redress of an individual citizens grievance against government agencies and political leadership. Against this background, the Administrative Reforms Commission(ARC, 1966) made following observation:

"… We are of the view that the special circumstances relating to our country can be fully met, by providing for two special institutions for the redressal of citizens' grievances. There should be one authority for dealing with complaints against the administrative acts of ministers of secretaries to government both at the centre and in the states. There should be another authority in each state and the centre for dealing with complaints against the administrative acts of other officials. All these authorities should be independent of the executive as well as the legislature and judiciary". The ARC called the first authority the Lokpal and the second authority the Lokayukta.

In spite of several attempts the Lokpal Bill has again and again fallen through in

Parliament. It appears that both the Congress and non-Congress Governments have not been sincere and serious enough about the enactment of the Lokpal Bill despite their public pronouncements to that effect and promise to give to the people a clean administration. There are two fundamental issues involved. Firstly, there is clearly the hidden unwillingness of political leadership to submit themselves for enquiry by an independent authority other than Parliament to which they are already responsible in a parliamentary democracy. Secondly, the functional jurisdiction of the proposed Lokpal is also debatable. Should the Lokpal take up the cases of corruption only or it should also be entrusted with the task of redressing citizens' grievances in respect of injustice caused by maladministration of officials. The citizen is interested in redressal of his little problems and individual grievances and the existing avenues do not provide him easy, speedy and cheap redressal. Hence, what is needed is an agency independent of government control to redress the common grievances of people.

The Lokayukta: Although no institution of Lokpal has yet been established at the Centre, there are states like Maharashtra, Madhya Pradesh, Rajasthan, Karanataka, Bihar, Orissa, Himanchal Pradesh and National Capital Territory of Delhi which have appointed Lokayukta for dealing with the public grievances on the lines suggested by the ARC. Maharashtra was the first state to enact legislation in 1971. The other state legislation were based more or less on the Maharashtra line which provides the Lolkayukta with exclusive power to look into complaints against state ministers, secretaries and other senior officers. Section 12 of the Himanchal Pradesh Lokayukta Act, 1983, provides, "If, after enquiry in respect of a complaint, the Lokayukta is satisfied that all or any of the allegations made in the complaint have or have been substantiated either wholly or partly, he shall, by report in writing, communicate his findings and recommendations to the competent authority and intimate the complaint and the public servant concerned about his having made the report". The competent authority examines the report and has to communicate to the lokayukta within a period of three months of the receipt of such report, action taken thereon. It may be noted that the Lokayukta is only a recommending authority. Its recommendations have no legal sanctity, nor are these binding. The final judgement in respect of the offence lies with the competent government authority.

Q4. Write a short note on following: [June-08, Q.10]
(1) Central administrative tribunal
(2) MRTPC
Ans. (1) Central Administrative Tribunal (CAT)
1. Central Administrative Tribunal: The Central Administrative Tribunal has been established for adjudication of disputes with respect to recruitment

and conditions of service of persons appointed to public services and posts in connection with the affairs of the Union or other local authorities within the territory of India or under the control of Government of India and for matters connected therewith or incidental thereto. This was done in pursuance of the amendment of Constitution of India by Articles 323A. In the statement of objects and reasons on the introduction of the Administrative Tribunals Act, 1985, it was mentioned that the setting up of such Administrative Tribunals exclusively would go a long way in reducing the burden on the various courts and reduce pendency and would also provide to the persons covered by the Administrative Tribunals a speedy and relatively cheap and effective remedy. In addition to Central Government employees, the Government of India has notified 45 other organisations to bring them within the jurisdiction of the Central Administrative Tribunal. The provisions of the Administrative Tribunals Act, 1985 do not, however, apply to members of paramilitary forces, armed forces of the Union, officers or employees of the Supreme Court, or to persons appointed to the Secretariat Staff of either House of Parliament or the Secretariat staff of State/Union Territory Legislatures.

A Chairman who has been a sitting or retired Judge of a High Court heads the Central Administrative Tribunal. Besides the Chairman, the authorised strength consists of 16 Vice-Chairmen and 49 Members. The conditions of service of Chairman, Vice-Chairmen and Members are governed by the provisions of the Central Administrative Tribunal (Salaries and Allowances and Conditions of Service of Chairman, Vice-Chairmen and Members), Rule, 1985, as amended from time to time. As per Rule 15-A, notwithstanding anything contained in Rule 4 to 15 of the said Rules, the conditions of service and other perquisites available to the Chairman and Vice-Chairmen of the Central Administrative Tribunal shall be same as admissible to a serving Judge of a High Court as contained in the High Court Judges (Conditions of Service) Act, 1954 and High Court Judges (Travelling Allowances) Rules, 1956, as amended from time to time.

(2) MRTPC (The Monopolies and Restrictive Trade Practices Act, 1969): Objectives and Policy: The Monopolies and Restrictive Trade Practices Commission has been constituted under Section 5(1) of the MRTP Act, 1969. The Commission is empowered to enquire into Monopolistic or Restrictive Trade Practices upon a reference from the Central Government or upon its own knowledge or information. The MRTP Act also provides for appointment of a Director General of Investigation and Registration for making investigations for the purpose of enquiries by the MRTP Commission and for maintenance of register of agreements relating to restrictive trade practices.

The MRTP Commission receives complaints both from registered consumer and trade associations and also from individuals. Complaints regarding Restrictive Trade Practices or Unfair Trade Practices from an association are required to be referred to the Director General of Investigation and Registration for conducting preliminary investigation. The Commission can also order a preliminary investigation by the Director General of Investigation and Registration when a reference on a restrictive trade practice is received from the Central/State Government, or when Commission's own knowledge warrants a preliminary investigation. Enquiries are instituted by the Commission after the Director General of Investigation and Registration completes preliminary investigation and submits an application to the Commission for an enquiry.

Monopolistic Trade Practices: Four enquiries under Section 10 (b) were pending with the MRTP Commission at the beginning of the year 1996-97; one enquiry was instituted during 1996-97. These 5 enquiries were pending as on 31 December 1996.

Restrictive Trade Practices: 905 enquiries under Section 10(a)(i), 10(a)(ii), 10(a)(iii) and 10(a)(iv) were pending before the Commission as on 31st March, 1996. During the period 1 April 1996 to 31 December 1996, the Commission instituted 166 fresh enquiries. Out of 1071 enquiries under this Head, the Commission disposed off 81 enquiries leaving a pendency of 990 enquiries at the end of December, 1996.

Unfair Trade Practices: Provisions relating to Unfair Trade Practices were incorporated in the MRTP Act in 1984. Unfair Trade Practices have been defined as trade practices which for the purpose of promoting the sale, use or supply of any goods or for provision of any services, adopt one or more of the practices mentioned therein and thereby cause loss or injury to the consumers of such goods or services, whether by eliminating or restricting competition or otherwise.

700 Unfair Trade Practices enquiries under Section 36B(a), 36B(c) and 36B(d) were pending before the Commission for disposal as on 31 March 1996. During the period from 1 April 1996 to 31 December 1996, 225 fresh enquiries were instituted raising the total to 925. Of these, 44 enquiries were disposed off leaving 881 enquiries pending before the Commission as on 31 December 1996.

Temporary Injunction: 408 applications for grant of temporary injunction under Section 12A were pending with the Commission on 31st March, 1996. During the period ending on 31st December, 1996, the Commission received 328 fresh applications raising the total number of applications to 736. 54 applications were disposed off during this period leaving 682 applications pending as on 31 December 1996.

Award of Compensation: There were 857 applications pending before the Commission for award of compensation under Section 12B on 31st March, 1996. During the period from 1st April, 1996 to 31st December, 1996, the

Commission received 438 more applications making the total number of applications to 1295. The Commission disposed off 60 applications during the period. Therefore, 1235 applications were pending as on 31 December 1996.

Registration of Agreements: Section 35 of the MRTP Act requires every agreement relating to Restrictive Trade Practices falling within one or, more of the categories enumerated in Section 33(1) of the Act to be furnished for registration within 60 days of the making of such agreement. In pursuance of this provision, during the period April, 1996 to December, 1996, 68 agreements were considered for registration and 55 agreements were registered and entered in the Register of Agreements while 13 agreements were pending for registration as on 31 December 1996.

Q5. Discuss about the advantages and disadvantages of administrative tribunals. Examine the safeguard in the working of administrative tribunals.   [June-09, Q.11][Dec-08, Q.15][June-07, Q.5]

The main advantages and disadvantages of administrative tribunals are as follows:

Advantages: The ordinary courts as at present could not cope with the enormous number of cases now dealt with by administrative tribunals, and any attempt by them to do so would cause inordinate delays. Tribunals, therefore, help prevent delays, and their proceedings do not last so long. As a result, the cost of bringing a case before a tribunal is much less than the cost of proceedings in the ordinary courts.

• The tribunals are usually composed of experts in the matters with which they deal.

• Tribunals are not bound so rigidly by precedent as the ordinary courts, although they do aim to secure consistency in their decisions.

• The tribunals assist the efficient conduct of public administration and promote a policy of social improvement.

• Tribunals are usually local by nature, and can therefore acquaint themselves with local conditions and carry out inspections of property and sites (particularly in the case of the Lands Tribunal) where this will assist them in their decisions.

Disadvantages: The lack of publicity where hearings are in private and no reasons are given for decisions.

• The poor quality of investigation of facts where the rules of evidence are not observed.

• The possibility of political interference by the government preventing the tribunal from giving an impartial decision. There is, however, little or no evidence of this having ever occurred.

• The danger that important judicial functions may be exercised by unqualified persons.

• With the exception of the Lands Tribunal and the Employment Appeal Tribunal, legal aid is not available for persons appearing before tribunals, and they may therefore not be properly represented. This applies particularly to bodies such as mental health review tribunals.

In November 1955, a Committee on Administrative Tribunals and Enquiries was established to consider the constitution and working of tribunals. The Committee reported as follows:

• The principles of openness, fairness, and impartiality had not always been manifest, but in general the tribunal system worked well.

• Proceedings should be given publicity, steps should be taken to ensure that people knew their rights and were able to present their cases properly, and tribunals should be free from outside influences, especially government influence.

• Tribunals are essential in modern society, but they should be demonstrably good reasons for setting up a tribunal, and in any case ultimate control should be exercised by the ordinary courts.

The position has been improved by the passing of the Tribunals and Inquiries Acts 1958 and 1966, now consolidated in the Tribunals and Inquiries Act 1971. These Acts provide for a Council on Tribunals, which keeps under review the working of certain tribunals, and reports to the Lord Chancellor on matters relevant to administrative tribunals which they may refer to him. The Lord Chancellor nominates the members of the Council, and the dismissal of members of certain tribunals can take place only with his approval, which gives the tribunals a great measure of independence. As has been seen from the examples of tribunals given above, there is very often a right of appeal from the decision of a tribunal to the High Court and in some cases even to higher courts, and all tribunals are subject to the supervisory jurisdiction of the High Court by means of the prerogative orders of certiorari, prohibition and mandamus.

All tribunals are also subject to the ultra vires doctrine, that is, any decision which they make or any action which they take must be within the powers conferred on them, or at least must be reasonably incidental to such powers. A person who is aggrieved by an ultra vires decision or action of a tribunal may appeal to the High Court for a declaration that the decision or activity is void.

It is now much more common than it used to be for tribunals to have public hearings and to allow people appearing before them to be legally represented, and the reports of inspectors who have conducted inquiries are very often made public.

Administrative adjudication suffers from many shortcomings that cannot perhaps be denied. But, like delegated legislation, it is an inescapable necessity in a modern complex society. Therefore, to overcome the shortcomings, few safeguards are suggested to make administrative adjudication impartial and certain. These safeguards include:

(1) Administrative tribunals should be manned by persons possessing legal training and experience. To inspire public confidence, the appointment of members should be made in consultation with Supreme Court.

(2) A code of judicial procedure for administrative tribunals should be devised and enforced. This is important in view of the prevalence of varying procedures of administrative adjudication in India.

(3) Reasons should invariable accompany decisions by the tribunals. "Good Laws", observed Jeremy Bentham, "are such laws for which good reasons can be given". A reasoned decision goes towards convincing those, who are affected by it, about its innate fairness and is a check against misuse of power.

(4) The jurisdiction of Supreme Court (as well as the High Courts) should not be curtailed. In other words, the right to judicial review on points of law must remain. Some, however, seek to ban judicial review altogether by making decisions final. According to M.C. Setalvad, former Attorney General of India, the need for judicial review is greater in a nascent democracy like India.

Q6. Write few words about the judicial system in India.

Ans. India, the largest representative democracy of the world, possesses a well-structured and independent judiciary. The three-tiered system of Indian judiciary comprises of Supreme Court (New Delhi) at its helm, high courts standing at the head of state judicial system followed by district and sessions court in the judicial districts, into which the states are divided. The lower rung of the system then comprises of courts of civil (munsifs, sub-judges civil judge) and criminal (first and second class judicial magistrate) jurisdiction.

The Supreme Court:

Supreme court of India

The apex court of the country enjoys original, appellate and advisory jurisdiction. The extensive original jurisdiction of the court ranges from matters like enforcement of fundamental rights (enumerated in the constitution), to disputes between the states as well as between the union and the states, the appellate jurisdiction of the apex court can be invoked through a certificate of leave of the high court or by special leave granted by the supreme court in respect of any judgement, order or decree from high court. Writs (mandamus, certiorari etc.) can be filed by any person against the violation of fundamental rights or against the orders of administrative tribunals.

The High Court: Working under the direct guidance and supervision of the Supreme Court, the High Courts are generally the last court of regular appeal. The High Courts of Mumbai, Chennai, Kolkata and Delhi enjoy original jurisdiction beyond a certain financial limit (For instance, Rs.20 lakhs and above in case of Delhi). Besides, for invoking writ jurisdiction, the High Courts can be approached for enforcement of other rights. It has the power to supervise the subordinate courts falling within its territorial jurisdiction. In certain cases, High Courts also has original jurisdiction, for expeditious remedy.

The Subordinate Courts: This segment of the Indian judicial system comprises of **(a)** District Courts, empowered to hear appeals from courts of original civil jurisdiction besides having original civil jurisdiction under many enactments **(b)** Sessions Court, are courts of criminal jurisdiction, having the similar scope of powers. The courts of specific original jurisdiction are courts of Civil judges, of Judicial Magistrates; Small Causes courts and Courts of Metropolitan Magistrates.

Quasi-Judicial System: This appendage to the Indian judicial system is a recent and sincere attempt on the part of the government to expedite the judicial process through dilution of procedural formalities and avoidance of litigation. Tribunals form an indispensable part of this system, which are appointed by the government and comprise of judges and experts on the particular field, for which the tribunal has been constituted. Industrial tribunals, pertaining primarily to labour disputes, may be taken as an instance.

Alternative Dispute Resolution: The advent of Alternative Dispute Resolution system in India, which comprises of methods like Arbitration, Conciliation and Negotiation, has simplified the concept and procedure of justice delivery system in India. In consonance of the UNCITRAL agreement, Parliament came out with a central act (Arbitration and Conciliation Act, 1996) to consolidate the law relating to domestic arbitration, international commercial arbitration and enforcement of foreign arbitral awards as also to define the law relating to conciliation and matters connected therewith.

Arbitration may be defined as a private determination of controversial issues by a third neutral party (arbitral tribunal), who is empowered to make a binding award. Conciliation refers to a voluntary process in which an impartial third party helps the parties in reaching a mutually satisfactory and agreed settlement of the dispute. Negotiation is carried on with the same objective in mind, with a voluntary negotiation on the part of the parties.

The process of arbitration may be initiated by a reference to the court of law of the matter in dispute, if there is specific arbitration agreement to that effect or the parties straightway going in for arbitration proceedings, on their own. The arbitral tribunal would comprise of members in odd numbers, which are appointed by the parties. Appointment of arbitrator may be challenged on grounds of partiality and doubts over his independence. The jurisdiction of the arbitral tribunal is conditioned by the arbitration agreement itself. The arbitral award is binding on the parties, unless recourse is taken for setting it aside. The statute also elaborates upon the procedure of enforcement of foreign arbitral awards and conditions in which they are binding.

Q7. What do you understand by judicial control over administration? Discuss the scope of judicial control over administration.

Ans. By judicial control is meant the power of the courts to examine the legality of the officials act and thereby to safeguard the fundamental and other essential rights of the citizens. The underlying object of judicial review is to ensure that the authority does not abuse its power and the individual receives just and fair treatment and not to ensure that the authority reaches a conclusion, which is correct in the eye of law. The role of judiciary in protecting the citizens against the excess of officials has become all the more important with the increase in the powers and discretion of the public officials in the modern welfare states. But the courts cannot interfere in the administrative activities of their own accord. They can intervene only when they are invited to do so by any person who feels that his rights have been abrogated or are likely to be abrogated as a result of some action of the public official. Secondly, the courts cannot interfere in each and every administrative act, as too much of Judicial action may make the official too much conscious and very little of it may make them negligent of the rights of citizens. In the words of Mr. L.D. White, "At one extreme, the vigour of judicial control may paralyse effective administration, at the other the result may be offensive bureaucratic tyranny, exactly where the balance may be best struck is a major problem of judicial administrative relationship.

Scope of Judicial Control over Administration: In the context of ever-expanding activities of government and discretionary powers vested in the various administrative agencies and public officials, the need to protect and safeguard the citizen's rights assumes significance and priority. In developing societies where the state is playing an important role in development, judiciary has a special responsibility to ensure social justice to the underprivileged sections of the community. However, it must be admitted that the courts can not interfere in the administrative activities on their own accord even if such activities are arbitrary. They act only when their intervention is sought. Judicial intervention is restrictive in nature and limited in its scope. Generally judicial intervention in administrative activities is confined to the following cases:

a) Lack of Jurisdiction: If any public official or administrative agency acts without or beyond his/her or its authority or jurisdiction the courts can declare such acts as ultra-vires. For instance, according to administrative rules and procedures, all organisations, the competent authority is identified for taking decisions and actions. If any authority or person other than the competent authority takes action, the court's intervention can be sought under the provisions of lack of jurisdiction.

b) Error of Law: This category of cases arises when the official misconstrues the law and imposes upon the citizen obligations, which are absent in law. This is called misfeasance in legal terminology. The courts are empowered to set right such cases.

c) Error of Fact: This category of cases is a result of error in discovering cases and actions taken on basis of wrong assumptions. Any citizen adversely affected by error of judgment of public official can approach courts for redressal.

d) Error of Procedure: "due procedure" is the basis of governmental action in a democracy. Responsible government means a government by procedure. Procedure in administration ensures accountability, openness and justice. Public officials must act in accordance with the procedure laid down by law in the performance of the administrative activities. If the prescribed procedure is not followed the intervention of the courts can be sought and legality of administrative actions can be questioned.

e) Abuse of authority: If a public official exercises his/her authority vindictively to harm a person or use authority for personal gain, court's intervention can be sought. In legal terms, it is called malfeasance. The courts can intervene to correct the malfeasance of administrative acts.

Q8. Write a short note on followings:
1. Judicial review
2. Criminal and civil suits against public officials
Ans. 1) Judicial Review: The judicial review implies the power of the courts to examine the legality and constitutionality of administrative acts of officials and also the executive orders and the legislative enactments. This is very important method of judicial control. This doctrine prevails the countries where Constitution is held supreme, for example, in U.S.A. India, Australia, etc.

In India, judicial review is restricted by certain provisions of the constitution as well as of Act declaring finality of administrative decisions in particular matters. However, it can be stated that the Legislature in India, being non-sovereign body cannot exclude judicial review in certain cases unless there is a provision to that effect in the Constitution. Generally, the courts do not interfere with purely administrative action unless it is ultra-vires as regards its scope or form.

Even in Britain, where judicial review is not applicable, the courts can use this system of controlling administrative actions within the scope of parliamentary statutes. In view of the parliament's sovereignty in Britain, many administrative acts and decisions are excluded from judicial review by the courts themselves under what is called 'judicial self-limitation'. However, it must be noted that administrative actions can be challenged for want of jurisdiction.

In the U.S.A, judicial review, at least in theory extends to the entire field of administrative action. However, in practice, the courts in the U.S.A have, by self-denial, restricted their power in several ways. For instance, courts usually do not review certain type of decisions particularly those concerning administrative discretion. The power of the courts as regards judicial review, although not crystallised in potentially great.

2) Criminal and Civil Suits Against Public Officials: The position regarding the public officials' personal liability in respect of acts done by them in their official capacity varies from country to country. In India, civil proceedings can be instituted against a public official for anything done in his official capacity after giving two months notice. When criminal proceedings are to be instituted against an official for the acts done in this official capacity, previous sanctions of the Head of the State i.e., the President or the Governor is required. Some functionaries like the President and the Governor are immune from legal proceedings even in respect of their personal acts. Ministers, however, do not enjoy such immunity. The Monarch in Britain and President in the U.S.A. are also immune from legal liability.

Q9. Discuss about the constitutional remedies/writs.

Ans. Any piece of legislation or law, which tends to interfere with the power of Supreme Court under Article 32 shall be declared as void. Hence, there is no way that the legislative or the executive authority can by-pass the power and responsibility entrusted to the Supreme Court by the Constitution. In a famous case titled as "Gopalan Vs State of Madras", the Supreme Court declared Section 14 of the Preventive Detention Act of 1950 as void, because as per the Supreme Court, the said Section acted as an iron curtain around the acts of the executive authority making the order of preventive detention.

WRITS:

1. Writ of *Habeas corpus:* It is the most valuable writ for personal liberty. *Habeas Corpus* means, *"Let us have the body."* A person, when arrested, can move the Court for the issue of *Habeas Corpus*. It is an order by a Court to the detaining authority to produce the arrested person before it so that it may examine whether the person has been detained lawfully or otherwise. If the Court is convinced that the person is illegally detained, it can issue orders for his release.

2. The Writ of *Mandamus:* *Mandamus* is a Latin word, which means "We Command". *Mandamus* is an order from a superior court to a lower court or tribunal or public authority to perform an act, which falls within its duty. It is issued to secure the performance of public duties and to enforce private rights withheld by the public authorities. Simply, it is a writ issued to a public official to do a thing which is a part of his official duty, but, which, he has failed to do, so far. This writ cannot be claimed as a matter of right. It is the discretionary power of a court to issue such writs.

3. The Writ of *Quo-Warranto:* The word *Quo-Warranto* literally means "by what warrants?" It is a writ issued with a view to restraining a person from acting in a public office to which he is not entitled. The writ of *quo-warranto* is used to prevent illegal assumption of any public office or usurpation of any public office by anybody. For example, a person of 62 years has been appointed to fill a public office whereas the retirement age is 60 years. Now, the appropriate High Court has a right to issue a writ of *quo-warranto* against the person and declare the office vacant.

4. The Writ of *Prohibition:* Writ of *prohibition* means to forbid or to stop and it is popularly known as 'Stay Order'. This writ is issued when a lower court or a body tries to transgress the limits or powers vested in it. It is a writ issued by a superior court to lower court or a tribunal forbidding it to perform an act outside its jurisdiction. After the issue of this writ, proceedings in the lower court etc. come to a stop.

5. The Writ of *Certiorari:* Literally, *Certiorari* means to be certified. The writ of *certiorari* is issued by the Supreme Court to some inferior court or tribunal to transfer the matter to it or to some other superior authority for proper consideration.

Q10. Discuss the limitation of judicial control over administration.

[Dec-08, Q.11]

Ans. The effectiveness of judicial control over administration is limited by many factors. Some of these limitations are:

i) Unmanageable volume of work: The judiciary is not able to cope with the volume of work. In a year the courts are able to deal with only a fraction of cases brought before it. Thousands of cases have been pending in Supreme Court, High Courts and Lower Courts for years together for want of time. There is an increase in the cases of litigation without a commensurate expansion of judicial mechanism. The old adage of 'justice delayed is justice denied', still holds good. This excessive delay in the delivery of justice discourages many to approach the court. The feeling of helplessness results in denial of justice to many.

ii) Post-mortem nature of judicial control: In most of the cases the judicial intervention comes only after enough damage is done by the administrative actions. Even if the courts set right the wrong done, there is no mechanism to redress the trouble the citizen has undergone in the process.

iii) Prohibitive Costs: The judicial process is costly and only rich can afford it. There is some truth in the criticism of pro-rich bias of judicial system in India. As a result, only rich are able to seek the protection of courts from the administrative abuses. The poor are, in most cases, the helpless victims of the administrative arbitrariness and judicial inaction. As V.R. Krishna Iyer pointed 'the portals of justice are not accessible to the poor'.

iv) Cumbersome procedure: Many legal procedures are beyond the comprehension of common man. The procedural tyranny frightens many from approaching the courts. Even though the procedures have a positive dimension of ensuring fair play, too much of it negatives the whole process.

v) Statutory limitations: The courts may be statutorily prevented from exercising jurisdiction in certain spheres. There are several administrative acts, which cannot be reviewed by courts.

vi) Specialised nature of administrative actions: The highly technical nature of some administrative actions act as a further limitation on judicial control. The judges, who are only legal experts, may not be able to sufficiently appreciate the technical implications of administrative actions. As a result, their judgments may not be authentic.

vii) Lack of awareness: In developing societies, most of the people who are poor and illiterate are not aware of judicial remedies and the role of the courts. As a result they may not even approach the court to redress their grievances. The courts deprivation of people also results in deprivation of justice to them.

viii) Erosion of autonomy of judiciary: There is executive interferences in the working of judiciary. The quality of judiciary mostly depends on the quality of the judges. The Law Commission made many recommendation to ensure the judicial standards of the bench. The suggestion to create Judicial Commission with responsibility for judicial appointments deserves serious consideration. In recent years, there are many allegations of corruption against judges. This undermines the prestige and the effectiveness of the judiciary.

Many steps have been initiated to overcome some of the limitations mentioned above. In the succeeding paragraphs, we shall discuss some of these measures, in particular, Public Interest Litigation, Legal Aid and Nyaya Panchayats.

Q11. What is public Interest Litigation?

Ans. Public Interest Litigation means "a legal action initiated in a court of law for the enforcement of public interest or general interest in which the public or a class of the community have pecuniary interest or some interest by which their legal rights or liabilities are affected," (From the S.C. judgement in Janata Dal vs. H.S. Chowdhury, 1982). PIL is a "strategic arm" of the legal aid movement and is intended to bring justice within the reach of poor masses. It is a devise to provide justice to those who individually are not in a position to have access to the courts. It was initiated for the benefit of a class of people, who had been denied their constitutional and legal rights because they were unable to have access to the court on account of their socioeconomic disabilities. "Millions of persons belonging to the deprived and vulnerable sections of humanity are looking to the courts for improving their life conditions and making human life meaningful for them. The time has now come when the courts must become the courts for the poor and struggling masses of this country. Fortunately, this change is gradually taking place and Public Interest Litigation is playing a large part in bringing this change."

A Public Interest Litigation (PIL) can be filed in any High Court or directly in the Supreme Court. It is not necessary that the petitioner has suffered some injury of his own or has had personal grievance to litigate. PIL is a right given to the socially conscious member or a public spirited NGO to espouse a public cause by seeking judicial for redressal of public injury. Such injury may arise from breach of public duty or due to a violation of some provision of the Constitution. Public Interest Litigation is the device by which public participation in judicial review of administrative action is assured. It has the effect of making judicial process little more democratic.

According to the guidelines of the Supreme Court any member of public having sufficient interest may maintain an action or petition by way of PIL provided:

• There is a personal injury or injury to a disadvantaged section of the population for whom access to legal justice system is difficult,

• The person bringing the action has sufficient interest to maintain an action of public injury,

• The injury must have arisen because of breach of public duty or violation of the Constitution or of the law.

It must seek enforcement of such public duty and observance of the constitutional law or legal provisions.

• This is a powerful safeguard and has provided immense social benefits, where there is essentially failure on the part of the execute to ameliorate the problems of the oppressed citizens. Considering the importance of this subject, three articles from the web on the subject are reproduced hereunder.

Emerging Issues

Q1. Write a short note on division of power between the centre and the state as per constitutional provisions. [Dec-08, Q.4]

Ans. The constitution of India provides that the country would be a democracy. The decision was taken before its independence that the administrative system of India will be liberal democratic system. India became a republic nation on the 26th day of January 1950 and it is the day when the constitution came into force. Since then division of power in Indian Administration existed between the centre and the state. According to the administrative divisions, India has 28 states and 7 union territories. Each of these regional administrative divisions has an elected government headed by a chief minister. A Governor is appointed by the President of India, as the representative head of the federal authority in each state.

The form, structure, functions and the organs of government are related to the type of the political system adopted and the nature of the distribution of powers among the units of government and organs of the state. Nation-states are categorised as unitary and federal systems. The form of government in India is the quasi- federal form, with federal structure and strong unitary spirit. In the federal form of government, Division of power in Indian Administration occurs; the power is divided between a central authority and constitutional political units such as the states and the provinces. The two levels of government are interdependent and share sovereignty. The federal system also provides that the constitution is the supreme power of the land. However, though a federal structure and a clear division of powers exist in India with an independent judiciary, yet there is a strong bias towards making the Central Government more powerful than the state governments. Hence, based on the distribution of powers between the Central Government and the State Government, there are three lists - Union list, State list and Concurrent list (powers entertained by both centre and state).

Divisions in Indian Administration is the distribution of power between the executive and the legislative powers between the centre and the state and certain residuary powers vest in the Union under article 249. The polity of India can turn into a complete unitary character during emergency on the ground of failure of the constitutional machinery. The relation between Union and States is the foundation of the Indian Federal system. There is autonomy in the legislative, executive as well as the judicial powers for the states of India. Both the Union and the States are moreover subject to the limits imposed by the Constitution. The Fundamental rights cannot be violated by either the Union or the States.

The Legislative powers of the government, such as powers to make laws upon a specific subject, are separated in India by means of three lists - union list, state list and concurrent list. Divisions in Indian Administration among the central government include the Parliament and the state government that is the state legislature. The division of the powers of the Union and the State can be traced by the three lists laid down by the Indian Constitution. This feature of distribution of powers are derived from the Australian constitution, these lists clearly divide the powers vested on the State and the Union.

Among the divisions in Indian Administration, Union list consists of subjects on which the Central government or the Parliament can make laws. The subjects included in the list are of nation importance. These include subjects such as defence, foreign affairs, atomic energy, banking, post and telegraph. The Central government has the power of making laws on these subjects at all times also during emergencies. There are 100 subjects on which the Central government can make law. The State list contains 66 subjects of local or state importance. The state governments have the authority to make laws on these subjects. These subjects include police, local governments, trade, commerce and agriculture. However, during national and state emergency, the power to make laws on these subjects is transferred to the Parliament.

Concurrent list, according to the Divisions in Indian Administration, contains 47 subjects on which both the Parliament and the state legislatures can make laws. These subjects include criminal and civil procedure, marriage and divorce, education, economic planning and trade unions. Yet, in case of conflict between a law made by the Central government and a law made by the state legislatures, the law made by the central government will prevail. There are certain changes regarding the authority of making laws. Education was shifted from the state list to the concurrent list by the 42nd Amendment Act of 1976.

However, constitution makers provide distribution of powers between the governments, after providing for the three lists, they provided for residuary subjects. These residuary subjects are matters which are not included in any of the three lists and the right to make laws on these subjects is called residuary power. The central government has been given rights to legislate on these subjects.

Q2. Discuss the financial relations between Centre and State governments. [Dec-09, Q.2]

Ans. Financial Relations between Centre and state government:

Division of financial powers and functions among different levels of the federal polity are asymmetrical, with a pronounced bias for revenue taxing powers at the Union level while the States carry the responsibility for subjects that affect the day to day life of the people entailing larger expenditure than can be met from their own resources. On an average, the revenue of States from their own resources suffices only for about 50 to 60 percent of States' current expenditure. Since the insufficiency of the States' fiscal resources had been foreseen at the time of framing the Constitution, a mechanism in the shape of Finance Commission was provided under article 280 for financial transfers from the Union. Its function is to ensure orderly and judicious devolution that is deemed necessary from the point of view of avoiding vertical or horizontal imbalances.

The Finance Commission is only one stream of transfer of resources from the Union to the States. The Planning Commission advises the Union Government regarding the desirable transfer of resources to the States over and above those recommended by the Finance Commission. Bulk of the transfer of revenue and capital resources from the Union to the States is determined largely on the advice of these two Commissions. By and large, such transfers are formula-based. Then there are some discretionary transfers as well to meet the exigencies of specific situations in individual States.

These institutional arrangements served the country well in the first three decades after independence. Testifying to the strength of these institutions neither the Union nor the States suffered from any large imbalance in their budgets, although the size of the public sector in terms of proportion of government expenditure to Gross Domestic Product had nearly doubled during this period.

Imbalances have become endemic during the last two decades and have assumed alarming proportions recently. For this state of affairs, the constitutional provisions can hardly be blamed. Broadly, the causes have to be sought in the working of the political institutions. There are shortcomings in the transfer system. For example, the 'gap-filling' approach adopted by the Finance Commission and the soft budget constraints have provided perverse incentives. The point, however, is that these deficiencies are capable of being corrected without any change in the Constitution.

Enlargement of the Scope of the Finance Commission

The institution of the Finance Commission has been one of the major success stories of the Constitution. The broad terms of reference as laid down in article 280(3) are unexceptionable. However, other matters in the interest of sound finance can also be referred to the Finance Commission. These would constitute additional terms of reference. It has been suggested that it would be desirable to associate the States more actively in deciding the additional terms of reference, preferably by having the National Development Council (comprising the Prime Minister and the Chief Ministers of States) to endorse the additional terms of reference. The Commission is not in favor of an amendment of article 280(3)(d) to enable such enlargement of the scope of the Finance Commission, However, it is recommended that terms of reference of the Finance Commission should be broader and comprise of matters which would take care, in a comprehensive way, aspects of the financial relations between the Union and the States. The broadening of such terms of reference could also be discussed earlier by the National Development Council.

Under article 281, the recommendations of the Finance Commission are laid before the Houses of Parliament along with an explanatory memorandum as to the action taken on them. The recommendations are not theoretically binding, although there has been no case so far when the Government of India has deviated from recommendations of successive Finance Commissions. It has been suggested that the Constitution itself should describe the recommendations as an award binding on both the Union and the States. This has been urged in the context of the mechanism of the State Finance Commissions which are set up under articles 243-I and 243-Y which too make only recommendations and not awards. The State Finance Commissions are a comparatively new constitutional mechanism. They would take some time to strike roots in the constitutional soil. Politicians at the State level have also to find their bearings in the new landscape where the old landmarks of patronage at the State level have yielded place to a non-discriminatory passage of resources from the State exchequer to the local government institutions. Keeping in view the factors pointed out above the Commission does not consider it necessary to recommend the amendment of the Constitution to provide for the recommendations of either the Finance Commission constituted under article 280 or of the State Finance Commissions constituted under articles 243-I and 243-Y being treated as awards.

Share of States in taxes, cesses and surcharges

The Constitution was amended to provide a prescribed percentage of the revenue receipts to be transferred to States (article 270(2)). However, surcharges and cesses do not form part of the divisible pool. Cesses are intended for specific purposes and the States can have no complaint if the money is spent on predetermined purposes. Surcharges can be regarded as a not so thinly veiled device to deny the States their share in receipts from such surcharges. Keeping in view the complexity of the present national and international situation which has placed additional burden on the Union, the Commission would not recommend any constitutional amendment to make surcharges shareable but would expect public policy to move decisively in the direction of doing away with the surcharges as part of the Union's fiscal armory.

Tax on services

In recent years, services have emerged as the dominant component in the gross domestic product (GDP). Yet there is no mention in the Constitution in any of the three lists (Union List, State List, Concurrent List) enabling any level of government to tax services. The Union has used the residuary power in the last entry of the Union List (entry 97) to levy taxes on selected services. The efforts have not succeeded in tapping the full potential of the service sector of a vast range of services which are primarily local in nature. It is necessary to enhance the revenue potential of the States in view of their major responsibilities for social and physical infrastructure. It might be worthwhile to provide explicitly for taxing power for the States in respect of certain specified services. For the Union also an explicit entry would be helpful, rather than leaving it to the residuary power of entry 97. However, it may be better to first let a consensus list of services to be taxed by the States come into force to be treated as the exclusive domain of the States, even if the formal taxing power is exercised by the Union. In other words, the golden rule here would be to hasten slowly. A *de facto* enumeration of services that can be taxed exclusively by the States should get priority from policy makers with a view to augmenting the resource pool of the States. The Commission recommends specific enumeration of services that may become amenable to taxation by the States. This is necessary with a view to augmenting the resource pool of the States. The Commission recommends an appropriate amendment to the Constitution in this behalf to include certain taxes, now levied and collected by the Union, to be enabled to be levied and collected by the States. Illustratively a list of such subjects in respect of which service tax is levied under the relevant section of the Finance Act, 1994 (Act 32 of 1994) as amended from time to time is given below:

(1) Section 65(48)(e): "To a client, by an advertising agency in relation to advertisements in any manner". Corresponding Entry in List-II of the Constitution – Entry 55 – "Taxes on advertisements published in the newspapers [and advertisements broadcast by radio or television]"

(2) Section 65(48)(f) – "to a customer, by a courier agency in relation to door-to-door transportation of time-sensitive documents, goods or articles". Corresponding Entry in List-II of the Constitution – Entry 56 – "Taxes on goods and passengers carried by road or on inland waterways".

(3) Section 65(48)(m) – "to a client, by a mandap keeper in relation to the use of a mandap in any manner including the facilities provided to the client in relation to such use and also services, if any, rendered as a caterer".

Corresponding Entry in List-II of the Constitution – Entry 49 – "Taxes on lands and buildings"

(4) Section 65(48)(o) – "to any person, by a rent-a-cab scheme operator in relation to the renting of a cab" Corresponding Entry in List-II of the Constitution – Entry 57 – "Taxes on vehicles, whether mechanically propelled or not; suitable for use of roads, including tram-cars subject to the provisions of Entry 35 of List III.

(5) Section 65(48)(za) – "to any person, by a mechanized slaughter house in relation to the slaughtering of bovine animals."

Status of Central Bank

A question has been raised whether any constitutional or legislative safeguards are needed to uphold the autonomy of the Reserve Bank of India (Entry 38, List I) in conducting monetary policy. An advisory group set up by the Reserve Bank of India (RBI) has recommended that legislative changes should be made to facilitate the emergence of an independent and effective monetary policy. However, the Commission sees no need for a change in the Constitution to specifically provide for independent conduct of monetary policy. The existing legislation has broadly succeeded in maintaining a suitable environment of security and continuity for the key personnel and of the autonomy of decision making by the top management. The Commission agrees that appropriate legislative changes would suffice for the proper and timely development of money, securities and exchange markets.

Q3. Explain the types of emergencies which can be proclaimed by the Union as stipulated in the Constitution.

Ans. In normal times, the Union and the states are expected to function separately within their constitutionally delimited spheres of activities. But our Constitution makes provisions for proclamation of emergencies to enable the Union government to acquire the strength of a unitary system in times of 'emergencies'. The Constitution envisages three different kinds of 'emergencies' or abnormal situations calling for a radical departure from the normal governmental machinery as set up by the Constitution.

The first kind of emergency, under Article 356, relates to the failure of constitutional machinery in a state. The President is empowered to make a proclamation when he is satisfied that the government of a state cannot be carried on in accordance with the provisions of the Constitution either on the report of the State Governor or otherwise. Under this provision President's rule has been imposed in several states at different points of time. It has proved to be a drastic coercive power which takes nearly, the substance away from the normal federal polity prescribed by the Constitution. The second kind of emergency is the 'national emergency'.

Under Article 352, a proclamation of emergency may be made by the President at any time when he is satisfied that the security of India or any part thereof has been threatened by war, external aggression or armed rebellion. Such a proclamation has far-reaching consequences for the fundamental rights and for the exercise of executive, legislative and financial powers of the Union government. The nation virtually slips into a unitary system in times of national emergencies.

A third type of emergency - the financial emergency - may be proclaimed by the President under Article 360. This is done when the President is satisfied that a situation has arisen whereby the financial stability or credit of India or any part of the territory thereof is threatened. During the financial emergency, the union executive has powers to direct any state to observe some specific cannons of financial propriety as well as taking measures such as reduction of salaries and allowances of persons service the state or the Union.

The emergency provisions are so drastic that when the proclamation of either of the emergencies is in operation, the government is carried practically on a unitary basis and during the crisis the state governments are, in effect merely subordinate governments and function as a part of a union structure.

Q4. What do you understand by decentralisation? Discuss the importance and types of decentralisation.

Ans. Decentralisation is the process of dispersing decision-making governance closer to the people or citizen. It includes the dispersal of administration or governance in sectors or areas like engineering, management science, political science, political economy, sociology and economics. Decentralisation is also possible in the dispersal of population and employment. Law, science and technological advancements lead to highly decentralised human endeavors.

A central theme in Decentralisation is the difference between hierarchies, based on: authority: two players in an unequal-power relationship; and an interface: a lateral relationship between two players of roughly equal power.

The more decentralised a system is, the more it relies on lateral relationships, and the less it can rely on command or force. In most branches of engineering and economics, Decentralisation is narrowly defined as the study of markets and interfaces between parts of a system. This is most highly developed as general systems theory and neoclassical political economy.

Importance of Decentralisation

The urge for Decentralisation has come from many sources. Firstly, it has been prompted by the need to deliver the basic public goods like food, housing, water from local units of administration as soon as possible. Secondly, most people in the developing countries live in rural areas which are away from the National Capital located in distant urban area. Administration has to 'penetrate' the rural areas and link these up with the nation as a whole. Thirdly, in many countries sociological diversities manifest themselves in ethnic, linguistic and religious differences. Administration needs to be decentralised in response to regional diversities. Fourthly, regional and local resources can be utilised for area development purposes, only if administration would move out to the regions and localities. Decentralisation, therefore, facilitates local planning and development with the help of local resources. Fifthly, decentralisation has its own value in political and administrative terms. Politically, local participation in development activities, with intensive responses paves the way for meaningful articulation of local demands. Planning, thus, becomes much more realistic and receives ready political support. From the administrative point of view, local capability to govern local areas increases through sustained participation in local decision making. Decentralisation is expected to release local energies and enlist local support for development activities. In the process, the local community can steadily attain political and administrative maturity.

Types of Decentralisation

Four different types of decentralisation can be identified, viz., administrative, functional, political and geographical. Administrative decentralisation refers to decentralisation of authority to the lower officials in the administrative hierarchy of organisations. It may also mean decentralisation powers or functions to the subordinate units. Functional decentralisation implies that the functions are decentralised to the specialised units or departments like education or health. Political decentralisation involves that the political powers and functions concentrated in the hands of higher-level political organs are decentralised to lower level political organs. We are all aware that Panchayati Raj agencies are units of decentralisation wherein political powers of decision making are decentralised from state governments to panchayats, samitis and zilla parishads. Finally, in geographical decentralisation, the powers and functions of headquarters decentralised to the field departments of the state government, which are further decentralised to their field officers at the regional and district levels. This facilitates quick decision-making keeping in view the local requirements.

Q5. Examine the recent trends in Decentralisation.

Ans. Even with our development planning experience of more than four decades, there is no sign of abatement of poverty and social injustice in the form of oppression of the harijans and the rural poor. One important reason for this state of affairs that has been widely acknowledged in centralised administration and planning and languishing popular institutions at the grassroots level. At the end of 1985, this point was clearly brought out by the G.V.K. Rao Committee on Administrative Arrangements for Rural Development (CARD).

The Committee emphasised the importance of local initiative in local development and recommended revitalisation of the Panchayati Raj institutions. Research findings revealed that the developmental process had gradually been bureaucratised and divorced from the Panchayati Raj institutions leading to what has been aptly termed as "Grass without Roots". To quote one study: "The basic reason for the failure of rural development and poverty alleviation programmes is the exclusion of the people from participation in the development process and the abandonment of the institutions of democratic decentralisation and the related electoral process."

The G.V.K. Rao Committee came out with a blue print of a decentralised system of field administration with Panchayati Raj playing the lead role in local planning and development. Another novel decentralisation plan below the state level has been advocated by Nirmal Mukherji through devolution of political powers to directly elected "district governments" in India. Such a decentralisation plan will of course virtually affect the Panchayati Raj structure from the district to the village.

The other committee to bemoan the languishing of grassroots democracy is the L.M. Singhvi Committee on Revitalisation of PRIs for Democracy and Development (1986). The Panchayati Raj institutions, as the Committee has observed "have become moribund and ... they have been denuded of their promise and vitality". To revive Panchayati Raj, the Committee recommended that "local self-government should be constitutionally recognised, protected and preserved by the inclusion of a new chapter in the constitution". This has since been achieved through the 73rd Constitutional Amendment, 1992, that accords constitutional status to Panchayati Raj Institutions. At the same time, municipal bodies have been accorded constitutional status under the 74th Amendment, 1992.

Q6. Describe the principles which govern relationship of political and permanent executives. [Dec-08, Q.12]

Ans. Once the premise for separation of these two wings, political and permanent executives is agreed upon, the two wings must operate based on certain basic conditions. The conditions become all the more necessary when the distinction in activities is delicate and overlapping. It is this necessity that gave rise to two important norms, viz., Neutrality and Anonymity.

Norm of Neutrality

The norm of Neutrality assumes three conditions: **1)** changing of political parties in power, **2)** meritorious bureaucracy; **3)** permanent bureaucracy.

Firstly, in a liberal democracy with pluralistic nature of political parties, particularly with electoral mechanism, there is bound to be a change of parties in power. That is, in fact, the logic of the system. In United States, there used to be spoils system before the Pendleton Act was passed. Under spoils system the political parties coming to power had complete discretion to change the administrative personnel from top to the bottom. This means the political values of the party coincided with the values of the administrative system. For the administrative personnel were chosen mainly on the basis of their values. This system did pose its own problems giving rise to the passage of Pendleton Act which brought in the concept of merit. This leads to the second condition, viz., recruitment of the members of administrative system on the basis of merit of the individuals.

This leads to the third condition, viz., recruitment on a permanent basis. This means the persons chosen for the service become life members of the service. This implies that changes in the fortunes of political parties have nothing to do with the continuation or otherwise of the members of the civil service. In fact, it is these factors which have brought in the concept of permanent executive. The recruitment of the personnel on a permanent basis in a changing political climate calls for neutrality of the permanent members. This means the members are not supposed to commit themselves to any political values. They are expected to cooperate and assist any party in power irrespective of the political preferences. This implies that members of the permanent executive either do not have clear preferences or do not allow those values enter their day-to-day work. There have been several debates on this question. But the existing theoretical position is that the permanent executive and their individual value preferences cannot go together. With the result neutrality has come to be accepted as one of the governing norms of the relationship between the political and permanent executives.

Norm of Anonymity

The second principle - anonymity flows from the norm of neutrality. The principle of anonymity emphasises that permanent executive works from behind the screen. In other words, they should avoid public gaze. This implies that the political executive takes the total responsibility for omissions and commissions. The executive takes the credit for the achievements and discredit for the failures. The people through electoral mechanism punish or reward the political executive or the political party that the executive represents. The permanent executive has to work under the overall guidance and direction of the political executive. The political executive will have all the powers not only to extract work from the permanent executive but reward or punish them. Under this arrangement the pattern of accountability is so distributed that while the political executive is solely accountable to the people, the permanent executive is also accountable to the political executive. It is precisely the reason why anonymity has come to be considered as one of the governing norms of political-permanent executive relationship. The discussion on these two norms can raise the question: how do we reconcile these two norms? For while the first norm advocates neutrality, the second advocates accountability. If the permanent executive is totally accountable to the political executive, can the latter afford to be neutral? If it means that they should be committed to the political executive in power, is it possible for the permanent executive to go on changing its commitment from regime to regime? Otherwise the members of permanent executive should maintain neutrality in such a way that they may even grow indifferent to all the regimes. However, it is assumed that technical and managerial skills are not political. It is often noted that Lenin welcomed Taylorism which was the product of industrial development in America. The skills and the technical knowledge which are assumed to be non-political can be used by any political party in power.

Q7. Why in India, cooperation between Political and permanent executives is increasingly becoming less?

Ans. There are several reasons for cooperation between these two executives becoming less. The following are some of the important reasons for this deteriorating situation:

1) Firstly, the cooperation between the political and permanent executive depends upon the societal consensus on the goals pursued. This is the advantage of some of the western capitalist societies where there is considerable consensus on the goals of development. There is also a certain degree of homogeneity in the societal formations. This gives an added advantage to those systems. In other words the conditions existing in the society provide the base for a better pattern of relationship between the political and permanent executive. In the third world societies like India where the consensus on development goals has not yet been achieved, there are bound to be certain problems. The heterogeneity of the society is shared by both the political and the permanent executives. The political executives, in the absence of consensus on development and absence of socio-political homogeneity, are subjected to political uncertainty. The absence of long-range view of the society weakens the ideological base. This, in turn, leads to a lot of ambiguity in policy preferences. This leads to what has come to be popularly known as adhocism. Adhocism cannot provide direction to the permanent executive. On the contrary political processes start occupying even the technical and managerial space. This leads to narrowing down of the distinction between the political executive and permanent executive. This can strain the relationship.

2) Secondly, the conflict between these two executives, partly emanates from the historical process and partly from the socio-economic development. Historically speaking the permanent executive during the colonial period not only performed the administrative role but political too. In fact during the colonial phase these two functions converged to a point that to make a distinction between the two would be difficult. It was the anti-colonial movement, aiming at political power for elected representatives, which led to the demarcation of the roles. While the freedom movement presented the aspirations of the people, the bureaucracy appeared as a counter-force. Thus the political elite had their own doubts and suspicion. The bureaucratic elite, deeply rooted in the colonial administrative culture, had an exaggerated view of themselves. They suffered from ego and arrogance. The achievement of freedom should have resulted in redesigning the whole bureaucratic system so as to make them fit to perform the new tasks. But the political elite hesitated to recast the system. With the result the bureaucracy which was used by the colonial masters against the freedom fighters was the very game instrument which the elite of Independent India had to depend upon. The differences embedded in historical process rendered cordiality between the two branches a bit difficult.

3) Thirdly, there is another dimension which leads to conflict. The social origins of the political and administrative elite in India do present a difference. While both the elites do not come from the large masses, they differ in their middle class origins. The political elite have got to be relatively more heterogeneous than the middle and higher level administrative functionaries. While a bulk of the members of the political executive, particularly at the state level, have been drawn from the rural and agricultural background, the top and middle level administrators are from the urban middle and upper middle classes. These differences are manifest in their style of living, mode of communication, ways of looking at things and their mannerisms. Thus the differences get preserved and accentuated. Although the character of bureaucracy has been changing, it has been changing rather slowly. The nature of political elite is also undergoing change. Yet one cannot say that they are comparable or identical. In other words the urban, industrial middle class on the one hand and rural agrarian upper or middle strata on the other dominate the permanent and political executives respectively. The relationships are also partly shaped by these factors.

4) Fourthly, there are also institutional mechanisms which accentuate or widen the areas of conflict. The political institutions normally are empowered with greater discretion and flexibility. They have to be relatively more responsive as they are in constant touch with the social system. The political executive, in parliamentary system of government takes even the legislature for granted. In a number of instances they take the decisions to the legislature or Parliament only for ratification. In fact, in the parliamentary form of government, the initiative does not rest with the legislature. The whole process is reduced to either the ratification or rejection of what has been brought before the legislative houses. Thus, the political executive has become quite strong. In fact it is observed that parliamentary governments over a period of time have become the cabinet system of governments which in turn are turning into prime ministerial governments. Thus, the executive branch has appropriated the powers of the legislative organs and became quite powerful. With this enormous power, they want the matters to move faster. They feel no constraints in exercise of power. The permanent executive has also gained greater power by virtue of being an integral part of the executive branch of the government. However, due to long colonial background and the rules and regulations and established procedures, the permanent executive tends to be less flexible. They also do not appreciate the political expediency. For them precedent is very important. The very nature of the institution is such that their authority is located in the law. As a result they do not feel enthusiastic about experiments and innovations. The political executive does attempt to change these institutions through administrative reforms. There are a number of instances to show that the permanent executives do not welcome the reforms. In fact at the first instance they try to hold back the reform measures. The strong habit of clinging to the rules and regulations continue to influence their approach. Thus, the conflict arises between flexibility and rigidity, expediency and experience, purpose and the process.

5) Lastly, in developing countries like India where there is scarcity of resources and intense competition, for those limited resources, the political executive is subjected to enormous pressure. The political executive in turn puts pressure on the bureaucracy. In a number of cases the tendency is to violate the norms, which they themselves formulate. The norms become necessary for lawful governance but pressures are built in scarce situation. As a result the permanent executive is pressurised to violate the norms and the other rules and procedures. They resist these trends as they are rooted in the rigid rules and regulations. This gives rise to tensions. A section of them may make compromises. This process may end up in public offices being used for private purposes. This may land these officers in various controversies and sometimes enquiries etc. These are some of the important reasons that had given rise to a number of tensions in the relationship within the executive branch of the government.

Q8. What do you understand by Pressure Group? Analyse the characteristics of Pressure Groups in India. [June-07, Q.8]

Ans. Pressure groups are forms of organisations, which exert pressure on the political or administrative system of a country to extract benefits out of it and to advance their own interests. The term 'pressure group' refers to any interest group whose members because of their shared common attributes make claims on the other groups and on the political process. They pursue their interests by organising themselves and by influencing the governmental policies. Their aim is to see that laws or government's actions are favourable to their interests. Pressure groups have been in existence in different forms ever since governmental machinery became capable of delivering certain benefits to either individuals or groups. They did take more concrete form in the wake of industrial revolution and the rise of market oriented economies. The emergence of trusts and monopolies and the struggle over tariffs led to the formation of pressure groups. With the advancement of technology and agricultural skills new problems, desires and needs arose and therefore new groups and organisations came into being to advance their common interests. State assumed various welfare functions in addition to its earlier regulatory activities. All this entrusted considerable power and discretion in the hands of state apparatus and the need to exert more pressure on the State became stronger. The dominant sections of the society needed the help of the State in promotion of the economic activities and the weak and the deprived needed its help for meeting their basic requirements. To articulate their interests, and exert pressure on the State apparatus these groups gained prominence. Pressure groups in mobilising and organising masses have widened the base of political participation as well as creating a responsive political and administrative system. They help in social integration, political articulation and act as catalysts for change.

Finer has characterised pressure groups as 'anonymous empire'. Richard D. Lambert views it as unofficial government. These groups influence both public policy as well as administration. They also contribute towards determination of political structure of society and the form of government. Any social group which seeks to influence the, behaviour of any political officer, both administrative as well as legislative, without attempting to gain formal control of the government can be called a pressure group.

Characteristics of Pressure Groups in India

Based on Certain Interests:

Each pressure group organises itself keeping in view certain interests and thus tries to adopt the structure of power in the political systems. In every government and political party there are clashing interest groups. These groups try to dominate the political structure and to see that groups whose interests clash with theirs are suppressed. Thus, each political party and system is pressurised by certain interest groups which may be similar or reactionary to each other.

Use of Modern as well as Traditional Means

Another characteristic feature of pressure groups is that they try to follow modern means of exerting pressure, without fully giving up the traditional or old ways of operation. They adopt techniques like financing of political parties, sponsoring their close candidates at the time of elections and keeping the bureaucracy also satisfied. Their traditional means include exploitation of caste, creed and religious feelings to promote their interests.

Resulting Out of Increasing Pressure and Demands on Resources

As the resources of developing countries are usually scarce, there are claims and counter claims on their resources from different and competing sections of the society. In such a situation, there has to be a process of allocation. The public policies thus become the devices through which allocation takes place. However, the allocation process has to be accompanied by certain amount of authority for the demands of all the groups cannot be satisfied. In the process certain other groups are denied the benefits. Those who are denied the benefits are found to be unhappy and do express their resentment through different forms. This may range from mild protests to violent outbursts. In such a situation, the allocator of values, viz., the State employs different techniques to contain the movement or meet the protest. At ideological level the State would claim legitimacy of its authority to allocate the values. If the legitimacy claim is accepted then the conflicts get resolved in a more orderly fashion. If the claims for the legitimacy are rejected, the State employs force and justifies it on the grounds of legitimacy and maintenance of order in the general interest of the society. The pressure groups take birth in this process.

In every society there is a continuous generation of demands. In developing countries like India, where around forty per cent population is below the poverty line, the demands emanate from the basic physical requirements of human beings. There are demands not only for food and basic needs but demands for work and opportunities. It is significant to note that the pressure for these demands has come more from the elite than the poor people themselves. Although there is restlessness, it has not acquired a concrete form in terms of poor peoples' organisation. The poor continue to be one of the most unorganised segments of the society with the result their problems do not get articulated sufficiently and pressure applied is not adequate to extract the share that is due to them.

Alternative to Inadequacies of Political Parties

Pressure groups are primarily a consequence of inadequacies of the political parties. The political parties are expected to articulate the demands of different deprived and dominant interests in the system. They are also expected to organise and mobilise the support structure to various demands. In India, the spectrum of political parties indicates that while all of them do talk of the poor and other deprived sections and give prominent place to their problems in their manifestoes, a larger number of them neither have the capacity nor the political will to organise the poor. Thus, the political parties leave a wide gap in the system. This gap is not filled by the pressure groups either. This is due to the inability of the poorer sections to organise themselves. The political parties have not been able to present the interests of the dominant groups as adequately and fully as one would expect them to do. Most of the political parties compete for the same social base. With the result there is not much difference between one party programme and the other. This has left enormous gaps in the socio-economic system of the country. These gaps have come to be filled up by the pressure groups. In a mixed economy where the state has opted for planned development, the dominant interests are always suspicious of the intentions of the state. This gives rise to organised pressure groups as a counter-check to politics and political parties. For instance, the Acts like Monopolies Restrictive Trade Practices (MRTP) or land reforms can always be a source of doubt about the real intentions of the policy formulators. That is the reason why the dominant interests are alert through pressure groups. Another reason why political system leaves considerable space for pressure groups is the continuous regulations and restrictions imposed by the political system. From obtaining a licence to selling a product in the market, there is presence of the State. This is a highly bureaucratised process. The interest or pressure groups not only need to have a highly organised pressure system but maintain middlemen, liaison officer, hidden persuaders and so on. They adopt several methods to extract the favours from the system on the one hand and circumvent highly impending procedures, rules and regulations on the other. The political parties because of their dependence on the poor voters do not publicly plead for the course of the dominant interests. On the contrary their rhetoric is anti-dominant social groups. This gives rise to pressure groups.

Represent Changing consciousness

Pressure groups are a sign of changing consciousness. The consciousness of different groups go on changing as the result (i) changing material conditions; and (ii) increasing politicisation. The change in the material conditions leads to higher level consciousness. For instance the increase in the food production or industrial goods does bring a change in the way individuals and groups look at the world.

The stagnation in production leads to fatalism but increase in the production leads to demands, protests and formation of new pressure groups. This is the initial expression of the changes in material conditions. This also leads to sharpening of the political processes. The political parties and political groups try to mobilize various groups by raising new demands or articulating the new aspirations. The people at large respond to those processes as they enter a new phase of consciousness. Thus, the changing material conditions and consciousness create a new situation for the rise of pressures and in turn the pressure groups. The pressures arising from competition are, in fact, the real arena of pressure group phenomenon. The poor and the deprived sections lack the capacity to organise themselves, therefore, they are usually organised or represented by the elite for upper strata. That is why the nature of pressure that is applied on behalf of the poor would be different from the pressure that the better off sections apply on the society. The better off sections who are locked up in competition from the limited resources of the society employ all the methods possible to extract maximum benefits from the system. In present times, the role of some movements, for protection of rights of people, has become significant. They are playing the role of a pressure group.

Q9. In what ways are pressure groups different from political parties?
[June-08, Q.16(a)]

Ans. Pressure groups have to be differentiated from political parties. Political parties, in the strict sense of the term, are associations of individuals sharing common values and preferences. They are organised on ideological lines and present a vision for the future. They have well trained cadres who are engaged in continuous political mobilisation of the masses. They use all the political means available to capture the power and consolidate their position to attain or realise their ideological goals. In a broader sense they are also interest groups. They have a social base whose interests it must protect and promote. They may adopt pragmatic approach and operate only in the immediate context. They may, sometimes, degenerate to the level of a pressure group to extract benefits for their group. In such a situation the distinction between a pressure group and political party may even disappear. The pressure groups unlike the political parties are formed to solve their immediate problems. They are relatively more temporary than political parties. A pressure group may appear for a short time if it does not present any long-range programme. However, where the interests of the group are of long-range, the pressure group may also last longer. In such cases it may even project the sectarian interests as general or universal interests. It depends on the imagination of their leadership. The pressure groups may have a well-knit organisation and organised membership. Generally they do not have cadres and do not directly deal with people. In most of the cases they deal either with the political parties or governmental apparatus. The pressure groups have far greater flexibility compared to political parties as they do not go to people and stake their claims for power. It is precisely this process that distinguishes political parties from pressure groups.

Q10. Explain the difference between lobbying and pressure groups.
[June-08, Q.16(b)]

Ans. Pressure groups and lobbying is not one and the same thing. Lobbying takes place when a few members of pressure groups loiter in the lobbies of the legislatures with a view to securing an opportunity to interact with legislators and to influence the decisions of the legislators. Parity cannot be drawn between lobbying and pressure groups even though the lobbyists are the representatives of particular interest groups. Lobbying is a communication process used for persuasion; it cannot be treated as an organisation. Lobbying is used in governmental decision making and it aims at influencing the policy process. It acts as an instrument that links citizens and decision-makers. Lobbying is different from pressure groups in the sense that pressure groups are organised groups and they perform various functions including lobbying.

Q11. Describe the types of pressure groups in India. **[Dec-09, Q.14]**
Ans. The different types of pressure groups found in India are business groups, trade unions, peasant groups, student groups, teachers' association, caste and religious associations, women's associations, etc.

The Business Groups

The Business group is the most important and organised pressure group in India. They are also most effective. They are independent of the political parties that exist and they have enough resources with which they can safeguard their interests. Business associations have existed in India even before Independence. The important business groups include the Confederation of Indian Industry (CII), Federation of Indian Chambers of Commerce and Industry (FICCI) and Associated Chamber of Commerce. They exert varied kinds of pressures, they try to influence planning, licensing bodies and economic ministries. Some businesspersons are always there in different legislatures at the Central as well as State level. Every Ministry of the Government of India has some kind of consultative committee and business groups are represented there. During pre-budget meetings the Finance Ministry interacts with the groups, to secure suitable inputs which helps in budget formulation.

Trade Unions

The Indian Trade Union movement has rapidly developed. The trade unions were present prior to Independence. Under communist influence, the All India Trade Union Congress (AITUC) was established in 1920s. The emergence of the communist movement also played an important role in the growth of trade unions in India. In 1948, the Indian National Trade Union Congress (INTUC) was established. Trade Unions in India are closely affiliated with the political parties; many national political parties have got their own federations of trade unions. In fact no amount of independence from political parties exists in trade unions. They seem to have been able to exert significant pressure at the policy formulation level and their strength is well recognised by political parties and government. The trade unions when required can be very vocal and militant in their actions to meet their demands. They work through the weapon of strike and have been able to achieve monetary gains in terms of wage increase, bonus, change in wage structure, etc. These type of pressure groups have been able to encourage class consciousness and class solidarity among the workers. Over the past few years the trade unions resorting to demonstrations, during the disinvestment by the government in public sector undertakings over the past few years. In spite of certain institutional limitations, such as, ideological differences, internal splits, external pressures, lack of international backing, the trade unions exert significant pressure at various levels of policy formulation.

Peasants Organisations

The rise of peasants groups in India has been mainly due to abolition of Zamindari System, implementation of Panchayati Raj, land reform measures, Green Revolution Movement. They gained power since 1960s. In 1936, the All India Kisan Sabha was established and after 1942 the Communist Party of India acquired control over it. Different parties have got their own peasant organisations. Like the trade unions, there is no peasant organisation which may be independent of party control, though at the State level, their organisations are non-political, independent of the political parties and homogenous. The agriculturists are mainly organised more in regional or local class unions than on all-India basis. Even though there are some important All India Kisan Associations like All India Kisan Congress, All India Kisan Kamgar Sammelan, Akhil Bharatiya Kisan Sangh, peasant groups have been mainly organised on territorial basis. Their demands relate to procurement prices of agricultural products, fertilizer subsidy, tenancy rights, electricity charges, etc. The Bharatiya Kisan Party (BKP) in Western U.P. is considered the most significant pressure group.

Students Organisations

The student organisations in India have also acted as pressure groups both prior to Independence and after Independence. The All Bengal Students Association was formed in 1928. The All India Students Federation (AISF) was established in 1936. After Independence the political parties continue to be affiliated with student organisations. The All India Students Congress and later on the National Students Union of India (NSUI) are affiliated to the Congress Party. The All India Students Federation and Students Federation of India (SFI), are controlled by Communist Party of India. The Radical Students Union, Democratic Students Union, Akhil Bharatiya Vidyarthi Parishad (ABVP) etc. are all affiliated to different political parties. They try to pressurise governmental policy on various crucial issues, their activities are not just confined to educational issues.

Community Associations

Apart from these there are various community associations in India. These community groups are organised on the basis of caste, class and religion. Some examples of caste organisations are Scheduled Caste Federation, Backward Caste Federation, etc. Amongst other organisations there are some like Vishwa Hindu Parishad, Northern and Southern India Christian Conference, etc. which represent interests that are supposed to safeguard their respective religions.

Q12. What is the meaning of the term Generalists? What are the arguments advanced by the generalists in favor of their dominant position in administration?

Ans. A generalist is considered an administrator with no technical or specialist qualifications. A generalist entrant to the civil service would have graduated (passed B.A., B.Sc., B.Com., B.Tech. or M.B.B.S.) in literature or history or social sciences, or physical or biological science or mathematics, or commerce or accountancy, or a technical subject like engineering, or medicine. On the strength of his/her subjects at graduation, which may be different from the specialisation needed for job offered, he/she is not fit to be posted in a particular department engaged in performing specific function such as agriculture, health, social service, etc. The posting of a generalist civil servant in a department or at a regional level of administration has nothing to do with the subject of his/her education or of further training or administrative experience. His/her selection to the civil service through a competitive examination open to all graduates in any discipline, such as, arts, social sciences, sciences, commerce, engineering technology, medicine, is adequate to entitle his/her to occupy a position in a department or at a regional level such as a district or a division, (a group of districts) or in the secretariat. A generalist usually performs the POSDCORB functions (planning, organising, supervising, directing, coordinating, reporting and budgeting).

Arguments in Favour of the Generalists

Traditionally, the Indian public services have been structured on the British pattern of division of services into the higher "administrative class and other subordinate technical services". The origin of such dichotomy can be traced to the famous Northcote-Trevelyan Report on "Organisation of the Permanent Civil Service", 1853. The report recommended that the superior posts in the administration should be filled with educated and promising young men by a competitive examination.

This administrative class recruited on the basis of literary attainments in recent years has come to be called generalists. The Macaulay report in 1854 laid emphasis on the superiority of generalists over the specialists. This was the basis and the philosophy on which the Indian Civil Service was constituted. This philosophy continued to hold good till Independence. However, due to the increased welfare functions of the government, Trevelyan and Macaulay philosophy has been questioned and challenged seriously: The main idea in the selection of the generalist civil service and the placement of its entrants to the high level positions in any department including the secretariat is that the intelligent young university graduates would occupy these positions with distinction without a formal in-service training. Another idea behind the generalist civil service was that these young entrants would perform the functions of providing advice to the government in policy-making, formulating decisions for execution of government policies, whichever be the subject or function of administration. The technical experts in the respective subjects would help in these tasks. Various points are put forward in favour of the generalists. They have a broad outlook and flexibility of approach, to adjust themselves to any department and position at any level, and to reflect and judge on any issue in administration. As they shift the ability of the generalists to assimilate different experiences functional, public and political, their ability to occupy higher position in any department and post gets strengthened. Besides, it is argued that the generalist acts as a mediator, an umpire between the expert and the politician, the people and the government, the pressure groups and the public interest represented by the parliament/legislature and the political executive, and the conflicting points of view and aspects. The generalists are said to know the "minister's mind" better than the specialists. They tone down the angularities and extremities of the positions taken by the technocrats or the specialists.

Q13. What do you understand by the term Specialists? What are the arguments put forth by the specialists in favour of their position in administration?

Ans. Specialists are those civil servants who have acquired proficiency in terms of their education and experience in administration of specific subjects. They include medical doctors, engineers, scientists, etc. Generalists are selected in administration on the basis of their having obtained a University degree irrespective of the subjects at it. They are selected, unlike the specialists, for having reached a certain (minimum) level of education *per se* indicating the essential minimum extent of intellectual and mental development. The Generalists are not chosen in administration for their proficiency in a particular discipline or branch of study or for further training or experience in that branch. It is said that administration *per se* becomes a matter of specialisation of the generalists.

Arguments in Favour of the Specialists

During the nineteenth century when the generalist civil service was founded in Britain and India, highly specialised knowledge was not required in administration as its functions were limited to the maintenance of law and order and looking after regulatory activities. The general criticism of the generalists is that they have not developed the essential professionalism or adequate knowledge in depth of the work of any department due to the absence of specialised education or post-service entry training in the work of that department. This has resulted, it is pointed out, in defective policy-making and had made basic evaluation of the policies difficult. The methods adopted for execution of policies are also ineffective. Effective communication with the sources of expert advice in and outside the administration is not established. Because most of the policies and the decisions flowing from them are executed by the specialists or officials under their charge, the generalists are away from the perception regarding the extent of the effective execution of the policies and the decisions and the reasons for it. The specialists feel that generalists misunderstand technical advice or do not obtain it at all. The generalists cannot undertake forward planning because they are not equipped with the necessary knowledge of the developments in particular subjects like engineering, agriculture, education, health, etc., as they move from one department to another, and even out of a department to a public enterprise or a university, or an auxiliary body like the National Book Trust or the National Council of Educational Research and 'Training (NCERT). Further, the 'intelligent amateur' theory underlying the constitution of the generalist civil service would not be applicable to the recent times when the functions of administration have become complex, more technical, scientifically oriented and subject specific.

The specialists advance their case for being placed on an equal footing with the generalists on various grounds. The shortcomings in the administration by the generalists are cited in their own favour. The chief merit of the specialists claimed by them for occupying the highest positions of headship of executive departments and secretaryship of secretariat departments in advance on the strength of their knowledge and experience of respective specialties. It is also actively canvassed by the specialists that, on the one hand, the generalists become better qualified to hold higher positions in different departments because they themselves have fashioned the system in their own favour, and on the other hand, the specialists are deprived of occupying highest positions even though they are better equipped. Scientific training inculcates an objective spirit among the specialists which reduces the alleged functional bias in them. Nor are the generalists completely free from a personal bias in the course of administration. The charge on the specialists of not being cost-conscious and of being too close to own department's clientele, is answered with a similar argument. The dual hierarchical structures of the cadres of the generalists and the specialists respectively not only mar administrative efficiency but also create discontent among the specialists. Easier and more cordial communication between them would result. Better expert advice from the specialists would be evoked.

Q14. Highlight the possible way out to bridge the existing gulf between the generalists and specialists.

Ans. Of late, certain steps have been initiated towards inducting specialists into administrative positions both at the centre as well as the states. For example, the Department of Atomic Energy is headed by a nuclear scientist, Ministry of

Law by a member belonging to the legal profession or service. Similarly, scientists preponderate in the scientific research departments. The Planning Commission is exclusively manned by specialists and professionals.

There is another method in vogue of giving a specialist head of the department ex-officio status of Joint/Additional Secretary to the government. For instance, at the union level, the members who are heads of operating departments are ex-officio secretaries in the Union Ministry. At the state level too, specialists are appointed as secretaries - ex-officio or in own right - in departments like law, public works, etc. The Director General of Indian Council of Agriculture Research (ICAR) is the ex-officio Secretary of the Department of Agricultural Research and Education in the Ministry of Agriculture. Similarly, the Director General of Council for Scientific and Industrial Research (CSIR) is the ex-officio Secretary of Department of Scientific and Industrial Research in Ministry of Science and Technology.

An independent Personnel and Administrative Reforms Department has been constituted at the centre in accordance with another recommendation of the ARC. Similarly, imparting of training in managerial techniques and reforms in administration as suggested by the Commission is under way. But the concept of overall career planning and development seems to have been stuck up. In the public enterprises, prior to the report of the ARC on public enterprises, government secretaries most of whom were generalists used to be appointed either in ex-officio capacity as part time Chairman/Managing Directors or Directors or on a full time substantive basis. The recommendation of the ARC to discontinue the practice was accepted and implemented by the Government. Another possible way out to bridge the existing gulf between the generalists and specialists could be the formation of any one of the following hierarchies like:

i) Separate Hierarchy: The system is prevalent in Australia, Sweden where there is common pay and greater respect for specialists.

ii) Parallel Hierarchy: This is a system where a specialist will be working with a generalist like for example Director General (Specialist) will be working with Deputy Secretary (Generalist).

iii) Joint Hierarchy: Here both a generalist as well as a specialist report jointly to a permanent Secretary who is a generalist.

iv) Unified Hierarchy: This implies creation of a unified civil service merging both central and All India Services. This requires common competitive examination of uniform standard and uniformity in emoluments and conditions of service. The generalist Indian Administrative Service, with all its shortcomings, has proved to be an asset to the administration both at the national and state level. Its alleged omniscience, overbearing outlook towards the specialists, its inadequate 'professionalism' and outdated knowledge in scientific and technological sectors of administration are known and have been discussed in scholarly works and current journals, magazines and newspapers. But its national outlook has helped to keep the State administration into the national mainstream. Its integrated approach has kept the national administration alive to the requirements of fostering interrelations among different sectors of administration as well as between the centre and the state.

At the same time, the value of the specialists' contribution and role in the administration at both the central and the state levels has to be appreciated. India has progressed tremendously in scientific, industrial, transport, communication, agricultural, educational and other fields. The specialists' role in this multisided national progress and the administrative infrastructure and processes for it, should be recognised. The complexion of administration is undergoing a change with the tasks getting more and more specialised in recent times. The discharge of functions by the administration in present times needs more professionalisation. While in the USA, the public service places emphasis on some specialist inputs, Indian system modeled on the British pattern gave importance to generalism. But now the gap between the generalists and specialists is getting reduced through suitable measures. Now generally a freshly appointed officer of IAS shall gain experience in the field as well as in regulatory and welfare departments in the initial 11 to 12 years. In the next few years opportunities are being made available to specialize in their areas of preference. Policy formulation, and implementation are the key components of administration. The contribution of generalists and specialists in this process cannot be assessed in rigid watertight compartments. The present times call for a blend of detailed knowledge of administrative activity as well as specialized knowledge along with proficiency in skills of organisation and policy making.

Q15. Discuss the meaning and importance of administrative reforms.
Ans. Administrative reform is a continuing necessity in a society, more so when the society confronts a quantum jump in its basic framework of governance including, of course, its goals. Administrative reforms can, in short, be defined as artificial inducement of administrative transformation against resistance. This definition highlights three distinct elements, namely:
-Administrative reform is artificially stimulated;
-It is a transformatory process; and
-There is existence of resistance to change process.
Obviously, reforms do not take place by themselves. They are pre-meditated, well studied and planned programmes with definite objectives in view. Reform is an induced and manipulated change, for it involves persuasion, collaboration and generation of conviction for betterment. Reform is more than a series of incremental changes or marginal adjustments, though it may result from the

cumulation of small changes, which periodically creates requirement for comprehensive and systematic efforts.

Need for Administrative Reforms

The distinguishing characteristic of modernised social system is its ability to deal with continuous systematic transformation. Society has to change in order to free itself from the shackles of traditionalism, cope with the changes in environment, adopt fresh innovative culture, adopt new knowledge and technology and crave for a new order through elimination of the old structures and system. Administrative reform is but a part of the universality of this change, for administration is nothing but a sub-culture, a social sub-system reflecting the values of the wider society. Administration must also correspondingly change to be in step with the outer modernisation process. Or else, disequilibrium would set in, resulting in imbalances, dysfunctionalities, maladjustments and goal displacement According to Fred W.Riggs administrative reform is a "problem of dynamic balancing ". Since public administration functions within a political context, its basic character, content and style of functioning is greatly influenced by the political environment, its institutional dynamics and process, in not merely setting national goals, priorities, or deciding between competing values, and allocating resources but also in devising the most effective instrument for translating these policies into successful programme realities. Added to this, the advances in Information and Communication Technology (ICT), and the state pervasive role in managing national assets and resources, controlling the entire economy through regulation and development, ensuring a just and equitable economic order, correcting age old social imbalances through newer forms of institution-making, and ushering in an egalitarian social system, has thrown up new tasks for administration. This requires fundamental and foundational improvement in the administrative capabilities. The latter in turn, requires proper planning, educational re-arrangement, skill-generation, attitude-formation and a host of other structural-functional reorganisation. With the nineties came the market reforms, and there was an emphasis on structural adjustment. Good governance is the stress of the governments of the day, with focus On accountability, efficiency, effectiveness, transparency and decentralisation. With focus on good governance today, there has been a greater change in the conventional role of the State, the government and the bureaucracy. Today, there is shift from responsiveness to partnership and collaboration. The importance is given to people's participation in governance and the involvement of the multiple actors. With citizen's participation and collaboration taking centre stage, the government have to act as partners with the citizens. Administration cannot fulfill the newer roles with the traditional organisation and methods. It has to be people friendly and work on public trust. Hence, the bureaucracy has to change to adapt to the new role. This need for change in turn necessitate reforms

Q16. Briefly describe the different types of administrative reforms since Independence. [Dec-08, Q.16]

Ans. When India became independent in 1947, it faced problems of partition, refugees, migration, retirement of a great number of administrative personnel, problem of integration of the princely States, etc. The new government adopted the ideology of welfare of the people through socio-economic development, which led to a greater proliferation of tasks and functions. To take up the welfare programmes and challenges, the administrative machinery, which was inherited from the colonial regime and rendered weak by erosive circumstances and stressful situations accompanying Independence, had to be revamped and reinforced. Administration, as the instrument for designing and implementing all the developmental programmes had to be restructured, reformed and renewed.

Secretariat Reorganisation Committee, 1947

The Government of India set up the Secretariat Reorganisation Committee in 1947, which was headed by Girija Shankar Bajpai. The Committee enquired into the matters of personnel shortages, better utilization of the available manpower and improvement of methods of work in the Central Secretariat.

Shri N. Gopalaswamy Ayyangar Report, 1950

Shri N. Gopalaswamy Ayyangar conducted a comprehensive review of the working of the machinery of the Central Government, which was presented in his report on 'Reorganisation of the Machinery of Central Government'.

A.D. Gorwala Committee, 1951

In July 195 1, a Committee. headed by Shri .A.D. Gorwala in its Report on Public Administration underlined the need for having a clean, efficient and impartial administration.

Paul. H. Appleby Reports, 1953 & 1956

In continuation of these efforts, the Government of India invited an American expert, Mr. Paul. H. Appleby to suggest reforms in Indian administration. Appleby submitted two reports. His first report namely 'Public Administration in India: Report of a Survey', 1953, dealt with administrative reorganisation and practices. His second report namely, 'Re-examination of India's Administrative System with special reference to Administration of Government's Industrial and Commercial Enterprises', 1956, dealt with matters pertaining to streamlining organisation, work procedures, recruitment, training in these enterprises. Among the twelve recommendations made, the Government of India accepted two of his recommendations. First, related to the establishment of a professional training institute, namely the Indian Institute of

Public Administration for promoting research in public administration. The second related to the setting up of a central office to provide leadership in respect to organisation, management and procedures. As a result, an Organisation and Methods (O&M) Division was set up in March 1954, in the Cabinet Secretariat for improving the speed and quality of the government business and streamlining its procedures. O&M units and work-study units were set up in the Ministries / Departments. The focus was on improving the paper work management and methods. A Manual of Office Procedure was prepared for all Ministries and Departments.

Committee on Plan Projects, 1956

In 1956, the Planning Commission set up a 'Committee on Plan Projects' to evolve organisation norms, work methods and techniques, with a view to achieve economy and efficiency in the implementation of the plan projects. In 1964, a Management and Development Administration Division was also established as a part of this Committee to promote the use of modem tools of management. It also undertook studies on problems related to development administration at the district level.

Committee on Prevention of Corruption, 1962

The Committee was set up under the chairmanship of K Santhanam to study the causes of corruption, to review the existing set up for checking corruption and to suggest measures for improvement. The Committee stressed on the need for streamlining the procedures relating to prevention of corruption and recommended the setting up of Central Vigilance Commission(CVC).

Administrative Reforms Commission (ARC), 1966

The Administrative Reforms Commission was set up in January 1966 under the chairmanship of K Hanumanthaiya. Its terms of reference was the widest as it covered the entire gamut of public administration at the Centre as well in the States. The 'Commission submitted 20 reports containing more than 500 recommendations. These led to major and minor changes in administration as well as paved the way for further thinking, which led to more reforms. The major recommendations of the ARC are mentioned below:

1) It spelt out the tasks for the Department of Administrative Reforms. The Commission suggested that the Department should concentrate on:

· Undertaking studies on administrative reforms that are of a foundational nature;

· Creating O&M expertise in the ministries and departments and providing training to the staff in their O&M units in modern managerial techniques; and

· Providing guidance to the O&M units in implementing the improvements and reforms.

2) It recommended the reactivating of the O&M units in different ministries and departments.

3) It called for setting up of a special cell in the central reforms agency to give effect to the reports of ARC; and

4) It stated that the central reforms agency should be research based in matters dealing with the methods of work, staffing pattern and organisational structure.

Kothari Committee, 1976

The Committee on recruitment and selection methods under the chairmanship of Shri Kothari was set up in 1976 by the UPSC to examine and report on the system of recruitment to All India Services and Central Group A and B Services. The committee in its report recommended for single examination for the IAS and Central Group A non-technical services.

National Police Commission, 1977

The Commission was set up under the chairmanship of Shri Dharam Vira to examine the role and functions of police with special reference to control of crime and maintenance of public order, the method of magisterial supervision, the system of investigation and prosecution and maintenance of crime records. The Commission made over five hundred recommendations extending to a wide area of interest relating to police administration.

Economic Reforms Commission, 1981

The Commission was set up with L K Jha as the chairman. The main functions assigned to the Commission related to the study of the important areas of economic administration with a view to suggest reforms. The Commission submitted a number of reports to the Government of India, which advocated the rationalisation and modernisation of the economic administrative system to pave way for a new economic order.

Commission on Centre-State Relations, 1983

Mr. R S Sarkaria, was the chairman of this Commission. Its term of reference was to examine and review the working of the existing arrangements between the union and states with regard to powers, functions and responsibilities in all spheres and make recommendations as to the changes and measures needed. National Commission to Review the Working of the Indian Constitution, 2000-03, under the Chairmanship of Chief Justice (Retd.) Venkatacheliah, was set up to examine the working of the Indian Constitution.

Question
Papers

SECTION I

Answer any two of the following questions in about 500 words each. Each question carries 25 marks.

Q1. Discuss the structure of the Moghul administrative system.
Refer to Chapter-1, Q.No.-5

Q2. Analyse the role of various constitutional commissions in India.
Refer to See Chapter-1

Q3. Discuss the role of the Governor in State administration.
Refer to Chapter-3, Q.No.-2

Q4. Explain the nature of Divisional administration. Examine the role of Divisional Commissioner.
Refer to Chapter-4, Q.No.-2

SECTION II

Answer any three of the following questions in about 250 words each. Each question carries 10 marks.

Q5. What are administrative tribunals? Bring out the reasons for their growth.
Refer Chapter-5, Q.No.-5

Q6. Discuss the impact of religion and caste on administration.
Refer to Chapter-5, Q.No.-1

Q7. Highlight the recent trends in Panchayati Raj Institutions in the light of the 73rd Constitutional Amendment.

Ans. The constitutional status of 'self-Government' has been accorded to the Panchayats under the 73rd Constitution Amendment Act, 1992. With the enactment and enforcement of the Act from 24th April 1993, the States were asked to amend this respective legislation pertaining to Panchayats to bring them in conformity with the Act by 24th April 1994. The main features of the Act are discussed below.

The Constitution of India provides for uniform system of three-tier Panchayats at the village, intermediate and district levels. But the Panchayats at the intermediate level may not be constituted in a State having a population not exceeding twenty lakhs.

All the seats in a Panchayat are filled by persons chosen by direct elections from territorial constituencies in the Panchayat area. The Legislature of a State may, by law, provide for the representation of the Panchayat area. The Legislature of a State may, by law, provide for the representation of the Chairpersons of the village panchayats at the intermediate level and district level. This will create an organic link among the three-tier panchayats.

One of the major reasons, which hampered the development of the Panchayati Raj Institution, has been the absence of regular and periodic elections within a time frame. Hence, these institutions had unstable tenures. That is why the Act has provided for a uniform term of five years and the elections are mandatory before the expiry of the term. In the event of dissolution, it has been made obligatory for the State to conduct the election within six months for the constitution of a new body. This will provide continuity and strength to these institutions and they will be able to establish themselves as an effective and strong people's institutions.

In order to ensure a genuine and meaningful participation of weaker sections of the society, the Act provide reservation for scheduled castes and scheduled tribes in the membership to these bodies at all the three level in proportion to their population. Mere participation at the membership level may not prove to be meaningful. Therefore, the Act provides for reservation in the offices of the Chairpersons also for these categories in proportion to their population in the State. It is a unique provision and would go a long way in according a proper voice to these weaker sections in the decision-making at all levels.

Women constitute half of our population. In order to give them an opportunity of participation in the local offices, not less than one-third of the posts of Chairpersons have been reserved in their favour. These provisions would make women and weaker sections equal partners in rural development.

The Amendment has assigned an important role to the Gram Sabha. All the votes in a village panchayat area are its members. It will exercise such power, and perform such functions at the village level as the legislature of a State may, by law, provide. The Gram Sabhas existed in all States even before the 73rd Amendment but they exist on paper and their role is insignificant. But the institution of Gram Sabha should be revitalized to involve the people to evolve the programme from the base.

Panchayati Raj Institutions can grow and develop if they are provided with a strong financial base. It is for this purpose the Act provides for a system of financial transfers on a mandatory basis. A State Finance Commission has been set-up in every State, once in every five years, to review the financial position of the Panchayats and make appropriate recommendations for strengthening the resources base of these institutions.

Free and fair elections in a democracy constitute the most important step in securing trust and respect from the people for any institution. Therefore, the Act provides for a State Election Commission for superintendence, direction and conduct of all panchayat elections.

The 11th Schedule containing 29 items, e.g. agriculture, minor irrigation, fisheries, rural housing etc. is to serve as a guide to the State Government for delegating functions to the PRIs. Panchayat have to prepare plans for economic development and social justice. Plans prepared by t he Panchayats are to be consolidated by the District Planning Committee.

Another important provision of the Amendment Act is the constitution of the District Planning Committee to consolidate the plans prepared by the Panchayats and Municipalities in the district.

The net effort of the 73rd Constitutional Amendment Act, 1992 is **(a)** constitutional status of Panchayati Raj Institutions; **(b)** widening of the social base of these institutions; **(c)** making Panchayats the foundation stone of planning; and **(d)** provision for constitutionally allocated fund for development work to be undertaken by the Panchayati Raj Institutions.

Panchayats in Scheduled Areas

(Extension to the Scheduled Areas) Act, 1996

The provisions of the 73rd Constitutional Amendment Act did not apply to the Scheduled Areas located in – Andhra Pradesh, Madhya Pradesh, Rajasthan, Gujarat, Maharashtra, Himachal Pradesh, Orissa and Bihar-vide Clause (i) of Article 244 of the Constitution. Parliament extended the Seventy-third Amendment Act of these areas on December 24, 1996 by legislating the Panchayats (Extension to the Scheduled Areas) Act, 1996. The basic premise of the provisions of the Panchayats was to facilitate participative democracy in tribal areas by empowering Gram Sabha, restore the power to community to manage natural resources like land, water, forest and minerals and evolve an effective delivery system for development within its territorial jurisdiction. However, the disturbing trends is widespread apathy on the part of the State Government as the number of States diluted the intent of the Act by assigning more power to the Gram Panchayat over the Gram Sabha. The State Government do not appear to have clear idea about the term Local Self-Government specially, "to what extent the panchayats in the Scheduled Areas are to be given administrative and financial autonomy need to be clarified to the states". In such circumstances the Government, NGOs and people's organisation have to play a significant role to make these provisions a reality.

Q8. What are Pressure Groups? Analyse the characteristics of Pressure Groups in India.

Refer to Chapter-6, Q.No.-8

Q9. Discuss the important recommendations of the Sarkaria Commission.

Ans. Sarkaria Commission was set up in June 1983 by the central government of India. The Sarkaria Commission's charter was to examine the relationship and balance of power between state and central governments in the country and suggest changes within the framework of Constitution of India. The Commission was so named as it was headed by Justice Rajinder Singh Sarkaria, a retired judge of the Supreme Court of India. The other two members of the committee were Shri B.Sivaraman and Dr.S.R.Sen.

The Commission submitted its final 1600-page report in 1988. The final report contained 247 specific recommendations. In spite of the large size of its reports - the Commission recommended, by and large, status quo in the Centre-State relations, especially in the areas, relating to legislative matters, role of Governors and use of Article 356.

It is widely accepted that to whatever extent the Commissions suggested change, the recommendations were not implemented by the government.

The Commission after conducting several studies, eliciting information, holding discussions and after detailed deliberations submitted its report in January 1988. The report contains 247 recommendations spreading over the following 19 Chapters.

Key Recommendations of the Sarkaria Commission are as follows-

· It made the strong suggestion that Article 370 was not a transitory provision. This appears to have been made specifically in response to "one all-India political party" that demanded the deletion of Article 370 "in the interests of national integration."

· It recommended that the residuary powers of legislation in regard to taxation matters should remain exclusively in the competence of Parliament while the residuary field other than that of taxation should be placed on the concurrent list.

· That the enforcement of Union laws, particularly those relating to the concurrent sphere, is secured through the machinery of the states.

· To ensure uniformity on the basic issues of national policy, with respect to the subject of a proposed legislation, consultations may be carried out with the state governments individually and collectively at the forum of the proposed Inter-Governmental Council. It was not recommended that the consultation be a constitutional obligation.

· Ordinarily, the Union should occupy only that much field of a concurrent subject on which uniformity of policy and action is essential in the larger interest of the nation, leaving the rest and details for state action.

· On administrative relations, Sarkaria made the following observation: "Federalism is more a functional arrangement for cooperative action, than a static institutional concept. Article 258 (power of the Union to confer powers

etc on states in certain cases) provides a tool by the liberal use of which cooperative federalism can be substantially realised in the working of the system. A more generous use of this tool should be made than has hitherto been done, for progressive decentralisation of powers to the governments of the states."
· On Article 356, it was recommended that it be used "very sparingly, in extreme cases, as a measure of last resort, when all other alternatives fail to prevent or rectify a breakdown of constitutional machinery in the state.

Q10. Discuss the major characteristics of the Government of India Act, 1935.
Refer to Chapter-1, Q.No.-14

SECTION III

Answer all the questions. Each question carries 2 marks. Select the correct answer for each question.
Q11. Which Moghul ruler could be singled out as the one with administrative abilities of high order?
(a) Babur   **(b) Akbar**
(c) Shahjahan   **(d) Aurangzeb**
Ans. (b)

Q12. The Secretariat was reorganized by
(a) Lord Clive   **(b) Lord Hastings**
(c) Lord Cornwallis   **(d) None of the above**
Ans. (c)

Q13. The Supreme Court
(a) protects the Fundamental Rights
(b) acts as a check on executive authority
(c) enforces the rule of law   **(d) All the above**
Ans. (d)

Q14. The Comptroller and Auditor General is appointed by the
(a) President   **(b) Prime Minister**
(c) Parliament   **(d) All the above**
Ans. (a)

Q15. Which one of the following is not a Central Service?
(a) Indian Foreign Service   **(b) Indian Economic Service**
(c) Indian Forest Service   **(d) Indian Audit and Accounts Service**
Ans. (d)

Q16. The Secretary is the
(a) administrative head of the ministry/department
(b) principal adviser to the minister
(c) representative of his ministry/department before the Parliamentary committees
(d) All the above
Ans. (d)

Q17. The Lal Bahadur Shastri Academy of Administration, Mussoorie is an example of
(a) Attached office   **(b) Subordinate office**
(c) Link office   **(d) None of the above**
Ans. (d)

Q18. The Chairman and members of State Public Service Commission can be removed by the
(a) Chief Minister   **(b) Governor**
(c) Prime Minister   **(d) President**
Ans. (d)

Q19. The directorate is a
(a) Line agency   **(b) Staff agency**
(c) Auxiliary agency   **(d) None of the above**
Ans. (a)

Q20. The executive branch of the Government consists of
(a) Political executive   **(b) Bureaucracy**
(c) Legislature   **(d) Both (a) and (b)**
Ans. (d)

SECTION I

Answer any two of the following questions in about 500 words each.
Each question carries 20 marks.

Q1. Enumerate the major characteristics and structure of the Moghul administrative system.
Refer June-2007, Q.No.-1

Q2. Discuss the evolution, organisation and functions of cabinet Secretariat in India.
Refer to Chapter-2, Q.No.-12

Q3. Examine the role of Governor in State administration.
Refer to Chapter-3, Q.No.-2

Q4. Bring out the role and functions of the institutions dealing with corruption.
Refer to Chapter-5, Q.No.-3

SECTION II

Answer any four of the following questions in about 250 words each.
Each question carries 12 marks.

Q5. "The involvement of the political parties and groups in the administrative processes of decision-making is implicit in a democratic political system." Analyse.
Refer to See Chapter-6

Q6. Explain the important functions of the Union Public service commission.
Refer to Chapter-2, Q.No.-16

Q7. Highlight the principal functions of the Chief Secretary.
Refer to Chapter-3, Q.No.-9

Q8. Illuminate the classification of State Public Services.
Refer to Chapter-3, Q.No.-15

Q9. Describe the components of District administration.

Ans. The district is an important geographical unit where the people come into direct contact with the apparatus of public administration. The actual pattern of administration varies from state to state, even than there is a large measure of uniformity in the broad pattern of district administration. Because of proximity of the community to the District Administration one finds a large number of State level agencies functioning in the district undertaking a variety of functions. These functions can be categorized as law and order, revenue, agriculture and animal husbandry, welfare, public distribution, elections, administration of local bodies, functions relating to emergencies and natural calamities and residuary functions.

A major concern of District Administration is maintenance of public safety, law and order, crime control and administration of justice. District Collector and the Superintendent of Police undertake these functions. They are responsible for maintenance of peace and tranquility in the district. Administration of jails, though a separate department, is closely related function in this category. As a District Magistrate, Collector has supervisory role in the administration of jails.

The second group of functions is related to revenue administration. Assessment and collection of land revenue, collection of other public dues and taxes like sales tax, maintenance of land records, adjudication of land disputes between private individuals and Government, implementation of land reforms, consolidation of agricultural holdings, etc. constitute revenue functions at the district level. District Collector is basically responsible for all these functions and to support him there is an elaborate network of revenue and other departmental officials. After Independence, development administration has become all pervading and Government has begun to deal with wide area of development functions. Because of the rural nature of the society agricultural development is an important function of district administration. This includes Irrigation, Cooperativ.es, Animal Husbandry, Fisheries, etc. A different subject matter specialist working under the supervision and control of the District Collector looks after each of these functions. In some States, most of these functions are undertaken by the Panchayati Raj Institutions.

Welfare is another component of development functions in the district. Public health, Welfare of Weaker Sections and Backward Classes, Education etc, come in this category. Each of these functions is entrusted to separate officers at the district level. Public distribution is an important function particularly in the context of scarcity and black-marketing. This is a delegated function assigned to the Collector.. Separate organization, however, exist under his control. Articles of daily consumption like food grains, kerosene, sugar, etc. come under this category. In a democratic system, elections to various bodies at the National, State and Local levels are conducted periodically. The process of election beginning from the registration of voters to the conduct of elections and the declaration of results is a vital function to be carried out at the district level under the supervision of the District Collector.

Local administration is 'a vital link between District administration and the local community. Rural and Urban Local Bodies play a pivotal role in district administration. The State Governments have entrusted the supervisory and controlling role to the Collector in the district. Natural calamities and emergencies is another vital area, which needs to be taken care of whenever required. The entire administration has to be geared to meet the threat of emergencies during natural calamities. As Head of District Administration the Collector plays a significant role in managing the crisis.

Apart from the important functions listed above there may be many areas/ functions of the Government, which can neither be precisely defined nor explained. These residuary functions like small savings, contribution to public loans etc. are equally important in the district administration.

Q10. Briefly explain the various types of Administrative Tribunals.
Ans. Refer to Chapter-5, Q.No.-4 and
Customs and Excise Revenue Appellate Tribunal (CERAT)
The Parliament passed the CERAT Act in 1 9 6 The Tribunal adjudicate disputes, complaints or offences with regard to customs and excise revenue. Appeals from the, orders of the CERAT lies with the Supreme Court.
Election Commission (EC)
The Election Commission is a tribunal for adjudication of matters pertaining to the allotment of election symbols to parties and similar other problems. The decision of the commission can be challenged in the Supreme Court.
Foreign Exchange Regulation Appellate Board (FERAB)
The Board has been set up under the Foreign Exchange Regulation Act, 1973. A person who is aggrieved by an order of adjudication for causing breach or committing offences under the Act can file an appeal before the FERAB.
Income Tax Appellate Tribunal
This tribunal has been constituted under the Income Tax Act, 196 1. The Tribunal has its benches in various cities and appeals can be filed before it by an aggrieved personals against the order passed by the Deputy Commissioner or Commissioner or Chief Commissioner or Director of Income'~ax. An appeal against the order of the Tribunal lies to the High Court. An appeal also lies to the Supreme Court if the High Court deems fit.
Railway Rates Tribunal
This-Tribunal was set up under the Indian Railways Act, 1989. It adjudicates matters pertaining to the complaints against the railway administration. These

may be related to the discriminatory or unreasonable rates, unfair charges or preferential treatment meted out by the railway administration. The appeal against the order of the Tribunal lies with the Supreme Court.

Industrial Tribunal

This Tribunal has been set up under the Industrial Disputes Act, 1947. It can be constituted by' both the Central as well as State governments. The Tribunal looks into the dispute between the employers and the workers in matters relating to wages, the period and mode of payment, compensation and other allowances, hours of work, gratuity, retrenchment and closure of the establishment. The appeals against the decision of the Tribunal lie with the Supreme Court.

Q11. Describe the important approaches to the concept of Decentralisation.
Refer to Chapter-6

Q12. Suggest the important measures to bridge the existing gulf between the Generalists and Specialists.
Refer to Chapter-3, Q.No.-14 (2)

SECTION III

Answer any two of the following question in about 100 words each. Each question carries 6 marks.
Q13. Discuss the role of National Commission for Scheduled Castes.
Refer to Chapter-2, Q.No.-4 (7)

Q14. What is the typical pattern of departmentalisation in the state Secretariat?
Refer to Chapter-3, Q.No.-8

Q15. Highlight the various sources of income of the urban local self-government bodies.
Refer to Chpater-4, Q.No.-15

Q16. Make a distinction between
(a) Pressure groups and political parties
Refer to Chapter-6, Q.No.-9

(b) Pressure groups and Lobbying
Refer to Chapter-6, Q.No.-10

SECTION I

Answer any two of the following questions in about 500 words each. Each question carries 20 marks.

Q1. Discuss the basic features of the Indian Constitution.
Refer to Chapter-2, Q.No.-1

Q2. Analyse the emerging patterns of relationship between the Secretariat and Directorates.
Refer to Chapter-3, Q.No.-14

Q3. Describe the important features of Divisional Administration and the role of the Divisional Commissioner.
Refer to June-2007, Q.No.-4

Q4. Examine the various facets of the Centre – State administrative relations.
Refer to Chapter-6, Q.No.-1

SECTION II

Answer any four of the following questions in about 250 words each. Each question carries 12 marks.

Q5. Write a note on the revenue administration during the Moghul period.
Refer to Chapter-1, Q.No.-3, Q.No.-4 +& Q.No.-5

Q6. Highlight the important features of the Indian Councils Act 1861 and the Indian Councils Act 1892.
Refer to Chapter-1, Q.No.-11

Q7. Bring out the relationship patterns between the Executive agencies and the Secretariat.
Refer to Chapter-2, Q.No.-8

Q8. Discuss in brief the role of the Chief Minster in State administration.
Refer to Chapter-3, Q.No.-6

Q9. Describe the functions of the District Collector.
Refer to Chapter-4, Q.No.-5

Q10. Examine the important issue pertaining to urban policing.
Refer to See Chapter-5

Q11. "The effectiveness of judicial control over administration is limited by many factors." Elucidate.
Refer to Chapter-5, Q.No-10

Q12. Analyse the principles governing the relationship between political and permanent executive.
Refer to Chapter-6, Q.No.-6

SECTION III

Answer any two of the following questions in about 100 words each. Each question carries 6 marks.

Q13. Explain the meaning of tenure system. What are its disadvantages?
Refer to Chapter-2, Q.No.-7

Q14. Bring out the features of recruitment to State Civil Services.
Ans. Features of civil services at state level
• Recruitment to State Civil Services is made at the age level of 21-25.
• Age relaxation is available for the members of scheduled castes, scheduled tribes and backward communities.
• Recruitment is made through an open competitive examination administered by the PSC; higher level posts are filled up by promotion.
• Vacancies to be filled up are advertised by the PSC every year and applications invited from candidates all over the country.
• Minimum qualification required is a Bachelor's Degree from a recognized university.
• The competitive examination through which selections are made has two components. *First*, a written, essay-type examination. *Second*, a personality test. Candidates obtaining certain minimum marks in the written examination are invited for a personality test, which is but an interview of about half an hour's duration.
• Marks secured by each candidate in written examination and personality test are totalled up. Depending upon the number of vacancies, a list of successful candidates is finalised. This list is in order of merit.

Q15. Highlight the advantages of administrative tribunals.
Refer to Chapter-5, Q.No.-5

Q16. Describe in brief the different types of administrative reforms since Independence.
Refer to Chapter-6, Q.No.-16

SECTION I

Answer any two of the following questions in about 500 words each. Each question carries 20 marks.

Q1. Discuss the characteristics and structure of Moghul Administrative System.
Refer to June-2007, Q.No.-1

Q2. Explain the role of the Governor in state administration.
Refer June-2007, Q.No.-3

Q3. Write a note on evolution and functions of the office of Collector.
Ans. The office of the District Collector in India has a long history. Its origin is related to the concept of a territorial unit of administration. During the Mauryan period the kingdom was divided into convenient territorial units and each unit was placed under the charge of an imperial authority. The authority that was important to the District Collector during that period was known as 'Raja'. Though they were essentially revenue officers, they exercised judicial functions also. Rajukas collected land revenue, maintained roads, promoted trade and industry and carried out public works like irrigation. During the Gupta period they were called 'visayapathis', who were Heads of 'visayas', which were equivalent to the modern districts. The visayapathi was responsible for the general administration including collection of taxes and other revenues. They also commanded military force to maintain law and order in the visaya. The Mughal rulers followed the system of administration of Hindu Kings.

Under the Mughal system the 'circar', which is comparable to the modern district had three officers viz. Amalguzar, Amir Zuazi and Faujdar. The Amalguzar was a principal revenue functionary of the circar and was responsible for the collection of revenue and proper utilisation of land. He also exercised certain administrative functions like punishing the robbers and some quasi-judicial functions like settlement of disputed claims on land. However, he was basically responsible of the collection and management of land revenue. Though, during, Mughal period Faujdar enjoyed a dominant position in the district administration, Amalguzar performed all revenue functions. Thus, before the advent of the British, there were territorial divisions and officers of these divisions were responsible for realisation of land revenue. These revenue officials were generally invested with several power and functions. It was, no doubt, considered a feudal form of territorial organisation. The territorial gradation of administrative areas more br less remained the same notwithstanding the changes that were brought about in the system by the British. The British built on the oriental system and established the present system of field administration. The creation of a district as unit of administration and the appointment of the District Collector as Head of District Administration laid the foundation for stable administration in India. Granting of 'diwani' (civil administration) in Bengal, Bihar and Orissa to the East India Company in 1765 marks the beginning of British revenue administration in India. In 1769 the Company launched a scheme of English supervision over the local revenue collecting institutions. East India Company appointed covenanted servants as supervisors during 1769-70 in the districts of the diwani provinces. The supervisors were expected to report on the production and capacity of the lands; amount of revenues and other taxes levied; and manner of collection etc. They were expected not only to be concerned with revenue collection but also to have an overall knowledge of all the factors that affected the district. But the system failed and the company decided in 1772 to take over the entire executive management of public revenues. Accordingly, Warren Hastings issued a proclamation. On May 14th, 1772 the supervisors were appointed as Collectors. Thus, the institution of Collector was created for the first time in 1772 during the period of Warren Hastings. From then onwards collection of revenue became the most important duty of the company's civil servants. The office of the District Collector became an important institution of the British local administration. They were entrusted with the executive power of management and collection of revenue and other duties of enquiry and investigation. From then onwards the Collector's role has gone through several changes that is period of strength, neglect etc. By the time India gained independence the District Collector had become **an** important functionary heading the District Administration.

Now Refer to Chapter-4, Q.No.-5

Q4. Examine the administrative relations between the centre and the States.

Refer to December-2008, Q.No.-4

Q5. Highlight the Provisions of Morley Mintoreformes.

Ans. The Indian Councils Act (1909) substantially increased the strength of legislative councils - the Imperial and provincial. For the Imperial, the Supreme Council, the number of additional members was raised from 16 to 60. For major provincial councils, the number was raised to 50 and for minor provinces it was fixed to 30. The additional members were both nominated and elected. The principle of election was functional representation. In the Supreme Legislative Council, the official majority was maintained by in h e provincial councils, the non-officials formed the majority. The Act definitely expanded the functions of the legislative councils. These concerned discussions on the budget (The Annual Financial statement), discussion on any matter of general public interest and thirdly the power of asking questions. The Act also increased the number of Executive Councilors the three major Presidencies - Bombay, Madras and Bengal, Indians were now appointed as members of the Secretary of States' Council (1907) and members of the Governor-Generals' Council (1909). Some other important features of the Act of 1909 included: right of separate electorate to the Muslims; the Secretary of the state for India was empowered to increase the number of the Executive 43ouncils of Madras and Bombay from two to four; two Indians were nominated to the Council of the Secretary of state for Indian affairs; and empowering Governor-General to nominate one Indian Member to his Executive Council.

Q6. Explain the role of council of ministers.
Refer to Chapter-2, Q.No.-3

Q7. Describe the structure and functions of central secretariat.
Refer to Chapter-2, Q.No.-6

Q8. Discuss the Powers of chief ministers in relation to council of minister and governor.
Refer to Chapter-3, Q.No.-6

Q9. Discuss the main features of Seventy fourth (74th) Constitutional Amendment Act, 1992.
Refer to Chapter-4, Q.No.-13 (3)

Q10. Analyse the features of social structures and its impact on administration.
Refer to Chapter-5, Q.No.-1

Q11. Examine the advantage and disadvantages of Administrative Tribunals.
Refer to Chapter-5, Q.No.-5

Q12. Briefly discuss the administrative reforms in India since independence.
Refer to December-2008, Q.No.-16

SECTION III

Answer any two of the following questions in about 100 words each. Each question carries 6 marks.

Q13. Write a note on the functions of Union Public Service Commission.
Refer to Chapter-2, Q.No.-16

Q14. Discuss briefly the three-time structure of Panchayti Raj.
Refer to Chapter-4, Q.No.-17

Q15. Describe the functions of Central Vigilance Commission (CVC).
Refer to Chapter-5, Q.No.-3 (i)

Q16. Outline the areas of cooperation between Political and Permanent Executives.
Refer to December-2008, Q.No.-16

SECTION – I

**Answer any two of the following questions in about 500 words each.
Each question carries 20 marks.**
Q1. Discuss the Revenue the Justice administration in Moghul period.
Refer to Chapter-1, Q.No.-4 & Q.No.-5

**Q2. Explain the emerging patterns of relationship between the secretariat
and Directorates.**
Refer to December-2008, Q.No.-2

Q3. Discuss the issues confronting police administration.
Refer to Chapter-4, Q.No.-11

**Q4. Highlight the important devices for securing centre – state
cooperation.**
Refer to Chapter-6

SECTION – II

**Answer any four of the following questions in about 250 words each.
Each question carries 12 marks.**
Q5. Discuss the features of Montague Chelmsford reforms.
Refer to Chapter-1, Q.No.-12

Q6. Highlight the basic features of Indian constitutions.
Refer to Chapter-2, Q.No.-1

**Q7. Explain the relationship between the Executive agencies and the
Secretariat.**
Refer to December-2008, Q.No.-7

**Q8. Discuss the factors responsible for the emergence of strong central
government.**
Refer to Chapter-3

**Q9. Write a note on the powers and functions of Panchayati Raj
institutions.**
Refer to Chapter-4, Q.No.-17

Q10. Highlight the cultural context of Indian administration.
Refer to Chapter-5, Q.No.-2

Q11. Explain the centre – state financial relations.
Refer to Chapter-6, Q.No.-2

Q12. Examine the limitations of judicial control over administration.
Refer to December-2008, Q.No.-11

SECTION - III
Answer any two of the following questions in about 100 words each. Each question carries 6 marks.

Q13. Write a note on institutional channels of popular participation in rural and urban areas.
Refer to Chapter-4

Q14. Explain the type of pressure groups in India.
Refer to Chapter-6, Q.No.-11

Q15. Identify the problem areas in field administration.
Refer to Chapter-4, Q.No.-4

Q16. What are the common grievances of citizens against administration?
Ans. Some of the common grievances against administration may be listed as under:
i) Corruption: Demand and acceptance of bribery for doing or not doing things.
ii) Favouritism: Doing or not doing things for obliging people in power or people who matter.
iii) Nepotism: Helping the people of one's own kith or kin.
iv) Discourtesy: Use of abusive language or other types of misbehaviour.
v) Neglect of Duty: Not doing things that the law requires.
vi) Discrimination: Ignoring poor and uninfluential citizens' genuine complaints.
vii) Delay: Not doing things at the appropriate time.
viii) Maladministration: Inefficiency in achieving the targets.
ix) Inadequate Redressal Machinery: Failure to attend to public complaints against administration.

SECTION – I

Q1. Discuss the Revenue and Judicial administrations in Mughal Period?
Refer to Chapter-1, Q.No.-5 & Q.No-8

Q2. Discuss the role of the state council of Ministers and the Chief Minister?
Refer to Chapter-2, Q.No.-3 & Chapter-3, Q.No.-6

Q3. Describe the components and administrative organizations at the district level?
Ans. Refer June 2008, Q.No.-9; and

Administrative Organization: The wide variety of functions undertaken at the district level result in a complex administrative system. Apart from the office of the District Collector, there are several departments namely, Agriculture, Animal Husbandry, Irrigation, Cooperatives, Social Welfare, Education, Civil Supplies, Medical and Public Health, Industries etc. in the district. Collectively all these departments constitute the district administration. Every State level department has corresponding functional department at the district level. Various departments in the districts are structured separately. The revenue department comprises various officials - The Collector at the district level, Deputy Collector at the sub-division, Tahsildar at the Taluk, Revenue Inspector at the circle and Village Officers like Patwari at the village level. The Superintendent of Police, Deputy Superintendent of Police, Inspector, Sub-inspector, and the Constable work at various level Is as field functionaries. Similarly, there are the department officers of Health, Education, Agriculture, Co-operation, etc. In many cases their jurisdiction is coterminous with a district, but increasingly there is more than one district level officer for each district. The Panchayati Raj Institutions have a hierarchy of officials, some of whom have been integrated with development departments at Block and Village level. While working in the same district each department maintains a distinct identity of its own like their State counterparts. Despite task differentiation and maintaining distinct identity there is a certain degree of task sharing between the departments.

Q4. Examine the Administrative reforms in India since independence?
Refer to Chapter-6, Q.No.-16.

SECTION – II

Q5. Discuss the regulating Act of 1733.
Refer to Chapter-1, Q.No.-6

Q6. Briefly examine the basic features of the constitutions.
Refer to Chapter-2, Q.No.-1

Q7. Discuss the structure of Panchayati Raj institutions in the light of 73rd constitutional Amendment Act, 1992.
Refer to the Chapter-4, Q.No.-17

Q8. Highlight the impact of culture on Administration.
Refer to Chapter-5, Q.No.-2

Q9. Examine the role of Chief secretary in State Secretariat System.
Refer to Chapter-3, Q.No.-9

Q 10. Describe the functions of Union Public Service Commission.
Refer to Chapter-2, Q.No.-16

Q11. Discuss the role of collector in relation to Panchayati Raj institutions.
Refer to Chapter-4, Q.No.-6

Q12. Examine the role of Planning Commission.
Refer to Chapter-2, Q.No-20.

SECTION – III

Q13. Write a note on forms of Judicial control over administrations.
Refer to Chapter-5, Q.No.-7

Q14. Briefly discuss the role of Divisional Commissioner.
Refer to Chapter-4, Q.No.-2

Q15. Write a note on Central Secretariat.
Refer to Chapter-2, Q.No.-5

Q16. Discuss briefly the main features of 74th Constitutional Amendment Act,1922.
Refer to Chapter-4, Q.No.-13

SECTION – I

Answer any two of the following questions in about 500 words each. Each question carries 20 marks:

Q1. Discuss the Evolution and functions of the central secretariat.

Q2. Discuss the meaning of Regional Administration and also state the rationale behind it.

Q3. Examine the various facets of the centre state administrative relations.

Q4. Describe the organization of Police administrations at central and state level.

SECTION – II

Answer any four of the following questions in about 250 words each. Each question carries 12 marks.

Q5. Discuss the role of Governor in state administration.

Q6. Write a note on the constitutional commissions.

Q7. Discuss the various approaches to the concept of decentralization.

Q8. Highlight the major characteristics of Mughul Administration.

Q9. Examine the need and importance of All India service.

Q10. Describe the impact of social institutions on administration.

Q11. Discuss the impact of the relationship between generalists and specialists on administration.

Q12. Examine the machinery for redressal of citizen's grievances.

SECTION – III

Answer any two of the following questions in about 100 words each. Each question carries 6 marks.

Q13. Write a note on the 'Evolution of Public Service Commission,' in India.

Q14. Discuss the functions of cabinet committee.

Q15. Examine briefly the factors shaping the secretariat – Directorate relationship.

Q16. Write a note on Administrative reforms.

> **To be of real I have to be gentle and comprehend without interfering or creating dependence**
>
> Brahma Kumaris

SECTION – I

Q1. Discuss briefly the structure and characteristics of Mughal administration.
Refer to Chapter-1, Q.No.-2 and Q.No.-5

Q2. Write a note on the Regulating Act of 1773.
Refer to Chapter-1, Q.No.-6

Q3. Highlight the basic features of the Indian Constitution.
Refer to Chapter-2, Q.No.-1

Q4. 'The exercise of discretionary powers by the Governor has made his office the most controversial office of the country'. Discuss.
Refer to Chapter-3, Q.No.-2

SECTION – II

Answer any four of the following questions:
Q5. Discuss the Pitt's India Act of 1784.
Refer chapter -1, Q.No.-7

Q6. Examine the functions and limitations of Union Public Service Commission.
Refer to Chapter-2, Q.No.-16

Q7. Describe the role of Council of Ministers at the State level.
Refer to Chapter-3, Q.No.-4

Q8. Trace the historical evolution, need and importance of the All India services.
Ans. Need For All India Services
Commenting on the need for the setting up of all India Services, in a speech before the Constituent Assembly, B.R. Ambedkar, the Chairman of the Constitution -Drafting Committee, said: "It is recognized that in every country there are Certain- posts in its administrative getup which might be called strategic from the point of view of maintaining the standard of administration. There can be no doubt that the standard of administration depends upon the caliber of the civil Servants who are appointed to these posts. The Constitution provides that, there shall be All India Services, the members of which alone could be appointed to these strategic posts throughout the Union." Ambedkar, thus, emphasized the Contribution such a Service could make in bringing about greater efficiency in the administration of the Union as well as the States.

Secondly, there are others who Emphasized the cohesive aspect of such Services, which, it is claimed, will ensure the uniformity of the administrative system throughout the country, We, in India, are fortunate enough to be able to carry out, if we will, that experiment in large Measure, thus, providing an effective check to fissiparous tendencies and secure for its recruits attractions which no other Services can have. In the fifth place, since the responsibility for the administration of a Stare, in the event of the breakdown of the normal constitutional machinery, is vested in the President, the existence in the State of a certain number of officers of all 1ndia Services occupying key posts in the administration will certainly be helpful to him. He can count more on the Cooperation of officers, who, in the last analysis, are Union Government's Employees, than on the officers of the State Government proper.

Q9. Discuss the issues confronting the Police administration.
Refer to Chapter-4, Q.No.-11

Q10. Briefly explain the powers and functions of Panchayati Raj Institutions.
Refer to Chapter-4, Q.No.-6

Q11. Explain the advantages and disadvantages of Administrative tribunals.
Refer to Chapter-5, Q.No.-1

Q12. Discuss the division of Administrative powers between the Center and the State as power Constitution provisions.
Refer to Chapter-6, Q.No-1

SECTION – III
Answer any two of the following questions:
Q13. Discuss the importance of National Development Council in relation to formulation of five year plans.
Refer to Chapter-2, Q.No.-21

Q14. Describe the main function performed by the Chief Secretary.
Refer to Chapter-3, Q.No.-9

Q15. Enumerate the type of pressure groups prevalent in India.
Refer to Chapter-6, Q.No.-8

Q16. Briefly describe the importance of field administration in India.
Refer to June-2010, Q.No.-3

SECTION – I

Answer any two of the following questions in about 500 words each. Each question carries 20 marks.

Q1. Discuss the system of Revenue administration during the British rule.

Q2. 'The Montague Chelmsford Reforms 1919 were considered as the preamble of the Government of India Act 1919'. Examine.

Q3. Trace the evolution of the cabinet secretariat and highlight it's functions.

Q4. Examine the emerging patterns of relationship between the Secretariat and Directorates.

SECTION – II

Answer any four of the following questions in about 250 words each. Each question carries 12 marks.

Q5. Explain briefly the features of Regulating Act of 1773.

Q6. Describe the organization and role of planning commission.

Q7. Discuss the tools of Legislative control over administration in India.

Q8. Examine the role of District Collector in India.

Q9. Explain the importance of the 74th constitutional Amendment Act, 1992.

Q10. Discuss the broad features of social structures and explain their impact on administration.

Q11. Highlight the position and role of State secretariat in State Administration.

Q12. Briefly discuss the Administrative reforms in India Since Independence.

SECTION – III

Answer any two of the following questions in about 100 words each. Each question carries 6 marks.

Q13. Discuss the functions of the Divisional Commissioner in State Administratives.

Q14. Highlight the main advantages of Administration Tribunals.

Q15. Distinguish between the principles of Neutrality and Anonymity.

Q16. Write a note on relationship between Generalists and Specialists.

SECTION – I

Answer any two of the following questions in about 500 words each. Each question carries 20 marks.

Q1. Distinguish between the Mauryan and Mughal administration.

Q2. Describe the basic features of Indian constitution.

Q3. Discuss the significance and role of field administration.

Q4. Explain the features of social structures and their impact on administration.

SECTION – II

Answer any four of the following question in about 250 words each. Each question carries 12 marks.

Q5. Write a note on the Indian Councils Act, 1892.

Q6. Describe the role of Council of Ministers at the State level.

Q7. Briefly explain the powers and functions of Panchayati Raj Institutions in the light of 73rd Constitutional Amendment Act, 1992.

Q8. Explain the advantages and disadvantages of Administrative Tribunals.

Q9. Discuss the issues confronting Police Administrations.

Q10. Explain the provisions underlying the financial relations between the Union and the state.

Q11. Briefly explain the scope and forms of Judicial control over administration.

Q12. Describe the reform measures undertaken by government since Independence.

SECTION – III

Answer any two of the following questions in about 100 words each. Each question carries 6 marks.

Q13. Write a note on the National Commission for Scheduled Castes.

Q14. Enumerate the financial resources of urban local bodies.

Q15. Describe the characteristics of Pressure groups in India.

Q16. Explain the functions of Central Secretariat.

SECTION – I

Answer any two of the following questions in about 500 words each. Each question carries 20 marks.

Q1. Explain the structures and characteristics of the Mughal administrative system.

Q2. Briefly describe the role of various constitutional commissions.

Q3. Discuss the role of the Governor in the state administrations.

Q4. Explain the role of Municipal bodies as per the 74th constitutional Amendment Act, 1992.

SECTION-II

Answer any four of the following questions in about 250 words each. Each questions carries 12 marks.

Q5. Write a brief note on continuity and change in Indian Administration.

Q6. Explain the role of the Prime Minister's Office (PMO).

Q7. Enumerate the emerging patterns of relationship between the Secretariat the Directorates.

Q8. Describe briefly the functions of the District Collector.

Q9. "The Legislature also acts as an instrument of popular control over administration." Elucidate.

Q10. What was the need of All India Services and how did they evolve?

Q11. Discuss the cultural context of Indian Administrations.

Q12. Explain the various types of devices for securing centre-state cooperation.

SECTION – III

Answer any two of the following questions in about 100 words each. Each question carries 6 marks.

Q13. Write a note on the Government of India Act, 1935.

Q14. Discuss the genesis of planning in India.

Q15. Explain briefly the issues confronting police administrations.

Q16. Highlight the common grievances against administrations.

SECTION – I

Answer any two of the following questions in about 500 words. Each question carries 20 marks.

Q1. Discuss the basic features of Indian Constitution.

Q2. 'Evolution of Union Public Service Commission has passed through three primary phases since 1926'. Explain.

Q3. Discuss the status-quo, Bridging-The-Gulf and Amalgamation Approaches to the relationship between the Secretariat and Directorates.

Q4. Explain the meaning and characteristics of Pressure Groups.

SECTION – II

Answer any four of the following questions in about 250 words each. Each question carries 12 marks.

Q5. Write a note on the structure of Moghul Administrative System.

Q6. Discuss the meaning, need and genesis of planning in India.

Q7. 'Powers of the State Government are enshrined in the state and concurrent lists'. Comment.

Q8. Examine the arguments for and against Divisional Commissionership.

Q9. What are the different types of Administrative Tribunals?

Q10. Bring out the relationship between generalists and specialists.

Q11. Explain the nature of Centre-State Financial Relations.

Q12. Examine the principles governing the relationship between political and permanent executives.

SECTION – III

Answer any two of the following questions in about 100 words each. Each question carries 6 marks.

Q13. Write a note on Morley-Minto Reforms 1909.

Q14. Describe the structure of Panchayati Raj Institutions.

Q15. What are the different modes of corruption?

Q16. Explain the limitations of judicial control over administration.

SECTION – I

Answer any two of the following questions in about 500 words each. Each question carries 20 marks.

Q1. Examine the role of National Commission for scheduled castes and National Commission for scheduled tribes in India.

Q2. Trace the evolution, organisation and functions of Cabinet Secretariat in India.

Q3. Describe the organisation of Police at the State, District and Sub-district levels.

Q4. 'There is a clear constitutional division of administrative powers between the centre and the states'. Elaborate.

SECTION – II

Answer any four of the following questions in about 250 words each. Each question carries 12 marks.

Q5. Explain the nature of revenue administration at the advent of British rule in India?

Q6. Trace the evolution of Central Secretariat in India.

Q7. Explain the different functions of Union Public Service Commission.

Q8. 'Recruitment to All India Services follows a methodical procedure'. Discuss.

Q9. Elucidate the role of Chief Minister at the State Level.

Q10. Write a note on Regional Administration.

Q11. The effectiveness of judicial control over administration is limited by many factors. Comment.

Q12. Discuss the advantages and disadvantages of administrative tribunals.

SECTION – III

Answer any two of the following questions in about 100 words each. Each question carries 6 marks.

Q13. Write a note on Pitt's India Act 1784.

Q14. Discuss the structure of the Public Services at the time of Independence.

Q15. What are the common grievances against administration?

Q16. Highlight the different types of pressure groups.

SECTION – I

Answer any two of the following questions in about 500 words each. Each question carries 20 marks.

Q1. Discuss the major characteristics of the Mauryan and Gupta administrative systems.

Q2. Briefly describe the basic features of our Constitution.

Q3. Explain the inter-relationship between society and administration.

Q4. Discuss the division of administrative powers between the Centre and States.

SECTION – II

Answer any four of the following questions in about 250 words each. Each question carries 12 marks.

Q5. Highlight the important landmarks in the British East India Company administration.

Q6. Briefly describe the role of various Constitutional Commissions.

Q7. Explain the importance and need of the All India Services.

Q8. Discuss briefly the powers and functions of State Council of Ministers.

Q9. Examine the role of Divisional Commissioner.

Q10. Write a note on issues confronting police administration.

Q11. Explain the reasons for the growth of administrative tribunals.

Q12. Discuss the scope and the methods of judicial control over administration.

SECTION – III

Answer any two of the following questions in about 100 words each. Each question carries 6 marks.

Q13. Write a note on revenue administration in Mughal Period.

Q14. Explain briefly the advisory role of Union Public Service Commission.

Q15. Trace the evolution of the office of Collector.

Q16. Discuss the relationship between political and permanent executives.

SECTION – I

Answer any two of the following questions in about 500 words each. Each question carries 20 marks.

Q1. Describe the revenue administration in Mughal Period.

Q2. Elaborate the structure and functions of Secretariat.

Q3. Discuss the role of Governor in the State administration.

Q4. Explain the role of Panchayati Raj bodies as per the 73rd Constitutional Amendment Act, 1992.

SECTION – II

Answer any four of the following questions in about 250 words each. Each question carries 12 marks.

Q5. Discuss the characteristic features of the East India Company.

Q6. Write a note on continuity and change in Indian administration.

Q7. Discuss the evolution and role of Prime Minister's Office.

Q8. Enumerate the emerging patterns of relationship between the Secretariat and Directorate.

Q9. Explain briefly the role of municipal bodies as per the 74th Constitutional Amendment Act, 1992.

Q10. Highlight the features of social structures and its impact on administration.

Q11. Describe various forms of judicial control over administration.

Q12. Explain the various types of devices for securing Centre-State Cooperation.

SECTION – III

Answer any two of the following questions in about 100 words each. Each question carries 6 marks.

Q13. Discuss Morley Minto reforms 1909.

Q14. Write a note on independence of judiciary.

Q15. Describe the characteristics of pressure groups.

Q16. Highlight the grievances against administration.

SECTION – I

Answer any two of the following questions in about 500 words each. Each question carries 20 marks.

Q1. Write a note on Indian Councils Acts, 1861 and 1892.

Q2. "Constitutional Commissions provide teeth to the provisions enshrined in the Constitution." Elucidate.

Q3. Discuss the evolution of Cabinet Secretariat in India.

Q4. Examine the role of the Governor in India.

SECTION – II

Answer any four of the following questions in about 250 words each. Each question carries 12 marks.

Q5. Explain the pattern of Revenue Administration at the Supra-District level.

Q6. Write a note on emerging patterns of relationship between the Secretariat and the Directorates.

Q7. Discuss the nature of regional administration in India.

Q8. Describe the organisation of Police at Central, State and Range levels.

Q9. Elucidate the powers and functions of Panchayati Raj Institutions under the 73rd Constitutional Amendment.

Q10. "There is a strong relationship between Culture and Administration." Discuss.

Q11. Explain the role of vigilance machinery in the State and Districts.

Q12. Discuss the different types of Administrative Tribunals.

SECTION – III

Answer any two of the following questions in about 100 words each. Each question carries 6 marks.

Q13. What are the Constitutional Authorities in India?

Q14. Explain the changing role of the Prime Minister's office.

Q15. Write a note on the relationship between District Collector and Panchayati Raj Institutions.

Q16. Explain the features of Tenure System.

Note: Answer the questions as per the instructions given in each section.

SECTION – I

Answer any two of the following question in about 500 words each. Each question carries 20 marks.

Q1. "British rule in India depended on administration of Land Revenue". Elaborate.

Q2. Explain the relationship between Secretariat department and Executive department at the State level.

Q3. Critically examine the role and relevance of the office of Divisional Commissioner in India.

Q4. Explain the organisation of police at the state, range, district and sub-district levels.

SECTION – II

Answer any four of the following questions in about 250 words each. Each question carries 12 marks.

Q5. Write a note on classification of State Civil Services.

Q6. Describe the features of Seventy-fourth Constitutional Amendment.

Q7. Explain the different types of extraordinary remedies available to citizens in India.

Q8. Discuss the approaches to the concept of Decentralisation.

Q9. "Pressure groups in India differ in their constitution and objectives." Comment.

Q10. Describe the recommendations of Sarkaria Commission on Centre-State relations.

Q11. What are the limitations of judicial control over administration?

Q12. Examine the main features of social structures and their impact on administration.

SECTION – III

Answer any two of the following question in about 100 words each. Each question carries 6 marks.

Q13. Write a note on evolution of the office of Collector.

Q14. What are the problem areas in Field Administration?

Q15. Discuss the composition and functions of the Board of Revenue.

Q16. What is the pattern of Departmentalisation in State Secretariat?

SECTION – I

Answer any two of the following questions in about 500 words each. Each question carries 20 marks.

Q1. Discuss the areas of cooperation and conflict between political and permanent executives.

Refer to Chapter-6, Q.No.-7

Q2. Trace the genesis of Panchayati Raj System and evaluate its performance.

Ans. Gandhi, who led non-violent struggle for independence observed, 'my idea of village swaraj is that it is a complete republic independent of its neighbors for its own vital wants and yet, interdependent for many others in which dependence is a necessity'. Gandhi's ideas had pervading effect, which was reflected in the Constituent Assembly debates. The draft of the Constitution did not make any referen nomic and social development. After considerable debate and discussions, Article 40 was incorporated in the chapter on the Directive Principles of State Policy. This Article calls upon the State 'to take steps to organise village panchayats and endow them with such power and authority as may be necessary to enable them to function as units of self-Government'.

Community Development Programme was initiated in the country in October 1952. Development Blocks were established with limited staff and funds. The aim was coordinated development of the area with the help of an extension organisation consisting of technical specialists working under the leadership of Block Development Officer. At the grass-roots level, there were multipurpose workers. The finances were made available on the basis of matching contribution from the community. The intention was to use limited Government funds to stimulate action for self-help.

Advisory committees were constituted for every block for advice on the allocation of funds for development programmes. To review the working of the Community Development Programme, the Committee on Plan Projects constituted a team to study the programme and to report on the content and priorities of the programme to ensure greater efficiency in their execution. The Panchayati Raj in India is broadly based upon the recommendations of a committee popularly known as Balwantrai Mehta Committee named after its Chairman. The Committee believed that 'so long as we do not discover or create representative and democratic institutions and endow them with adequate power and finance, it is difficult to evoke local interest and excite local initiative in the field of development'. With this basic premise, the team made a large number of recommendations, which formed the basis for the establishment of three-tier structure of Panchayati Raj in the country.

Most of the State Governments had accepted the recommendations of the Balwantrai Mehta Committee, and Panchayati Raj Institutions were established. Both the Central and State Governments have appointed several committees and commissions for reviewing and recommending reforms to strengthen Panchayati Raj. The Committee of Panchayati Raj appointed by the Central Government under the chairmanship of Shri Asoka Mehta in 1978, is very important as it reviewed the system of Panchayati Raj in different States.

Evaluation of Panchayati Raj System

Panchayati Raj has/had its ups and downs. It has passed through the phases of ascendance, stagnation and decline. Protagonists argue that Panchayati Raj has become a democratic seed drilling by making the people conscious of their rights. It has bridged the gap between the bureaucracy and the people. It has also generated a new leadership, which is young, forward looking and modernistic. It has even cultivated a development psyche among the people. It has played a positive role in initiating and implementing the development programmes. At many places, political base has been used to provide the needed impetus to implement development programmes. It has opened a new type of leadership in the rural areas. These leaders trained in the art of democratic institutions have climbed the ladder and have become political executives at the higher echelons of democratic institutions.

The Acts creating Panchayati Raj Institutions have no doubt specified the power and functions of each of the tiers of Panchayati Raj. They were expected to formulate plans based on local needs and implement them. But unfortunately, local bodies began formulating plans in a mechanical and routine way without taking into consideration the local requirements. One reason attributed to this is the narrow resource base of the Panchayati Raj Institutions, which does not enable them to take all the local needs, and plan for their fulfillment. Asoka Mehta Committee went to the extent of commenting that the attitude of political elite at the higher level was lukewarm towards strengthening Panchayati Raj. This led to half-hearted approaches on the part of the Government to transfer power and responsibilities to the Panchayati Raj bodies. But a major criticism is that the leadership is drawn from a narrow social base. It is alleged that the majority of them come from dominant land owning castes and classes. Asoka Mehta Committee has noted in this context that the Panchayati Raj Institutions are dominated by economically and socially Privileged section of the society and as such has facilitated the emergence of oligarchic forces yielding no benefits to weaker sections.

Coordination is sine-qua-non for efficient administration of development programmes. Unfortunately, it appears to be one of the serious problems facing Panchayati Raj. The dual control over extension officers, absence of total integration of development departments and Panchayati Raj Institutions are some of the reasons attributed for the failure of coordination. Emphasis is on cumbersome administrative procedures, which affect the initiative and hamper the process of implementation. There appears to be more emphasis on rule mindedness than on roles to be performed. This has resulted in delays in the execution of development programmes. Red tape is dampening the initiative of people's representatives as well.

Identification of officials with the goals of the organisation is a pre-condition for the successful working of any programme. In Panchayati Raj Institutions, as we have noted, there are several officials coming from different Departments, their divided loyalties between Panchayati Raj and parent Departments also comes in the way of total identification of the officials with the goals and objectives of the Panchayati Raj Institutions.

Panchayati Raj Institutions, particularly, at the grass-roots level, concentrate on civic amenities than extension work. There appears to be enthusiasm in the construction of school buildings than running the schools effectively. Though civic amenities and infrastructure are important, extension cannot be totally ignored. Another problem area is that the welfare or weaker sections, which either for want of commitment or for wants of resources, does not seem to have received proper attention by the Panchayati Raj Institutions.

Panchayati Raj notwithstanding these limitations has provided the needed impetus in democratising rural-local institutions. It has generated interest and enthusiasm among the rural people. This enthusiasm unfortunately is not matched by support from the higher levels and is not supplemented by matching resources.

Q3. Describe the role of Governor in state administration.
Refer to Chapter-3, Q.No.-2

Q4. 'The office of the collector is an important institution transmitted by British rulers to Indian administrative system'. Examine.
Refer to Chapter-4, Q.No.-5

SECTION – II

Answer any four of the following questions in about 250 words each. Each question carries 12 marks.
Q5. Highlight the major characteristics of Mughal Administration.
Refer to Chapter-1, Q.No.-2

Q6. Discuss the changing role and functions of the Prime Minister's Office.
Refer to Chapter-2, Q.No.-10 and Q.No.-11

Q7. Discuss the principal functions of the Chief Secretary.
Refer to Chapter-3, Q.No.-9

Q8. Examine the patterns of relationship between the Secretariat and Directorates.
Ans. There are three possible pattern of relationship between the Secretariat and Directorates. Each adopts a different approach.
(i) The Status-quo 4pproach,
(ii) The Bridging-the-gulf Approach, and
(iii) The De-amalgamation Approach.
Now, Refer to Chapter-3, Q.No.-14

Q9. Explain the need and significance of village policing.
Ans. Maintenance of peace and tranquility is essential not only for the development of villages but also for national development. Village policing has been in existence for over centuries. In some form or other it consisted of Village Patel, Village Headman and the Village Chowkidar. In most of the states, they are hereditary functionaries. The responsibility for drawing the attention of police to any matter of importance in the villages vests in these functionaries. They are also responsible for preventing crime in the village. The 1902 Police Commission emphasised that they should function as servants of the village community rather than as subordinates to the regular police. The British Government recognized the need and importance of these hereditary village police officials. The same system, therefore, was allowed to continue. The same system continued even in independent India because of its historical roots, acceptability of the system to the community and its role in policing the village. Thus the system of Village Headman and Watchman prevailed in India before, during and after the British rule. These hereditary functionaries were given land as remuneration. They were also given some proportion of land revenue, collected at the village level. The village Headman was responsible to keep a watch on crime and criminals and report to the Police Station regularly. After independence, due to the emergence of democratic institutions at the grassroots level, the village functionaries moved increasingly towards development work. In some of the States, they are either wholly or partially brought under the Panchayats. But the system in actual working was found to be deficient in several respects. The National Police Commission identified some of these deficiencies as lack of attention, absence of perception of their responsibilities for collecting information or for reporting, low pay, and excessive control of police.

To overcome some of these problems and deficiencies alternatives to the hereditary system were introduced in some States. The National Police Commission recommended that the existing Chowkidari system in the country should be retained with some changes to make it more effective. The suggested reforms include prescription of age limits and educational qualifications, proper pay, etc. The Commission also recommended constitution of village defence parties with one of the members being designated as Dalapathi. Thus, the National Police Commission envisaged that the Dalapathi, village defence party and the former chowkidar should constitute the village police set-up.

Q10. Highlight the implications of cultural factors on administrative process.
Refer to Chapter-5, Q.No.-2

Q11. Explain the impact of relationship between generalists and specialists on administration.
Ans. The system of administration in India which has largely been generalist dominated has been due to the impact of administrative philosophy of England during 19th century where generalists formed the basic principle of administration.

The issue of the relationship between the generalists and the specialists has come to the fore on account of various factors. In the first place, they are organised in separate hierarchies, i.e. groups having supervisor-subordinate relations between various levels. That is why, the generalists and the specialists have lost contact with each other, and they look to each other with a kind of envy and suspicion. In the second place, the tasks of policy-making, control of administrative machinery and management at highest levels are allotted largely to the generalists in preference to the specialists, excluding few exceptions. In the third place, generalists are moved from one department to another, from one type of job to another, from a department to a public enterprise or local government and back, without hindrance. The specialists, on the other hand, are transferred or promoted within their respective departments. These contrasting situations have given rise to a feeling among the generalists of being 'administrators' *per* se and *par* excellence, and an inferiority complex and a feeling of being neglected among the specialists. Posts of secretaries in the government departments, and-even of heads of most executive departments are reserved for the generalists. There are also salary differences in favour of the generalists. This privileged position of the generalists tends to offend the self-image of the specialists, and in result their morale and confidence.

The generalists and the specialists also function in the private sector industries and business. But their relations do not suffer from bitterness or envy, as in Public Administration. This is so because in private administration specialists like engineers, accountants also occupy managerial and executive positions.

In India, the members of the Indian Administrative Service(1AS) occupy higher posts in various departments both in the field and the secretariat except those which are too technical, i.e. specialists that are occupied by the members of the Central Services. Apart from the Central Services which are included among the specialist services, scientists, legalists, engineers, economists and other cadres are also termed specialists. The **IAS** incumbents like those in the Indian Police Service(1PS) and the Indian Forest Service are posted in the State administration as well as in the Central administration. But, strictly speaking, members of the Indian Police Service and the Indian Forest Service are not generalists; the IAS is really considered the only genuine generalist civil service in India. The members of the 1AS begin their career in a State administration as an assistant collector/commissioner and rise to hold headship of an executive department like agriculture, social welfare, sales tax, etc., and secretaryship of a department in the State secretariat. After a stint of 10 years or so in the State administration, some of the IAS civil servants are transferred to the Central Secretariat, and in some cases finally elevated to secretaryship of a department, ministry there. Some of these are again deputed at times to the Central public enterprises RS managing directors and/or Chairmen. But this trend is diminishing in recent times.

Specialists occupy different positions in their own departments in the field and the Secretariat, A few of them rise to the secretaryship of the respective department.

Q12. Write a note on Urban Local Self Government.
Ans. Self-governing institutions which manage local administration of cities and towns are called 'Urban Local Self-Government' bodies. Urban local self-government generally includes Municipal Corporations, Municipalities, Town Area Committees, Improvement Trusts, Notified Area Committees, Cantonment Boards and Port Trusts. Unlike rural local self-government bodies, urban local self-government in India is not hierarchical, that is to say that the lower units of the local bodies do not work under the control of the higher units.

Following the 74th Constitutional Amendment Act, 1992 Urban Local Self-Government in India has been classified into three types - Municipal Corporations, Municipalities and Nagar Panchayats. Under the 74th Constitutional Amendment a Nagar Panchayat shall be set up in such 'transitional areas'. Indeed, an urban area, irrespective of its size, needs a local Government for the provision of civic services and facilities such as water supply, garbage clearance, construction and maintenance of roads. These are some of the important services that an Urban Government has to provide to sustain civic life in an area. The Municipal Corporation, Municipal Council and Municipal Committee as per the size of the area provides these services.

(i) Municipal Corporations: Municipal Corporations are set up in bigger towns and cities having several lakhs of people, where civic problems are complex. A Municipal Corporation is set up under a statute passed by the State

Legislature, If the Corporation is located in the State concerned. It is set up by the Union Parliament if it is located in a Union Territory. A Corporation enjoys more powers than a Municipality.

(ii) Municipal Council: Every State in the country has enacted legislation for the constitution of the Municipalities in the State specifying their functions, structure, resource and their role in civic administration.

Urban areas having towns with population ranging from above 50,000 to 500,000 are governed by elected municipal bodies known as Municipal Councils. Any municipal area with 3,00,000 population must form Ward Committees to ensure true people's participation in the governance of the area.

(iii) Municipal Committee: Those urban areas which are undergoing transition and have a population of less than 50,000 people are governed by municipal or town committees, the members of which are elected by the resident citizens of the area concerned.

SECTION – III

Answer any two of the following questions in about 100 words each. Each question carries 6 marks.

Q13. Discuss the role of Central Vigilance Commission in dealing with Corruption.

Refer to Chapter-5, Q.No.-3 (i)

Q14. Highlight the various forms of judicial control over administration.

Ans. The forms and methods of judicial control over administration vary from country to country, depending upon the type of the constitution and the system of law. Broadly speaking, there are two systems of legal remedies against administrative encroachments on the rights of citizens. One is called the Rule of Law system and the other is called the Administrative Law system. The Rule of Law means that everybody, irrespective of social and cultural differences, whether an official or a private citizen is subject to the same law and the ordinary law of the land. The official cannot take shelter behind state sovereignty in committing mistakes in his official capacity. Some of the forms of judicial control over administration in India, under the Rule of Law system are as follows:

1. Judicial Review: Refer to Chpater-5, Q.No.-8(i)

2. Statutory Appeal: The statutes made by Parliament and State Assemblies itself provide that in a particular or to a higher administrative tribunal. Sometimes, legislative enactment itself may provide for judicial intervention in certain matters.

3. Suits Against the Government: There are several limitations, varying from country to country, as regards filing suits against the government for its contractual liability. The contractual liability of the Union and the State Governments is the same as that of an individual citizen under the ordinary law of contracts, subject however, to any statutory conditions of limits, which the Parliament can regulate under the constitution. The State is liable for the tortuous acts of its officials in respect of the non-sovereign functions only

4. Criminal and Civil Suits against Public Officials: Refer to Chapter-5, Q.No.-8(ii)

5. Extraordinary Remedies: Apart from the methods of judicial control, there are the extraordinary remedies in the nature of writs of Habeas Corpus, Mandamus, Prohibition, Certiorari and Quo Warranto. These are called extraordinary remedies because the courts grant these writs except the writ of Habeas Corpus, in their discretion and as a matter of right and that too when no other adequate remedy is available.

Now, Refer to Chapter-5, Q.No.-9

Q15. Briefly discuss the advantages of Administrative Tribunals.
Refer to Chapter-5, Q.No.-5

Q16. Write a note on Election Commission.
Refer to Chapter-2, Q.No.-4 (3)

Change your life today. Don't gamble on the future, act now, without delay.

Lighten up, just enjoy life, smile more, laugh more, and don't get so worked up about things.

SECTION – I

Answer any two of the following questions in about 500 words each. Each question carries 20 marks.

Q1. 'Planning Commission has been performing the role of an advisory body to the government'. Discuss.
Refer to Chapter-2, Q.No.-20

Q2. Examine the various facets of the centre-state administrative relations.
Refer to Chapter-6, Q.No.-1

Q3. 'The Secretariat department must be distinguished from Executive department'. Comment.
Ans. The Secretariat Department must be distinguished from the executive department. The Secretariat has the function of aiding, assisting and advising the political executive in arriving at policy choices. The heads of executive departments – who are in the main known as director (although other nomenclatures are also used to refer to them) – have the responsibility of implementing policies formulated by the political executive. Therefore, the secretaries assist in policy formulation whereas the directors' role lies in executing policy. Long ago, the Simon Commission had observed, that executive department is an administrative unit separate from the Secretariat, which reaches its apex, usually, in a single officer like the Inspector General of Police, or the Chief Conservator of Forests, outside the Secretariat altogether. Such a head of a department will usually be concerned principally with a single secretary to Government and a single minister of his orders and the funds which he has to spend.

Each secretariat department is in charge of a number of executive departments. This number varies over a wide range with some departments taking charge of a much larger number of executive heads than others. There is an average of 6 to 7 executive departments in relation to one secretariat department. However, it must be carefully noted that not all secretariat departments have executive departments attached to them. Some of the secretariat departments are engaged in advisory and controlling functions and therefore do not have executive departments reporting to them. Examples are Departments of Law, Finance, etc.

The Secretariat and executive departments organisationally express the policy formulation and policy execution processes involved in the functioning of the government; the two may be looked upon as extensions of the personality of the Council of Ministers. The former is a policy-making organ, the latter a policy executing organ.

The secretariat department is normally headed by a generalist civil servant (drawn from the IAS), the executive department by a specialist. The specialist (the head of the executive department) function under the supervision of the generalist (the secretary or the head of the secretariat department). This can be illustrated with some examples, Director of Agriculture, who is a specialist, in that he is trained in and holds a formal degree in agricultural sciences, would function under the supervision of the Secretary, Agriculture (a generalist, an IAS). The latter represents agriculture department at the secretariat level, whereas the Director of Agriculture represents agriculture department at the executive level. The director is the executive head of the agriculture department – the Directorate of Agriculture. Likewise, the home department in the Secretariat has the Director-general of Police as its executive head of the department. Similar correlation obtains between education secretary and education director, industries secretary and industries director, social welfare secretary and social welfare director, and so on.

Q4. Explain the structure of Urban Local Self-Government.
Refer to June 2016, Q.No.-12

SECTION – II

Answer any four of the following questions in about 250 words each. Each question carries 12 marks.
Q5. Discuss the impact of National Movement on administration reforms.

Ans. Following is the impact of National Movement on administrative reforms:
(1) The National Movement and Constitutional Reforms: While the British established a regular system of government in India from 1857 to 1947, the slow pace of constitutional experiments showed uneasy compromises, the British Statesmen were making with the exigencies in the Indian situation. The policy of apparent association, therefore, went had in hand with the policy of oppression, and constitutional advances were always barbed with restrictive conditions so that the core of executive bureaucratic responsibility would remain untouched. Such contradictions seem to be inevitable with imperialism because imperialism itself is incompatible with democratic theory and practices.

The Indian National movement organised itself in the Indian National Congress (1885). Initially influenced by the Western educated upper middle class, it aimed at securing reforms through peaceful and constitutional means. The British rulers also felt that this would remove misunderstanding about the intentions of the government and would save the empire. The moderates had faith in the British sense of justice and fair play.

Their aim was gradual reforms with constitutional means. The Congress programme tossed between extremists and liberals till it became a mass movement, in the real sense and demanded nothing short of 'Purna Swaraj'.

(2) Demands for Administrative Reforms: The early Congress quested the British Government to reform administration by making it broad based and representative. Various issues that rose during its early phase revealed that the National Congress was concerned with wider interests and larger sections of the people. It advocated reduction in expenditure on military and home departments and establishment of military colleges in India. On the economic side, it advocated repeal of cotton excise duties, reduction of salt duties, reduction in land revenue and opening of agricultural banks. It proposed changes in tenancy laws to help peasants. On the industrial side, it advocated establishment of technical and industrial educational institutions, revival of old industries and establishment of new ones, protective tariff for new industries and extension of irrigation work In Social and individual field, it promoted temperance, repeal of various laws, restricting individual liberty and appointment of Indians to higher posts. In the political field, it advocated the abolition of Indian Executive Council and reforms in the Legislative Councils established under the Indian Councils Act 1861, more powers to local bodies, reducing official interference in their functioning and removing restrictions on press.

Q6. Discuss the role of Chief Minister.
Refer to Chapter-3, Q.No.-6

Q7. Explain the major functions of UPSC.
Refer to Chapter-2, Q.No.-16

Q8. 'Collectors face many problems in performing their duties'. Elaborate.
Ans. The Collector has become an increasingly important functionary in district administration. Both in, the regulatory and development functions, he has a very important role to play. In the performance of his functions, he faces a number of problems and constraints, which inhibit his work. Problems like frequent transfers, increasing workload, political pressures, crisis

situations, and individual orientation of Collectors are a few which need to be examined in this context.

The Civil Servants need to have a tenure, which is long enough to understand the environment, establish constructive relationships, and to implement the development programmes. A well-accepted policy is to retain an officer in a particular place for a period of three to five years. Unfortunately, this policy does not seem to be the practice in case of the Collectors. A few studies, conducted on this issue indicate that there are too frequent transfers inhibiting the proper performance of the Collector's functions. For example, in Rajasthan, the average tenure of Collectors was 14.2 months, which is not conducive to attain development objectives. This indicates that they are dislocated before they acquaint themselves with the problems of the district. Some of the Collectors have tenure of less than four months, and there are very few Collectors who enjoy three years of tenure. This type of frequent transfers apart from having a negative influence on the Collector would adversely affect district development administration.

One complaint often made is that the Collector is over-worked. Though studies are few in this area. These studies revealed the varied nature of the workload of the District Collectors. An analysis of the work of Collectors in the former Bombay State indicates that the Collector spends 54 per cent of his time on correspondence, 26 per cent on tours, and the remaining 20 per cent on meeting the visitors, attending to protocol duties, attending meetings and hearing cases. In another study conducted by Jack Gillespie, it was shown that the Collectors spend 36 per cent of time on correspondence, 18 per cent on tours, 11 per cent on receiving visitors and the remaining time to other functions like attending meetings, protocol duties, job related social activities etc. It was also revealed that the Collectors spend on an average 70 hours a week for official functions. This means, about 10 hours everyday including Sundays and holidays. This indicates the amount of pressure on his time and the increasing workload on the Collectors. These activities leave them with hardly any time for reflection or concentration on development activities.

Crisis administration is another important and a necessary function of the Collector. The crises may include communal disturbances, floods and famines, dacoity, terrorism, accidents and campus disturbances. These type of crises demand the Collector's immediate intervention. This affects their normal functions and the immediate casualty is neglect of development functions.

Q9. Examine the administrative structure of Panchayati Raj Institutions.
Ans. The need for efficient and competent personnel in Panchayati Raj Institutions has been recognised from the beginning. Local Self-Government agencies have to implement several development programmes, which require technical personnel. They provide continuity in the policies and programmes of these bodies because the political executives change periodically. Competent personnel are also essential to ensure non-partisan and objective decision-making.

There are two categories of personnel in Panchayati Raj Institutions, one is the State cadre officials placed under the control of Panchayati Raj Institutions, viz. Block Development Officers (BDOs) and other technical officers from State Departments. Their environment, transfers, promotions and discipline rest with the State Government. The second is the constitution of separate Panchayati Raj cadre. It is found in Maharashtra, Gujarat, Andhra Pradesh and Rajasthan. Broadly in Panchayati Raj, two types of officers can be identified, viz. generalist and technical officers. Chief Executive Officer, BDOs, Village Level Workers (VLWs) come under generalist category. District technical officers like district level officers, and extension officers constitute the technical category. Another classification is State Cadre official and Local Cadre officials. Chief Executive Officer, BDOs, Technical Officers, Extension Officers, etc. belong to the State Cadre. They belong to one of the State level Departments. The State Government regulates their conditions of service. VLWs, school teachers and ministerial staff broadly constitute local cadre officials. They are appointed at the district level and are considered as employees of Panchayati Raj Institutions.

There is a large measure of uniformity in the staffing pattern in the Panchayati Raj Institutions in the country. At the village level there is a Secretary or an Executive Officer looking after the administrative work of the panchayat. The VLW is appointed for a group of villages. He is mainly a multi-purpose functionary concerned with development programmes in the villages under his jurisdiction. At the block level, BDO acts as a Chief Executive officer and co-ordinates the work of officers under him. Extension officers for each development activity are posted at the block level. They work under the administrative control of the BDO as well as the technical control of district level officers. This dual control has led to several problems at the block level. In Zilla Parishads, Chief Executive Officer or District Development Officer is the Head of the Zilla Parishad. District technical officers assist him in the development work.

There are a number of personnel problems as different categories of functionaries work in Panchayati Raj. They are selected by different agencies and their conditions of service and channels of promotion are different. Often their compatibility to the Panchayati Raj system is questioned. A number of State level officers are on deputation, they function as birds of passage without any commitment with the Panchayati Raj Institutions. Frequent transfer of officers, increasing volume of paper work, inadequate opportunities for growth and advancement are some of the problems, which are effecting the functioning of Panchayati Raj Institutions. The Panchayati Raj staff exhibit a lack of unified pattern, unsatisfactory conditions of service and lack of effective training programmes.

Q10. Highlight the role of police in prevention of crime and maintenance of public order.
Refer to Chapter-4, Q.No.-8

Q11. Discuss the advantages and disadvantages of Administrative Tribunals.

Refer to Chapter-5, Q.No.-5

Q12. Examine briefly the factors shaping Secretariat - Directorate relationship.

Ans. The Secretariat and the Directorate constitute two wheels of the governmental machinery. Unless they achieve a certain measure of coordination and cooperation, the ability of the machinery to deliver goods is hampered. Two sets of factors have played a dominant role in shaping the Secretariat-Directorate relationship at the state level. Of these, one concerns the functioning of the Secretariat at a practical plane. The second is concerned with the expansion that has lately come about in the Secretariat – its role, personnel, number of administrative units of which it is comprised, and so on. Of course, the two factors are closely inter-related; it is to facilitate academic understanding of the matter that these are being dealt with separately here. It may be noted, it is these very factors which – as they work themselves out – generate situations, which tend to build up tension in the Secretariat-Directorate relationship.

Factors Responsible for Expansion in the Secretariat

The foremost of these is the parliamentary system of government. The principle of legislative accountability - under which the minister is, inter alia, supposed to answer questions, concerning his department, on the floor of the house - has brought about centralisation of functions in the Secretariat. Also, easy access of ministers to their constituents generates pressures on ministers in regard to matters such as appointments, promotions, transfers, and so forth. Now, clearly, these are matters of executive nature. The ministerial desire to nurture his constituency (and therefore, respond to demands for appointments, etc.) results in the minister's involvement in executive matters. This is how the Secretariat, a policy making body, becomes involved, in the matters of policy execution.

The second factor, which has been responsible for a steady and substantial increase in the volume of work in the Secretariat is the governmental policy to develop the economy through planning and state intervention and a whole host of welfare functions with the government in recent years has assumed. Every effort at directing and administering the economy leads to increased volume of work in the government. Secretariat, in particular, has gained in stature and influence from this situation. The reason for this is that more important work as well as decisions commanding wide impact have devolved on the Secretariat.

Two factors account for this: First, the generalist secretaries are thought to possess a breadth of vision and a well-rounded experience, which comes from the varied job placements that an IAS officer is typically exposed to in the course of his career. In contrast, the head of the department is considered narrow in vision and too theoretical in approach. Secondly, the ministerial staff in the Secretariat is considered to be of a higher caliber as compared to that in the Attached Offices. The result is that the Secretariat attracts more business. Thirdly, as noted above, not an insignificant portion of growth in the Secretariat is due to its taking over numerous executive functions and multifarious unimportant tasks, which do not properly belong to it. Finally, some expansion is also due to the tendency of the bureaucracy to proliferate in any situation. The Secretariat is, thus, today encumbered with non-essential work and has become unwieldy and overstaffed.

SECTION – III

Answer any two of the following questions in about 100 words each. Each question carries 6 marks.

Q13. Discuss the modes of corruption in administration.

Ans. The Central Vigilance Commission has identified the following modes of corruption:

(1) Acceptance of substandard stores/works.

(2) Misappropriation of public money and stores.

(3) Borrowing of money from contractors/firms having official dealing with officers.

(4) Show of favours to contractors and firms.

(5) Possession of assets disproportionate to income.

(6) Purchase of immovable property without prior permission or intimation.

(7) Losses to the government by negligence or otherwise.

(8) Abuse of official position/powers.

(9) Production of forged certificate of age/birth/community.

(10) Irregularities in reservation of seats by rail and by air.

(11) Irregularities in grant of import and export licenses.

(12) Moral turpitude.

(13) Acceptance of gifts

Q14. 'Judicial control over administration has limitations'. Elaborate.
Refer to Chapter-5, Q.No.-10

Q15. Discuss the Mayor-in-Council system.
Ans. In view of the importance of the city, the Mayor who is first citizen of the city is a Political Head. he presides over the meetings of the Corporation and generally exercises limited administration control over the working of the

Municipal Corporation. General pattern in India is that the council elects the Mayor for a term of one year and he can be re-elected. Normally, the Mayors are ceremonial Heads without any executive authority. The rural-urban relationship committee, which went into the problem of power for the mayor did not favour any substantial increase. If the mayor is to be elected by the voters of the entire city enjoying five years term in Andhra Pradesh, there is a need to reconsider the age-old practice of keeping the mayor only as a figure Head with ceremonial functions and a short term of one year.

Q16. Write a note on National Commission for Scheduled Castes.
Refer to Chapter-2, Q.No.-4 (7)

SECTION – I

Answer any two of the following questions in about 500 words each. Each question carries 20 marks.

Q1. Discuss the features of Indian Constitution.
Refer to Chapter-2, Q.No.-1

Q2. Explain the role of the Governor in State administration.
Refer to Chapter-3, Q.No.-2

Q3. Examine the administrative relations between the Centre and States.
Refer to Chapter-6, Q.No.-1

Q4. Describe the organisation of police at the State, District and Sub-district levels.
Ans. At the State level, the Police Administration is more or less uniform throughout the country. The Chief Minister or Home Minister is largely responsible for policy and supervisory functions. The Home Department coordinates and supervises the Police Administration in the State. It acts as a link between Central and State Governments. But the Inspector General of Police (IGP) or the Director General of Police (DGP) who is the Head of the State Police undertakes the real work. His office is called the Office of the IGP/ DGP popularly called Chief Office. This office collects information and feeds it to the Government; advises political decision-makers like the cabinet and the ministers; supervises and controls line agencies. It organises training and acts as a clearinghouse of special police services. The IGP/DGP aids and advises the Government and exercises general supervision and control over the police department. He exercises administrative, personnel, and financial power. He provides leadership to the Police Administration in the State. He is assisted in his duties of IGP by the Deputy Inspector General of Police (DIGS) and Superintendents of Police (SPs) and other staff. They Head the specialised branches like intelligence department, crime branch, transport department, training, armed forces, general administration, law and order, etc.
Now, Refer to Chapter-4, Q.No.-10

SECTION – II

Answer any four of the following questions in about 250 words each. Each question carries 12 marks.

Q5. Discuss the inter-relationship between society and administration.
Refer to Chapter-5, Q.No.-1

Q6. Trace the evolution of Central Secretariat in India.
Refer to Chapter-2, Q.No.-5

Q7. Elucidate the role of Chief Minister.
Refer to Chapter-3, Q.No.-5

Q8. Write a note on regional administration.
Refer to Chapter-4, Q.No.-1

Q9. Examine the advantages and disadvantages of administrative tribunals.
Refer to Chapter-5, Q.No.-5

Q10. Elaborate the functions of The Union Public Service Commission (UPSC).
Refer to Chapter-2, Q.No.-16

Q11. Discuss briefly the institutions in India for dealing with corruption.
Refer to Chapter-5, Q.No.-3

Q12. Out line the areas of cooperation between political and permanent executives.
Refer to Chapter-6, Q.No.-6

SECTION – III

Answer any two of the following questions in about 100 words each. Each question carries 6 marks.

Q13. Discuss the major characteristics of the Mauryan and Gupta administrative systems.
Refer to Chapter-1, Q.No.-1

Q14. Write a note on the evolution of the office of District Collector.
Refer to June-2009, Q.No.-3

Q15. Explain the concept of Public Interest Litigation (PIL).
Refer to Chapter-5, Q.No.-11

Q16. Describe the need for administrative reforms.
Refer to Chapter-6, Q.No.-15

Note: Answer the questions as per the instructions given in each sections.

SECTION – I

Answer any two of the following questions in about 500 words each. Each question carries 20 marks.

Q1. Discuss the characteristics and structure of Moghul administrative system.
Refer to Chapter-1, Q.No.-2 & Q.No.-5

Q2. Briefly describe the basic features of our Constitution.
Refer to Chapter-2, Q.No.-1

Q3. 'Evolution of UPSC has passed through three important phases since 1926.' Elaborate.
Refer to Chapter-2, Q.No.-14

Q4. Examine the administrative reforms in India since Independence.
Refer to Chapter-6, Q.No.-16

SECTION – II

Answer any four of the following questions in about 250 words each. Each question carries 12 marks.

Q5. Discuss the provisions of the Morley-Minto Reforms.
Refer to June-2009, Q.No.-5

Q6. Explain the role of Council of Minister at union level.
Refer to Chapter-2, Q.No.-3

Q7. Discuss the main features of Seventy Third (73rd) Constitutional Amendment Act, 1992.
Refer to Chapter-4, Q.No.-13 (3)

Q8. Briefly describe the role of various Constitutional Commissions.
Refer to Chapter-2, Q.No.-4

Q9. Explain the historical development and need of All India Services.

Ans. Ever since the creation of the Indian Civil Service in the days of the East India Company there has always existed in India an All-India cadre of service The All-India cadres were introduced almost in all departments of the Central Government. These services were, however, not under the control of the Governor-General they were directly under the Secretary of State for India and his Council No All-India service officer could be dismissed from his service by any other authority than the Secretary of State-in-Council. An officer had a right of appeal to that body if he was adversely dealt with in important disciplinary matters. His salary, pension, etc. were not subject to the vote of any Indian legislature.

These elitist Services, unresponsive and unaccountable to public opinion, found it difficult to adjust themselves to the reform-era introducing every limited responsible government under the Government of India Act of 1919. The Lee Commission in 1924 recommended the abolition of certain all India Services, particularly those dealing with departments that had been 'transferred' to Indian hands under the Act of 1919 namely the Indian Educational Service, Indian Agricultural Service, Indian Veterinary Service and the Roads and Building Branch of the Indian Service of Engineers. It, however, recommended the retention of the Indian Civil Service, Indian Police, Indian Forest Service, Indian Medical Service and the Irrigation Branch of the Indian Service of Engineers. It also recommended the increasing Indianisation of these Services. The Commission further recommended that any British officer should be free to retire on a proportionate pension if at any time the department in which they were employed should be transferred to the control of responsible Indian ministers. These recommendations were implemented in practice.

Now, Refer to June-2011, Q.No.-8

Q10. Discuss the cultural context of Indian administration.
Refer to Chapter-5, Q.No.-2

Q11. Highlight the various forms of Judicial control over administration.
Refer to Chapter-5, Q.No.-8

Statutory Appeal
The statutes made by Parliament and State Assemblies itself provide that in a particular type of administrative action, 'the aggrieved party will have a right of appeal to the courts or to a higher administrative tribunal. Sometimes, legislative enactment itself may provide for judicial intervention in certain matters.

Suits Against the Government
There are several limitations, varying from country to country, as regards filing suits against the government for its contractual liability. The contractual liability of the Union and the State Governments is the same as that of an

individual citisen under the ordinary law of contracts, subject however, to any statutory conditions of limits, which the Parliament can regulate under the constitution. The State is liable for the tortuous acts of its officials in respect of the non-sovereign functions only.

Extraordinary Remedies

Apart from the methods of judicial control already discussed, there are the extraordinary remedies in the nature of writs of Habeas Corpus, Mandamus., Prohibition, Certiorari and Quo Warranto. These are called extraordinary remedies because the courts grant these writs except the writ of Habeas Corpus, in their discretion and as a matter of right and that too when no other adequate remedy is available.

Q12. Examine the important recommendations of the Sarkaria Commission.

Refer to June-2007, Q.No.-9

SECTION – III

Answer any two of the following questions in about 100 words each. Each question carries 6 marks.

Q13. Describe the characteristic features of the East India Company.

Ans. The East India Company, established on 31st December 1600, was a monopoly, mercantile Company, which was granted by the British crown the right-to trade in the eastern parts. A trading station, with a number of factors was called Factory. A settlement (number of factories) was under an Agent Factor was the term applied to an agent transacting business as a substitute for another in mercantile affairs. Employees were graded as apprentices, writers, factors and merchants.

Recruitment of officials, their nomenclature, terms and conditions of service were governed by rules and practices appropriate to commercial business. Generally, patronage was the method of recruitment and promotion in the services. Patronage was in the hands of the Proprietors or Directors of the Company.

In the early years of Company rules, officials were frequently moved around, from one district to another. They had no training on the job and learnt the hard way by trial and error. They were ignorant of the laws, customs and languages of the local people. Given very low salaries, the Company's servants were known to be corrupt.

Q14. Write a note on the Prime Minister's Office.

Refer to Chapter-2, Q.No.-11

Q15. Discuss briefly the discretionary power of the Governor.

Ans. Some discretionary powers are as follows:

• Governor can dissolve the legislative assembly if the chief minister advices him to do following a vote of no confidence. Now, it is up to the Governor what he/ she would like to do.

• Governor, on his/ her discretion can recommend the president about the failure of the constitutional machinery in the state.

• On his/ her discretion, the Governor can reserve a bill passed by the state legislature for president's assent.

• If there is NO political party with a clear cut majority in the assembly, Governor on his/ her discretion can appoint anybody as chief minister.

• Governor determines the amount payable by the Government of Assam, Meghalaya, Tripura and Mizoram to an autonomous Tribal District Council as royalty accruing from licenses for mineral exploration.

Q16. Explain the Institution of Lokayukta.
Refer to Chapter-5, Q.No.-3 (2)

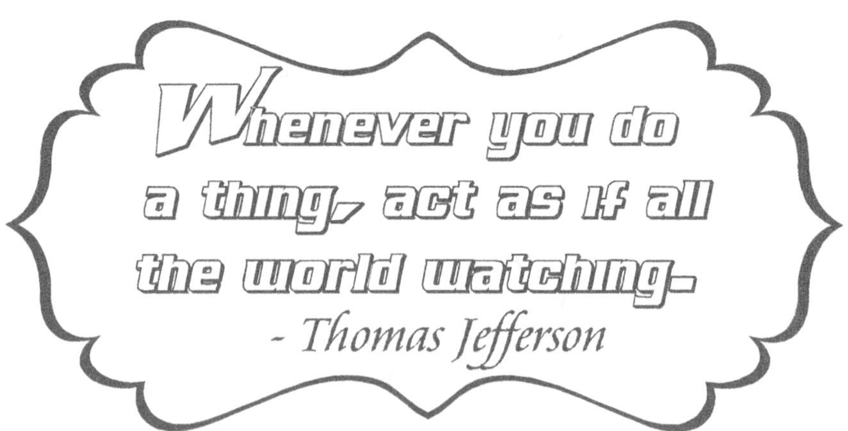

Note: Answer the questions as per the instructions given in each sections.

SECTION – I

Answer any two of the following questions in about 500 words each. Each question carries 20 marks.

Q1. Discuss the features and the changes brought by the Regulating Act of 1773.

Ans. The Regulating Act deserves special mention because it was the first action on the part of the British Government to regulate the affairs of the Company in India. The Company, through a Charter, had only been given trading rights by the British Crown. When it acquired territories in India and slowly but surely converted itself into a ruling body, the Parliament could not accept and regularise this development. Moreover, it was believed that whatever lands the Company acquired were in the name of and on behalf of the King. Therefore, the administration of these territories had to be controlled by the Crown.

Again, merchants and traders could hardly equal the task of administration. This was proved by the growing level of corruption and mismanagement of territorial acquisitions. While the shareholders of the Company were looking for bigger dividends because the Company was playing a double role of trading and ruling. the Company was making big losses and had to be bailed out. To tide over a critical period when finances were low because of Indian wars and growing demand for increased dividends, the Company asked the British Parliament for a loan of £ 1,400,000. This gave Parliament a long-awaited chance to assert its right to control the political affairs of the East India Company. They granted the loan on condition that administration in India would be according to directions of the British Parliament. Hence, the Regulating Act of 1773 was passed.

(1) Changes Introduced by the Regulating Act in England

The Court of Proprietors of the Company was reformed. Formerly, a shareholder, holding a stock of £ 500 and over, became a member of the Court of Proprietors. The Regulating Act raised it to the minimum to £ 1000. This made the Court of Proprietors a compact, better organised body to discharge both its duties and responsibilities.

Changes were also made in the Board of Directors. It was now to consist of 24 members elected by the Court of Proprietors every 4 years, 6 directors retiring every year– instead of all the Directors being elected every year as before. This gave the Board some continuity and facilitated better management.

(2) Changes Introduced by the Regulating Act in India

The Governor of Bengal was now designated as the Governor-General of Bengal and Governors of other provinces in India were subordinate to him. The Governor-General was to be assisted by a council of four members sent from England. Decisions were to be taken by majority vote and the Governor-General Warren Hastings had a casting vote. The British territories in India came to be controlled from Bengal and that in turn was subject to control from England.

The Regulating Act set up the Supreme Court at Calcutta with Lord Chief Justice and three judges. This was the Supreme Court of Judicature, the highest court in British India. It had power to exercise civil, criminal, admiralty and ecclesiastical jurisdiction. It had jurisdiction over British subjects and Company's servants. But its relations with the existing courts were not defined

(3) Effects of the Regulating Act

The changes in the Company's organisation in England made it more effective managing body at headquarters.

The Act created a centralised administration in India, making the Bombay and Madras Governors subordinate to the Governor-General of Bengal. There was a felt need for a uniform policy for the whole of British India, thus, avoiding much wasteful expenditure.

The creation of the Supreme Court made for better justice to British subjects. The Regulating Act brought in a system of checks and balances. It made the Governors subordinate to the Governor-General, the Governor-General subordinate to his Council and the Supreme Court effective in its control over the Governor-General in Council.

The Regulating Act laid the foundation of a Central administration and instituted a system of Parliamentary control. It marked the beginning of the Company's transformation from a trading body to a Corporation of a new kind, entirely administration in its object and subordinate to Parliament.

Q2. Examine the basic features of Indian Constitution.
Refer to Chapter-2, Q.No.-1

Q3. Describe the functions of the District Collector.
Refer to Chapter-4, Q.No.-5

Q4. Explain the various forms of judicial control over administration.
Refer to Dec-2017, Q.No.-11

SECTION – II

Answer any four of the following questions in about 250 words each. Each question carries 12 marks.

Q5. Bring out the important features of Montague-Chelmsford Reforms.
Refer to Chapter-1, Q.No.-12

Q6. Discuss the functions of the Union Public Service Commission.
Refer to Chapter-2, Q.No.-16

Q7. Elaborate the major functions of a State Chief Minister.
Refer to Chapter-3, Q.No.-5

Q8. Analyse the problem areas in field administration.
Refer to Chapter-4, Q.No.-4

Q9. Discuss the powers and functions of panchayati raj institutions.
Refer to Chapter-4, Q.No.-17

Q10. Examine the impact of culture on administration.
Refer to Chapter-5, Q.No.-2

Q11. Write a note on the types of administrative tribunals.
Refer to Chapter-5, Q.No.-4 & Refer to June-2008, Q.No.-10

Q12. Discuss the different forms of pressure groups in India.
Refer to Chapter-6, Q.No.-11

SECTION – III

Answer any two of the following questions in about 100 words each. Each question carries 6 marks.

Q13. What are the functions of central secretariat?
Refer to Chapter-2, Q.No.-6

Q14. Bring out the constitutional safeguards relating to the independence of State Public Service Commission.
Refer to Chapter-3, Q.No.-16

Q15. Explain the role of urban development authorities.
Refer to Chapter-4, Q.No.-14

Q16. List the types of Administrative reforms.
Refer to Chapter-6, Q.No.-16

Note: Answer the questions as per the instructions given in each sections.

SECTION - I

Answer any two of the following questions in about 500 words each. Each question carries 20 marks.

Q1. Discuss the key features of Montague-Chelmsford reforms.

Q2. Write a note on the powers and functions of the Governor.

Q3. 'Several issues which affect the organisation and working of the police'. Elaborate.

Q4. Define the 'Pressure Groups' and explain their methods of operation.

SECTION - II

Answer any four of the following questions in about 250 words each. Each question carries 12 marks.

Q5. Discuss the key features of Moghul administration.

Q6. Analyse the administrative implications of federalism.

Q7. Explain the principal patterns of relationship between the secretariat and Executive agencies.

Q8. Describe the important types of planning.

Q9. Explain the functions of Chief Secretary.

Q10. Describe the component parts of District administration.

Q11. Discuss the impact of social structure on administration.

Q12. Analyse the reasons for increasing conflict between political and permanent executives.

SECTION - III

Answer any two of the following questions in about 100 words each. Each question carries 6 marks.

Q13. What are the functions of Finance Commission?

Q14. Write a note on Cadre Management of All-India Services.

Q15. List the advantages of administrative tribunals.

Q16. Explain the factors impeding decentralisation.

Note: Answer the questions as per the instructions given in each sections.

SECTION – I

Answer any two of the following questions in about 500 words each.
Q1. Explain the relationship between secretariat department and executive department at the state level.
Refer to Dec-2016, Q.No.-3 (Pg. No.-247)

Q2. Describe the regulatory, executive and quasi-judicial functions of the Union Public Service Commission.
Ans. The functions of the UPSC as specified under Article 320 of the Constitution bear resemblance to those of the Federal Public Service Commission as specified in Government of India Act 1935. These functions may be broadly classified into three categories, viz., (1) regulatory; (2) executive and (3) the quasi-judicial.

(1) Regulatory: Among the regulatory functions the UPSC advises the government in matters relating to (i) methods of recruitment and (ii) the principles to be followed in making appointments, promotion and transfer from one service to another. However, unlike the regulatory jurisdiction vested in the United States Civil Service Commission (USCSC), the UPSC in India has hardly any such powers. The UPSC's jurisdiction is purely advisory. Article 320 (3) of the Constitution merely states that it is the duty of the Commission to advise the government on all matters relating to the methods of recruitment to civil services, promotions and transfers. Thus, unlike the USCSC, the UPSC cannot make regulations on personnel matters which will be binding on all government departments. Although certain functions of the UPSC are often described as being regulatory ones but in reality these are purely advisory functions.

(2) Executive Functions: The Commission has a specific constitutional duty of conducting examinations for appointments to the services of the Union. Under this provision the UPSC conducts many written examinations for different categories of post annually, besides the holding of interviews for selection of candidates for specialised and other categories of positions. Here too it may be noted that the Commission's jurisdiction is narrowly restricted to gazetted officers who constitute an insignificant proportion of the total number of government employees. This means that the executive jurisdiction of the Commission extends to only 1.9% of the total employees of the Central Government.

Another executive function of the UPSC is to present annually to the President a report of the work done by the Commission during the preceding year. The President is obliged to place the report before both houses of the Parliament with a memorandum explaining the cases, if any, where the advice of the Commission was not accepted and reasons for such non-acceptance.

(3) Quasi-judicial Functions: The quasi-judicial jurisdiction of the UPSC is limited both in scope and extent. In fact it has no true appellate jurisdiction. It can only advise on disciplinary actions taken against employees. According to the Constitution, the government should consult the Commission on the following matters:,

(i) All disciplinary actions affecting a government employee like censure, withholding of increments or promotion, reduction to a lower grade, compulsory retirement, removal or dismissal from service, etc. ii) Claims far reimbursement for costs incurred by an employee in legal Proceedings instituted against him in respect of acts done in the execution of his duty. iii) Claims for the award of pension in respect of injuries sustained by an employee and any question as to the amount of any Such reward (Constitution of India, Article 320(3)(C)).

The UPSC derives its functions, apart from the Constitution of India as discussed above, from other sources too like (a) the laws made by the Parliament, (b) rules, regulations and orders of the executive, (c) conventions. Under Article 321 of the Constitution, the parliament through legislation, can confer additional functions on the UPSC pertaining to the services of the Union or the States. If necessary, the Parliament can place the personnel system of any local authority, corporate body or public institution within the jurisdiction of the Commission.

According to Article 318 and 320 of the Constitution, the Central Government through certain regulations and orders entrust certain functions to the Commission. Also the President may define from time to time through regulations, the matters in which the Commission need not be consulted.

The Commission also discharges certain functions, which through conventions have been entrusted to it, though these are not stipulated in the Constitution. Under the Constitution, recruitment to the Defence forces is beyond the purview of the Commission, as the defence service is not a part of the Civil Service. But since 1948 the Commission has been conducting written tests for the selection of scientists and technicians for the pool of highly qualified scientists and technologists, who are deputed to Central Government, scientific institutions, national laboratories, universities etc. These functions are being discharged by the UPSC on the basis of conventions only.

Q3. Examine the role of the Governor in the state administration.
Refer to Chapter-3, Q.No.-2 (Pg. No.-96)

Q4. Write a note on the Urban Local Self-government.
Refer to June-2016, Q.No.-12 (Pg. No.-244)

SECTION – II

Answer any four of the following questions in about 250 words each.
Q5. Briefly describe the basic features of Indian Constitution.
Refer to Chapter-2, Q.No.-1 (Pg. No.-45)

Q6. Explain the changing role of the Prime Minister's office.
Refer to Chapter-2, Q.No.-11 (Pg. No.-68)

Q7. Write a note on components of civil services at the state level.
Ans. It first be clearly understood that at the state level in India, not one but two distinct sets of civil services operate. One of these is the civil services recruited by the respective state governments to handle a diverse range of governmental activity at the state level. These are known as the state civil services or simply state services. The second set of civil services serving the states is the All India Services. All India Services officers are recruited to perform a varied range of jobs, both at the state level as well as at the Centre. It is this feature of the All India Services, which renders them clearly distinguishable from the state services. Among the best known examples of the All India Services are the Indian Administrative Services (IAS) and the Indian Police Service (IPS). Thus, the civil service at the state level is composed of two distinct components. One, state services and two, All India Services.
All India Services: All India Services were constituted with the crucial purpose of creating an elite corps of officers who would man top positions both in the states as well as the Centre. Officers of the All India Services are recruited by the Union Government through the Union Public Service Commission. Upon recruitment, each officer is allotted to a specific state cadre. It is from the particular state, to which he is allotted, that the concerned officer moves to the Central government. The arrangement under which such movement takes place is known as the Tenure System. The officer is moved back and forth between the state (of his allotment) and the Centre during the first twenty years of his career (after which he finally lands up at the Centre). Officers of

the All India Services operate under the joint control of the Centre and the state to which they are allotted. The fact that the All India Services officers are centrally recruited (and then allotted to various states) guarantees that all states have a certain minimum and uniform level of talent in their administrative services and that the states' administrative machinery is adequately equipped. The existence of the Tenure System, under which officers of the All India Services move to the Centre periodically, ensures that the incumbents of the policy making posts at the Centre are backed by rich field experience.

State Services: These are recruited by the respective state governments through their public service commissions or other agencies. Members of these services are primarily meant for service in the states; only occasionally may a few members of some of the state services be borrowed by the Centre or some other organisations. States have well-organised services to cater to the needs of different sectors of governmental activity in non-technical and technical spheres. Typically, a state may have the following services: (1) Administrative Services; (2) Police Service;

(3) Judicial Service; (4) Forest Service; (5) Agriculture Service; (6) Educational Service; (7) Medical Service; (8) Fisheries Service; (9) Engineering Service; (10) Accounts Service; (11) Sales Tax Service; (12) Prohibition and Excise Service and (13) Cooperative Service.

Inter-relationship and Inter-linkages: The personnel of the state services operate in subordination to the members of the All India Services. State services occupy lower positions in the administrative hierarchy than those held by the personnel of the All India Services. They constitute the middle level of the state administrative system.

An attempt has been made to evolve - from out of those two sources of supply - a common stream. This has been achieved in two ways. One, by providing opportunities to the State Services' personnel to rise to higher posts, which are normally reserved for the All India Services officers. Two, by inducting a certain percentage of the State Services' personnel into the All India Services.

Q8. Examine the role of the District Collector in Panchayati Raj Institutions.

Refer to Chapter-4, Q.No.-6 (Pg. No.-134)

Q9. Explain the different types of administrative tribunals.

Refer to Chapter-5, Q.No.-4 (Pg. No.-162)

Customs and Excise Revenue Appellate Tribunal (CERAT): The Parliament passed the CERAT Act in 1986. The Tribunal adjudicate disputes,. complaints or offences with regard to customs and excise revenue. Appeals from the orders of the CERAT lies with the Supreme Court.

Election Commission (EC): The Election Commission is a tribunal for adjudication of matters pertaining to the allotment of election symbols to parties and similar other problems. The decision of the commission can be challenged in the Supreme Court.

Foreign Exchange Regulation Appellate Board (FERAB): The Board has been set up under the Foreign Exchange Regulation Act, 1973. A person who is aggrieved by an order of adjudication for causing breach or committing offences under the Act can file an appeal before the FERAB.

Income Tax Appellate Tribunal: This tribunal has been constituted under the Income Tax Act, 1961. The Tribunal has its benches in various cities and appeals can be filed before it by an aggrieved person/s against the order passed by the Deputy Commissioner or Commissioner or Chief Commissioner or Director of Income Tax. An appeal against the order of the Tribunal lies to the High Court. An appeal also lies to the Supreme Court if the High Court deems fit.

Railway Rates Tribunal: This-Tribunal was set up under the Indian Railways Act, 1989. It adjudicates matters pertaining to the complaints against the railway administration. These may be related to the discriminatory or unreasonable rates, unfair charges or preferential treatment meted out by the railway administration. The appeal against the order of the Tribunal lies with the Supreme Court.

Industrial Tribunal: This Tribunal has been set up under the Industrial Disputes Act, 1947. It can be constituted by' both the Central as well as State governments. The Tribunal looks into the dispute between the employers and the workers in matters relating to wages, the period and mode of payment, compensation and other allowances, hours of work, gratuity, retrenchment and closure of the establishment. The appeals against the decision of the Tribunal lie with the Supreme Court.

Q10. What are the limitations of judicial control over administration?
Refer to Chapter-5, Q.No.-10 (Pg. No.-172)

Q11. Describe the division of administrative powers between the centre and states.
Refer to Chapter-6, Q.No.-1 (Pg. No.-175)

Q12. 'Pressure groups differ in their constitution and objectives.' Discuss.
Refer to Chapter-6, Q.No.-9 and Q.No.-10 (Pg. No.-191)

SECTION – III

Answer any two of the following questions in about 100 words each.
Q13. Enlist the defects of the Regulating Act of 1773.
Refer to Chapter-1, Q.No.-6 (Pg. No.-18)

Q14. What are the modes of corruption in public services?
Refer to Dec-2016, Q.No.-13 (Pg. No.-253)

Q15. Elaborate the issues confronting police administration.
Refer to Chapter-4, Q.No.-11 (Pg. No.-141)

Q16. Explain the concept of public interest litigation.
Refer to Chapter-5, Q.No.-11 (Pg. No.-174)

> Whatever you do, do with determination. You have one life to live; do your work with passion and give your best. Whether you want to be a chef, doctor, actor, or a mother, be passionate to get the best result.

Note: Answer the questions as per the instructions given in each sections.

SECTION – I

Answer any two of the following questions in about 500 words each. Each question carries 20 marks.

Q1. Describe the organisational structure of police at the state, district and sub-district levels.

Q2. 'The Chief Minister is prime mover of the executive government of the state'. Examine.

Q3. What are the major forms of judicial control over administration?

Q4. Examine the areas of co-operation and conflict between political and permanent executives.

SECTION – II

Answer any four of the following questions in about 250 words each. Each question carries 12 marks.

Q5. Write a note on the national commission for scheduled castes.

Q6. Discuss the role and functions of the central secretariat.

Q7. What are the major functions of the Union Public Service Commission?

Q8. Explain the significance of the Lokpal and Lokayukta for dealing with corruption.

Q9. Examine the advantages and disadvantages of administrative tribunals.

Q10. Describe the powers and functions of the Panchayati Raj Institutions.

Q11. Discuss the financial relations between two centre and states.

Q12. Comment on the nature and types of pressure groups in India.

SECTION – III

Answer any two of the following questions in about 100 words each. Each question carries 6 marks.

Q13. How do the cultural factors affect the administrative processes?

Q14. Enlist the features of the Government of India Act 1935.

Q15. Explain the types of planning.

Q16. Discuss the significance of Lakhina experiment.

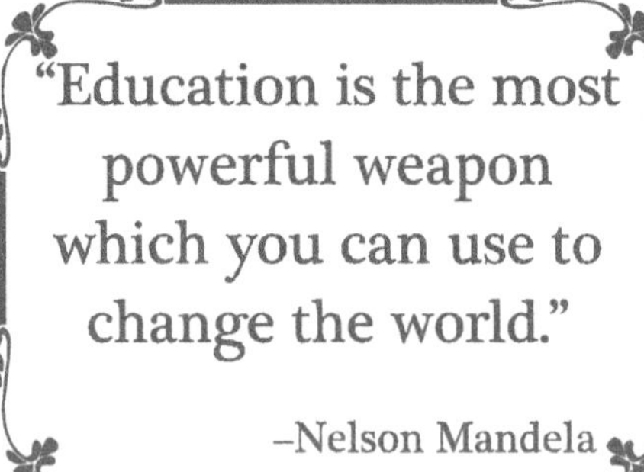